W9-AOE-677

ALCOA

☆ ☆ ☆ ☆ ☆ ☆ ☆ ☆ ☆

An American Enterprise

ALCOA

AN

AMERICAN

ENTERPRISE

By Charles C. Carr

☆ ☆ ☆ ☆ ☆ ☆ ☆ ☆ ☆

NEW YORK 1952 TORONTO

RINEHART & COMPANY, INC.

4633

First released in January, 1952

A Note of Explanation

☆ ☆ ☆ ☆ ☆ ☆ ☆ ☆ ☆

THIS IS THE STORY of an American enterprise during its first sixty-two years of existence. Aluminum Company of America, popularly known as Alcoa, has had many experiences similar to those found in the history of other industrial concerns. On the other hand, Alcoa has met with situations for which it would be difficult to find a parallel in the experience of any other American company. For this reason the story should be of interest not only to those intrigued with the romance of aluminum, but to others who are seeking a case history of a business which came to its fruition under our American system.

Searching Alcoa's files and checking data with many qualified Company people have been arduous but pleasant tasks. They were made easier by the fact that the author was for many years Director of Public Relations for the Company. During this period he gained a knowledge of what was needed for a book of this kind as well as a close personal acquaintance with many Company men who have participated in the making of Alcoa history. To name all those who rendered valuable assistance would make this preface too long. Only two will be mentioned—Junius D. Edwards, Assistant Director, Aluminum Research Laboratories, and J. G. Taylor, long-time editor of Alcoa employee publications. This preface affords opportunity to express deep gratitude to these two splendid assistants and to all other Alcoa people who took time and painstaking effort to be of help.

Joining Alcoa when he was fifty years old, after a long career as a newspaperman and a newspaper publisher, the author came to the Company with an objective viewpoint. When he retired at the age of sixty-five and undertook the writing of this book, he tried to keep that same approach to the subject. All phases of Alcoa's history, whether or not they involved controversy, are included. The Alcoa story is not ended with the closing chapter of this volume. As the book goes to press new expansions to meet the threat of war clouds are occurring on the part of Alcoa and other aluminum producers.

Since there was access to Alcoa's voluminous records and files and the source is frequently given in the running text, no further attempt has been made to identify this material in the footnotes. Notations included in the explanatory notes are largely references to published literature and published documents.

CHARLES C. CARR

St. Petersburg, Florida
July 1, 1951

Contents

☆ ☆ ☆ ☆ ☆ ☆ ☆ ☆ ☆

Contents

Illustrations

✩ ✩ ✩ ✩ ✩ ✩ ✩ ✩ ✩

ALCOA

☆ ☆ ☆ ☆ ☆ ☆ ☆ ☆ ☆

An American Enterprise

Aluminum

☆ ☆ ☆ ☆ ☆ ☆ ☆ ☆ ☆

ISCOVERY OF A CHEAP process for making aluminum was an industrial atomic bomb of the Nineteenth Century. The electrolytic fission of aluminum oxide by twenty-two-year-old Charles Martin Hall, in an Ohio woodshed in 1886, touched off an industrial chain reaction which, throughout its sixty-five-year progress, has been a classic example of American enterprise at work. From that first pellet of homemade aluminum and the knowledge which produced it was born the great aluminum industry of the United States, spearheaded by the pioneer producer, The Pittsburgh Reduction Company, now Aluminum Company of America.

Aluminum was already on the market at the time of Hall's discovery. It was not a new product. Expensive, yes, but available if anyone could use it at eight dollars a pound. Its properties of light weight, reasonable strength and stability had been known for some years, particularly to metallurgists and engineers. But young Hall's process for making low-cost aluminum was new, commercially untried and seemingly a risky investment, although the returns to venture capital could be ample if the process worked on a large scale.

He brought his great discovery to Pittsburgh in 1888 after trying for two years, without success, to instill into others the faith that was in him. In the City of Steel, Hall found a young man, a metallurgist who knew something of the metal aluminum and understood the problems which would confront a pioneering project to develop his process. This man, Alfred E. Hunt, and a group of young Pittsburghers, in the best traditions of American pioneering and enterprise, backed Hall with their dollars. Thus was opened the frontier of a new and strange business which was to be a continuation of man's efforts to produce aluminum cheaply enough to compete with other metals.

The record of these efforts starts with the year 1807, when Sir Humphry Davy, the great English electrochemist, decided that the earth, alumina, might well be the oxide of a new metal. In the following year he attempted to reduce, by electrolysis, alumina fused with potash.[1] Although he did not succeed in producing the new metal, he became convinced that alumina had a metallic base and suggested that the metal be called *alumium*. He later changed it to *aluminum* to correspond with the oxide, alumina, and to this day it has been called aluminum or aluminium. The latter spelling is still used abroad.

The first scientist to succeed in the dramatic struggle to wrest aluminum from the chemical combinations in which Nature had

[1] Philosophical Transactions, read before Royal Society on June 30, 1808.

2

tightly locked it was H. C. Oersted, a Danish physicist and chemist.[2] In 1825 Oersted heated potassium amalgam with aluminum chloride and then distilled the mercury from the resultant amalgam. This small lump was the first aluminum man had ever seen.

Frederick Wöhler, a German, improved Oersted's chemical method by using metallic potassium instead of the amalgam, and by 1845 had succeeded in making metallic particles of aluminum as large as big pinheads. He was the first to measure its specific gravity and show its amazing lightness—one of aluminum's outstanding properties in both peace and war. Nine years more elapsed before the French scientist, Henri Sainte-Claire Deville, in 1854 substituted sodium for potassium as the alkali-metal reducing agent, and introduced aluminum to the world.

Here at last was something to intrigue scientist and layman alike. The most plentiful metallic element on this terrestrial globe, having kept itself concealed since civilization began, was now yielding to man's ingenuity. It could be seen, touched, lifted. At the Paris Exposition of 1855, Sainte-Claire Deville placed on view a solid silvery bar—the first specimen of aluminum ever exposed to the gaze of the general public. The new metal proved a sensation. It weighed only one third as much as iron. Like copper, it resisted corrosion. It was a splendid conductor of heat, a fine reflector. Although not so strong as iron, it had sufficient strength for many practical purposes. Its silvery color appealed to the artistic.[3]

There was plenty of aluminum locked in Nature's combina-

[2] Oersted's description of this work, translated from the original Danish and appearing in *The Aluminum Industry*, by Edwards, Frary and Jeffries, McGraw Hill Book Company, 1930.
[3] Sainte-Claire Deville's book, *De l'Aluminium, ses Propriétés, sa Fabrication et ses Applications*, was the first important book published on aluminum (1859).

tions. In fact, 8 per cent of the earth's crust is the element aluminum, although it is combined with other elements, chiefly oxygen. The big problem of securing aluminum was the cost of the aluminum chloride and of the sodium used as a reducing agent. Hamilton Y. Castner, an American chemist, helped lower the price of sodium by discovering new methods for its manufacture. However, even with these improvements, eight dollars a pound in 1886 was a new low price for aluminum made by the Castner-Sainte-Claire Deville chemical process. This record of great names in science and invention brings us to Charles Martin Hall, the Ohio boy without a job, whose discovery created a million jobs!

This chronicle will deal with aluminum, the metal, only as the history of wresting it from Nature becomes a part of the story of Aluminum Company of America and its relationship with Industry and Government over the past sixty years. The Pittsburgh Reduction Company, founded in 1888, became Aluminum Company of America in 1907. In this record The Pittsburgh Reduction Company will appear as a corporate entity in the early portion of the narrative, and Aluminum Company of America, frequently termed "Alcoa," will be named many times. During the past decade the trade name "Alcoa" has been used by the Government, by the Courts, by the Company and by the general public to designate the Company. Because of the brevity of the expression and its common usage, Alcoa will be interchanged throughout the book with Aluminum Company of America.

CHAPTER ONE

Charles Martin Hall

☆ ☆ ☆ ☆ ☆ ☆ ☆ ☆ ☆

AFTER THE EPOCHAL DISCOVERY in 1886 by a young man
in America and a similar discovery at almost the
same time by a young man in France, aluminum
really came into man's possession. Its commercial history made
a greater advance in the next decade than had occurred in the
previous seventy-eight years following Sir Humphry Davy's attempt to separate the metal from its combination with oxygen.

Charles Martin Hall, a twenty-two-year old American, succeeded in his search for an economical method of making aluminum only after many experiments and many disappointments.
His every effort to find a cheap chemical process for the production of the metal was fruitless. He finally evolved a new plan to
reduce aluminum oxide to the metal by electrolysis. For success,
however, he needed a solvent free from water such as a molten
salt which would dissolve alumina, but chemists had not yet discovered such a solvent. His patient and persistent search led

5

him to the goal. His success was a landmark in man's effort to find an inexpensive way to produce aluminum. The process Hall discovered is still the basic method used today, but it did more than unlock a door. It opened up new vistas to men who are still hard at the task of making aluminum cheaper and more useful.

Today the layman is so accustomed to marvelous advances in science and technology that almost nothing seems to surprise. It is difficult, therefore, to visualize the stubborn problems which faced Sainte-Claire Deville, whose efforts to make aluminum an everyday metal preceded the great discoveries by an American and another Frenchman in the mid-Eighties. In the technicolor motion picture, "Unfinished Rainbows," a documentary history of aluminum during the past century, Napoleon III, who is anxious to aluminize his armies with lightweight equipment, becomes impatient with the metallurgist Sainte-Claire Deville and says, "But I thought you said this metal could be found most anywhere," and Sainte-Claire Deville answers, "In the raw state, yes, but it is so hard to separate from its compounds. . . ." Needless to say, Napoleon III, despite his vision of the future, did not equip his armies with aluminum—not at seventeen dollars per pound, the lowest cost his research men could achieve in those days.[1]

This chapter is the story of Hall, on whose invention the American industry is founded, but at the outset some mention should be made of Héroult. Hall's genius as an inventor found quick acceptance from the group of practical businessmen in

[1] "Unfinished Rainbows," documentary film in Alcoa film library, Wilding Picture Productions, 1941; viewed by more than 25,000,000 people in the past decade.

Pittsburgh to whom he finally came. The aluminum industry they founded, based on his process, had influence on the world-wide development of the metal. Paul L. T. Héroult, son of a French peasant, also influenced aluminum history in Europe through his inventions. At times in this chronicle his name will recur when he and his process affected the American scene.

The histories of Hall and Héroult are strangely parallel. Each was twenty-two years old when he made his discovery; death came to each in 1914. They were vastly different in temperament and in their research activities. Hall continued to improve his basic patent and to develop alloys with the aluminum which came from the reduction pots. Héroult, a metallurgist, did not at first sense the importance of his basic discovery and continued his development of aluminum alloys by another process. He was also interested in steel metallurgy, particularly the electric steel furnace which he developed. It is still in use today. Héroult furnaces were installed in the early days at the Illinois Steel Company and elsewhere in this country. Héroult made many trips to America on his various projects. His aluminum activities were largely confined to continental Europe where he was a figure in two companies, one in Switzerland and one in France.[2]

Charles Martin Hall, one of the great names in American industrial history! What about the family background, youth and traits of character of this lad who, on February 23, 1886, successfully solved a problem which had baffled scientists for three quarters of a century? What of this young man who, without training in an engineering school, living in the environment of a

[2] A more detailed history of Héroult is found in *The Aluminum Industry*, McGraw-Hill, 1930.

literary college in the Midwest, found a cheap and practical method of producing aluminum?

He was the son of a Congregational minister, Heman Bassett Hall, who took his young bride, Sophronia Brooks, to Jamaica, where they labored for ten years as missionaries. Older children in the Hall family were born in Jamaica, but Charles and two of his sisters first saw the light of day after the family had returned to the States and the father was filling various pastorates in this country. Charles Martin Hall was born at Thompson, Ohio, December 6, 1863. Until he was nine years old he lived in small Ohio towns where his father was called to preach. Then the family moved to Oberlin, Ohio, where the mother had decided a large family of children could be educated at least expense.

The Reverend Mr. Hall retired from the ministry but lived to a ripe age at Oberlin as friend and advisor of his children who grew to maturity about him. He died in 1911, but his wife lived only long enough to see her ambition realized with seven of her children either graduated or on their way to graduation from Oberlin College. She died in 1885, the year Charles was graduated but a year before he made his great discovery.

Charles Martin Hall mowed and trimmed the lawns of Oberlin citizens in summer, shoveled snow and built fires for them in winter. In the summer he was also a book canvasser. Letters written to his family during these canvassing days were full of confidence.[3] He was always sure he would "do better in the next town." Trying to make pin money this way has discouraged many a college boy. Setbacks acted as a challenge to him.

[3] Quotations from Hall letters are from correspondence preserved in Alcoa files.

Oberlin College has always been known for its classical, theological and music courses. However, for a liberal arts school, it did offer a broad curriculum ranging from mathematics and astronomy to physics and chemistry for those students interested in science. Young Hall took all of these courses which were offered. Naturally he studied chemistry; it was his passion and he had been intrigued with it from childhood. He tried to learn at home the chemistry he could not find in college textbooks and laboratories. Hall revealed the source of his "home reading" in 1911 in his address accepting the famed Perkin Medal, one of the highest honors American science bestows. He said his favorite reading was a torn and soiled textbook on chemistry which his father had used as a college student.

The book summed up all that was known about aluminum in 1841, the date of its publication. In essence, this was a brief description of the method Wöhler had used when he produced some particles of aluminum the size of pinheads. There were some other books on general science about the house and young Hall read them all. His next older sister, Julia, who became his confidante and co-worker in his home laboratory, had a mental picture of her brother stretched full length on the floor, face downward, head in hands, poring over these books.

Hall was a born inventor if such there be. The family residence, a two-story square brick house, had a cupola on the third floor which Charles sometimes used as a laboratory. His sister, Mrs. M. L. Stimson, recalled that, on one occasion, one of his experiments started a fire which caused much excitement but resulted in no greater damage than a burned-up tablecloth. Later on he was seriously experimenting on an aluminum reduction process in his woodshed laboratory, in reality a "summer kitchen" tied on to the back of the house and used for wood storage in winter. To keep the neighbors from becoming too inquisitive, he told his sisters to just say that "Charles is cooking something out there."

There is no doubt that Hall was dreaming of a way to make aluminum all through his college days. Hall himself said at the time of the Perkin Medal award, after telling about reading his father's chemistry book, "Later I read about Sainte-Claire Deville's work in France and found the statement that every clay bank was a mine of aluminum but that the metal was as costly as silver. I soon after began to think of processes for making aluminum cheaply." Prof. F. F. Jewett, his chemistry teacher, doubtless made the oft-quoted remark that fame and fortune awaited the man who would find an inexpensive way to separate the metal. However, Hall's sisters, reminiscing in later years, did not fully subscribe to the balance of that story which indicated it was a new idea to Hall, who promptly nudged a classmate and said, "I'm going after that metal." Prof. Jewett corroborated this in a statement he made before the Physical Science Club at Oberlin in 1916 where he said, "Even before he entered college, the subject of the extraction of aluminum from its ores had occupied his (Hall's) mind."

With a growing determination to find a new way of producing aluminum and undismayed by the failure of his first experiments, Hall set to work in earnest in his woodshed laboratory during his first year after graduation. His sister Julia had studied chemistry at Oberlin and was able to supply an understanding which stimulated Hall's thinking on scientific problems. In a more im-

Charles Martin Hall, the boy who was determined to become an inventor.
Working with homemade equipment in the family woodshed, he discovered
a low-cost process for separating aluminum from its oxide and thus started
America's gigantic aluminum industry.

portant way, she strengthened his determination when he was discouraged. Julia also worked with her hands, washing alumina and doing other things to assist in the experiments made tedious by lack of supplies and the necessity of making equipment at home.

In October of 1885 Hall reasoned that if he could find a liquid without water which would dissolve aluminum oxide, he might hope to separate the metal by electrolysis. On February 10, 1886, the young inventor discovered that cryolite, a sodium aluminum fluoride, in its molten state would dissolve aluminum oxide. What should have been the crucial test came on February 16th when he hopefully passed an electric current through the molten alumina dissolved in cryolite. When the experiment was finished, no aluminum could be found. Hall reasoned correctly that the fault was in the crucible and not in his process. Then followed days of feverish activity to replace the clay crucible with one made of carbon. On February 23, 1886, the carbon crucible was installed and again a direct electric current was passed through the molten cryolite-alumina for several hours. When the mixture had cooled and the mass was broken up, there were some shining buttons of aluminum! [4]

Miss Louie Hall, a younger sister, whom this writer interviewed in 1936 at the time of the fiftieth anniversary of her brother's discovery, recalled that great day as if it had been just the day before.[5] There was much excitement at home with

[4] A good reference for a description of Hall's invention of the electrolytic aluminum process is that which he gave in his Perkin Medal address:—Perkin Medal Address by Charles Martin Hall, *Journal Industrial and Engineering Chemistry*, March, 1911.

[5] These recollections and others in this chapter referring to the Hall family are contained in a biographical sketch "Charles Martin Hall as his Family Knew Him," by C. C. Carr, *Wearever News*, 1936.

Charles rushing over to the college to show Prof. Jewett what he had. It is not surprising that he thought of Prof. Jewett in that hour; his chemistry professor had given him encouragement and advice and had provided him with some equipment from the college laboratory. Jewett was always modest about his part in the affair. In 1920, at his fiftieth Yale reunion, the chemistry professor said, "My great discovery has been the discovery of a man—Charles Martin Hall."

The youthful Hall realized that he had made a great discovery but it took some time to find some money and hire a patent attorney to prepare the necessary patent papers. The actual application for a patent on the Hall process was filed on July 9, 1886. The patents were not actually issued by the Patent Office until April 2, 1889. During the long struggle to make his invention commercially valuable, Hall often told his sisters he guessed he would become a "broken-down inventor." He would point to other intelligent men of vision who had made no accumulation of worldly goods.

At times, he had reason to feel this way during the discouraging two years following his invention. His first shock came a few months after he had filed his patent application in July, 1886. The Patent Office reported that there was another application pending with a similar claim. The Frenchman, Paul L. T. Héroult, had filed a patent application in France slightly antedating that of Hall. While Hall had never heard of Héroult, neither had the latter ever heard of Hall. This "interference," formally entered in June, 1887, helped to delay the granting of Hall's patent for nearly two more years. Hall gained patent priority when he proved beyond question that he had reduced his invention to practice on February 23, 1886. Héroult had to rely on April 23, 1886, his patent filing date in France.

With patent pending and a reasonable assurance of prior recognition in this country, Hall began the depressing task of trying to find financial backing for what seemed to him almost an assured commercial success. His older brother George, who lived in New England, asked him to come to Boston. Nothing resembling financial support developed there. His precious globules of aluminum were looked upon as laboratory curiosities. They did not suggest to financiers the birth of a great industry.

Hall returned to Oberlin in October, 1886, still actuated by the same spirit he had displayed as a book canvasser in his college days when he thought he "would do better in the next town." He stayed in Oberlin until early in the next year, with occasional trips to Washington and elsewhere on his patent matter. He also spent those months negotiating with a chemical manufacturer in Cleveland who was willing to take the process only as a gift. Shortly thereafter, in the same city of Cleveland, there did appear at least a nod of recognition. Alfred and Eugene Cowles had done much in developing the electric furnace. The Cowles Electric Smelting & Aluminum Company was making quite a success of an aluminum alloy process which produced only alloys, chiefly a copper alloy with a small percentage of aluminum, known as "aluminum bronze." The Cowles plant was located at Lockport, N. Y., where water power was available. The Cowles brothers listened to Hall and admitted there might be something to his discovery.

Hall entered their employ at seventy-five dollars per month. He was to conduct his experiments for ninety days and then receive $750 if they decided to continue the investigation. The Cowles Company also took an option to purchase the Hall patents and process them within six months. If they exercised this option, they were to give Hall a one-eighth interest in a re-organized Cowles company. The Lockport experience was most unsatisfactory from Hall's standpoint. He always insisted they did not wish him to succeed.

The Cowles name will appear in subsequent chapters on early patent problems when some patents they acquired in connection with their alloy process came in conflict with the Hall process. In the lawsuits of that patent litigation, Hall charged that during his Lockport stay Cowles supplied him with virtually no facilities with which to work, did not keep their agreement on money matters, and showed only passive interest in what he was doing. That this indictment had a sound basis is evidenced by a letter written by Edwin Cowles and unearthed in one of the subsequent lawsuits. Cowles said in this letter, "We reasoned as follows: If some parties were to get hold of his process there might be great danger of its killing our process." [6] At any rate, the Cowles Company, whether or not they were playing a cat-and-mouse game, did not exercise their option. Hall's unfortunate stay at Lockport came to an end in a little more than six months.

While at Lockport, Hall met Romaine C. Cole, another young man without money but consumed with ambition to make a success of this fascinating aluminum business. Cole had been in-trigued with the possibility of aluminum manufacture and he knew a man in Pittsburgh, a successful metallurgist, who was

[6] Plaintiff's exhibit Cowles Electric Smelting & Aluminum Co. vs. Pittsburgh Re-duction Co., U. S. Circuit Court, Northern District of New York.

also interested in the same subject. This man was Capt. Alfred E. Hunt, for whose firm, Hunt & Clapp, Cole had done some experimental work on aluminum in connection with their materials testing business. "There are your real backers," said Cole to the somewhat discouraged and disillusioned Hall.

Hall sent Cole to Pittsburgh to interest Capt. Hunt in his new process. Cole was not an inventor, but he had the vision of the modern entrepreneur who can bring together the idea and the men who can see it through. He did just that when he introduced Hall to the small group of Pittsburgh men who also had vision and the courage of their convictions.

Cole proved himself a good negotiator in presenting to Capt. Hunt the possibilities of the Hall process. He so impressed the Pittsburgh metallurgist and his associates that a preliminary meeting was held on July 31, 1888, and it was decided to form a company. By August 8th, when the second meeting was held, Hall had arrived in Pittsburgh and both men were present at a gathering of the group on the afternoon of that date.

Capt. Hunt had come to Pittsburgh in 1880 to take charge of the open-hearth steel department for Park brothers at their Black Diamond Steel Works. In 1883 he and George H. Clapp had bought out their other partners in the Pittsburgh Testing Laboratory and were operating that business under the firm name of Hunt & Clapp. A chapter about Capt. Hunt and his associates will follow, but enough must be told here to show that Cole was right when he said to Hall, "Capt. Hunt is your man."

The decision to go along with Hall and Cole and to organize at once a company with $20,000 capital to equip a small pilot plant to demonstrate the feasibility of the Hall process was largely a one-man decision. Capt. Hunt called in some associates to help him organize The Pittsburgh Reduction Company and to raise the needed capital. However, he put George H. Clapp, his friend and partner, into the venture without even asking him. Mr. Clapp was touring Europe with his wife when Cole first interested Capt. Hunt in the Hall process. In later years, George Clapp, who was to have a long lifetime of association with Alcoa, often told, with a twinkle in his eye, how Capt. Hunt greeted him on his return from abroad. "Well, you don't know it, but you are in the aluminum business," said Capt. Hunt. Mr. Clapp promptly acquiesced and acted as temporary secretary at the organization meeting on July 31, 1888. Thereafter for many years Mr. Clapp gave his major attention to the operation of Hunt & Clapp while Capt. Hunt threw himself wholeheartedly into the aluminum business.

Hall's letters to his sister Julia give some interesting sidelights on the young inventor's thoughts before he finally fell in with the right people in Pittsburgh. In those early days he did not realize that he was to gain fame and fortune seldom vouchsafed a young man with a commercial idea. In a letter written to Julia from Cleveland on July 13, 1887, when he was still trying to do business with the Cowles brothers, he said:

> Dr. Brooks thinks I could go to the Cowles Company with an offer to sell out for $200,000 in money and stock, $10,000.00 to bind the bargain and the rest in six months or a year. That would give me time to test the thing and if it was of no use I would still have $10,000.00. . . . I would not expect to get $200,000.00, but by setting the figure high

would be more likely to get a good offer from them. I might also stipulate for a business position in their company. Do you have any advice? With $25,000.00 or $50,000.00 and a business position I could work out another invention.

Hall's early days in Pittsburgh also tell of the problems incident to making the pilot plant prove the commercial feasibility of his laboratory experiments. On September 16, 1888, he wrote Julia that the pilot plant building was nearly finished and he hoped to start making aluminum by October 15th. He and Cole roomed together. They lived over a saloon and received both room and board from a Mrs. Doyle for five dollars per week. On December 9, 1888, following the memorable Thanksgiving on which the first aluminum was produced at the pilot plant on Smallman Street in Pittsburgh, Charles wrote Julia, "Everybody is convinced of the success of the scheme—although we are not making sixty pounds a day right along as calculated." And to show how slowly the pilot plant progressed, he said in another letter to Julia written on February 3, 1889, "Capt. Hunt told me Friday we had made way with $18,000.00 already. It looks incredible and I hope he is mistaken, but it is a good deal."

First mention of Hall's lifelong friend and associate occurs in his letter to Julia December 18, 1888. He says, "Capt. Hunt got Davis to take my place when we work nights. He is the boy from Boston and fresh from Amherst College. He has a good deal of ability as well as grit to stand it working all night in the dirt and soot and worse." He was referring to Arthur Vining Davis, great genius of the aluminum industry, now Chairman of the Board of Aluminum Company of America, who took turns on the day and night shifts with Hall when they were proving to Capt. Hunt and associates that the Hall process would actually succeed.

An indication of the close friendship between the two men and a recognition of Arthur V. Davis's basic qualities may be found in the will of Charles Martin Hall probated after his death from a spleen disease at Daytona, Florida, in 1914. In that will, Hall gave the bulk of his considerable fortune to educational institutions, but he gave two hundred shares of Alcoa stock to Arthur V. Davis "as a token of esteem and respect for a long and pleasant business association." He also made Mr. Davis an executor and trustee of his estate.

Hall's own character is likewise revealed in this remarkable will. Aside from modest money gifts to one brother and sister and to several nephews and nieces, he left no cash to other family members close to him. He never married. He had already given his close relatives stock during his life. The records show that he started giving them stock as early as September, 1889. So, to his sisters, Edith, Julia and Louie, he gave no money with the following explanation: "They are already abundantly provided for (through stock) and any addition to their property would increase their anxieties and not add to their happiness."

Except for small bequests to such institutions as the Niagara Falls Memorial Hospital, the Niagara Falls Y.M.C.A., and the Village Improvement Society of Oberlin, Ohio, Hall's millions in money and stock were dispersed by the trustees, Arthur V. Davis and Homer H. Johnson, to Oberlin College, Berea College in Kentucky, the American Missionary Society and the cause of education in Japan, Asia, Turkey and the Balkan States. Oberlin got $800,000 and one third of the balance of the estate. Berea received one sixth, the American Missionary Society one sixth, and the cause of education in the Near East and the Far East one third. Although the son of a minister and a religious man himself, Hall stipulated that no part of the educational fund was to be used for instruction in theology. However, he had no objections to religious instruction being taught as a part of a general curriculum in whatever schools were established in the Near East and Far East.[7]

Hall's fortune when he died approximated thirty million dollars in value, a far cry from the $200,000 he thought he might get from the Cowles Company back in 1887 before he journeyed to Pittsburgh. Despite the rich financial reward he received for his patents and his demonstration that his process would work commercially, his tastes were modest, his habits simple. He was notoriously absent-minded. There is one story which Mrs. Alfred E. Hunt used to chuckle over that well illustrates it. Charles Hall was at the Hunt home for a Sunday midday dinner. During the meal a fire engine with galloping horses and clanging bell drew everyone away from the dinner table to the windows. The young inventor-genius, intent upon seeing the excitement, stuck his head through the window glass. Letters in old Company files contain frequent references to things Hall had left behind— umbrellas, overcoats, hats, galoshes. He was constantly writing his co-worker, Arthur V. Davis, to bring or send one of these items to whatever place he was in at the moment.

He remained a researcher and inventor until his death. His mind was active on ways to make aluminum and aluminum alloys

---

[7] The Hall will is published in part in Oberlin Alumni Magazine, Volume II, February, 1915.

better and cheaper rather than on personal matters or physical comforts. When he was at the Niagara Falls works of the Company in 1902, he wrote several letters asking for a purchase order for an electric fan. He had no thought of the fan for his personal benefit; he needed it to blow a blast of air down one of the bus lines which had been running hot.

His personal relaxation came from music, expressed in his case by piano playing. This diversion was a lifelong characteristic. Much as he needed every dollar in the early Pittsburgh days, he rented a piano. Next to his board and room, this expense seemed an essential to him. On one occasion the church located next door to his then rooming place found that his piano playing was interfering with church services. The elders waited upon him with the request that he time his playing so as not to interfere with Sunday School or church. He had one term of lessons in the Conservatory of Music at Oberlin. This devotion to the piano proved the type of diversion he needed. At his home in Niagara Falls he played regularly. He was always ready to spend money for concerts.

His cultural life also included much reading and he showed splendid taste in his library. He collected Oriental rugs, starting early in Pittsburgh and continuing the hobby after he began to travel abroad. He gave his fine collection of Orientals to Oberlin College. Hall did not touch liquor and did not smoke. Of Dr. Charles M. Chandler of Columbia University, one of his closest friends, Hall told his sisters, "Chandler is such a good friend I will permit him to smoke in my house, but he is about the only one."

The Pittsburgh Reduction Company which Capt. Hunt and

his associates formed to try out the Hall process was to become Aluminum Company of America. Arthur Vining Davis, the youngster who alternated with Hall in the schedule of long and arduous hours to nourish the struggling enterprise, was to become Chairman of the Board of Alcoa and a world-famous industrialist. Roy A. Hunt, son of Capt. Alfred E. Hunt, the founder of the enterprise, was a lad in knee pants when the Hall process was brought to Pittsburgh. Today Roy A. Hunt, after twenty-three years as President of Alcoa, is Chairman of the Executive Committee.

Charles Martin Hall, the lad who found an inexpensive way to produce aluminum, belies the adage that inventors usually die poor and unhonored. He had a rich, fruitful life, and a financial reward beyond his dreams. He is a shining example to disprove the theory that our free-enterprise system fails to create opportunities for any lad of ability and ambition, however humble his beginnings. Hall's life story would seem to prove that opportunities still exist under our American system, opportunities for young people to achieve both fame and wealth in the field of Industry.

CHAPTER TWO

Alcoa's Beginnings

☆ ☆ ☆ ☆ ☆ ☆ ☆ ☆ ☆

THE INVENTION of Charles Martin Hall was not the first discovery of how to produce metallic aluminum from its compounds. That discovery had been made sixty years earlier by Oersted, the Danish scientist. Hall's contribution was the finding of a way to get aluminum by a method inexpensive enough to make the commercial use of the metal possible. His method is the one in universal use today. In the more than sixty years since then, research workers the world over have not improved upon the fundamental character of his invention.

However, the effort to reduce the cost goes on unceasingly. The company which was founded on Hall's invention is still engaged in research on one phase or another of this cost reduction. The Hall process has had many improvements, as have the underlying steps in mining the ore and in refining bauxite to secure the white powder known as alumina. It may even happen that some method better than the Hall process for producing

23

metallic aluminum will someday come forth. If and when it does, it will be the fruition of countless hours which add up to many years of research by those who have followed in Hall's footsteps.

When the twenty-two-year-old college graduate discovered a way to produce aluminum by passing an electric current through a fused bath of cryolite and alumina, it is doubtful that he realized he was ushering into America a new and great industry. Yet he knew this before his untimely death in 1914. By then it had become apparent that the commercial production of aluminum would require large reserves of bauxite, great sources of low-cost power, preferably hydroelectric, and ample raw materials. To make one pound of refined *alumina* takes about two pounds of bauxite together with soda ash, lime, steam and fuel oil. To make one pound of *aluminum* there are needed two pounds of this refined alumina and substantial amounts of pitch, coke, coal, cryolite and fluorspar. The industry requires a vast investment in mills, machinery, dams, mines and transportation facilities—an investment which today averages nearly $15,000 for every employee in the far-flung Alcoa organization.

It was the summer of 1888 when Hall came to Pittsburgh and found the group of young men who were to see his process through to success. To understand the little company formed in Pittsburgh in 1888, we need a word picture of this group of business pioneers, typical Americans, who scraped the bottoms of their individual barrels to raise the $20,000 with which The Pittsburgh Reduction Company was started. This $20,000 was for the purpose of building and equipping a small pilot plant. If this experimental plant proved that Hall's process was commercially sound, a sizable corporation was to be formed in which

Captain Alfred E. Hunt, a leading metallurgist of the Eighties. With rare vision, he foresaw a great aluminum industry based on the Hall process, and became first president of The Pittsburgh Reduction Company.

the inventor and his associate, Romaine C. Cole, would receive 47 per cent of the capital stock. If the pilot plant failed, Capt. Hunt and his friends would be simply sadder and wiser.

At the organization meeting of the company on July 31, 1888, at Capt. Hunt's home, 272 Shady Lane (now Shady Avenue), Pittsburgh, the first chore was to pick a name.[1] Oddly, the name chosen that night was Pittsburgh Aluminium Company, a reflection of the confusion which then existed between the American spelling and that used abroad.

The American and European spelling of the word is mentioned in our Foreword, but this early use of "aluminum" by the Pittsburgh group gave rise to an apocryphal story told in later years. It was to the effect that the little company changed the word to "aluminum" because a printer had inadvertently left out the "i" on some Company stationery. When the printer went bankrupt, the Company decided to let the spelling stand rather than to spend $300 for new stationery. While the facts do not support this delightful tale, one point could be easily verified— the Company didn't have $300 to spend for stationery, let alone reprinting it.

The minute books of the Company show that as early as July 10, 1889, the word was being spelled "aluminum" in all correspondence. The corporate name omitted the word within two weeks after the organization meeting when the change was made to The Pittsburgh Reduction Company, by which it was called until 1907. The Pittsburgh Reduction Company then became Aluminum Company of America. Rumor has it that the founders were constantly embarrassed through the Nineties by having people

[1] Early minute books, The Pittsburgh Reduction Company.

25

confuse The Pittsburgh Reduction Company with some kind of a garbage disposal outfit. Legend has it that one of the officials was called up late at night and blasted to eternal damnation for not removing a dead horse that had been lying in a near-by alley.

The group got down to business at the second meeting on August 8, 1888, when a company with 200 shares of stock, par value $100 per share, was created. The company was to build and equip an experimental plant to try out the Hall process on a commercial basis. This $20,000 was not easy to raise, so it was arranged that the initial stockholders would pay it in, 5 per cent at a time, "on call." Subsequent events showed the calls coming in rapid succession as the money was needed for building and plant construction. If the organizers became satisfied that the Hall process could be worked "successfully and profitably," an ambitious corporate setup was planned—a company with 10,000 shares of stock.

This increase in capital structure did occur a little more than a year later, on October 2, 1889.[2] Hall and Cole received 47 per cent of the entire stock issue for the Hall patents and the charter members got 25 per cent for their pioneering in the initial venture.[3] In addition to their original investment of $20,000, the pioneers had put up another $10,000 of hard cash to complete the experimental project. The remaining 28 per cent was to be sold for improvements and expansions.

Thus the little company, early in its career, became a sizable financial project, disproving the oft-repeated statement that Alu-

[2] Capital stock increase filed with Secretary of Commonwealth of Pennsylvania, October 2, 1889.

[3] Exhibit 1004, Alcoa anti-trust case, Agreement between Charles M. Hall, Romaine Cole and The Pittsburgh Reduction Company.

minum Company of America, with its present capital running into hundreds of millions, operated in its initial years on a meager $20,000. The capital increase to 10,000 shares in 1889 meant a million-dollar concern if shares sold at par. After the pilot plant proved itself, the 28 per cent of the stock offered for sale did go at that figure. In fact, by 1895, there is a record of a private stock sale at $105 per share.[4]

Hall and Cole were not in the organizing group and had no part of the initial investment. This sum which the group of young Pittsburgh businessmen put up was vital to the early structure of Alcoa. Without it, there would have been no company and no proving of the merit of Hall's invention. It was merely the "seed money" these young men were willing to invest because they had faith in the future of aluminum. However, they continued to have faith and to invest their dollars after the pilot plant proved itself, so it may truly be said that Alcoa actually started with an investment of $20,000.

Who were these men to whom Romaine C. Cole introduced his young inventor friend, Charles Martin Hall? Capt. Alfred E. Hunt, thirty-three years of age, the spark plug of the group, was a steel metallurgist, one of the foremost of his day. As already stated, he had come to Pittsburgh in 1880 to take charge of the open-hearth furnace operation at the Black Diamond Steel Works owned by Park Brothers. He and George H. Clapp had gone into partnership in 1883 as proprietors of the chemical department of the Pittsburgh Testing Laboratory, founded two years earlier by William Kent [5] and William F. Zimmerman, two emi-

---

[4] Letter from Capt. Hunt to James C. McGuire, New York, November 11, 1895.
[5] William Kent was the author of Kent's Handbook for Mechanical Engineers.

nent engineers. In 1887, Hunt and Clapp became the owners of the corporation, operating it for a time as "Hunt and Clapp— Pittsburgh Testing Laboratory." The Pittsburgh Testing Laboratory later again assumed its corporate name and is a world-famous materials testing institution today.

Capt. Hunt was a New Englander, born in Massachusetts.[6] He was graduated from Massachusetts Institute of Technology in Metallurgy and Mining in 1876. His first job was in Boston with the Bay State Iron Works, which was then operating the only open-hearth steel furnace in the United States. For two years the young metallurgist was in charge of the Nashua Iron & Steel Company's open-hearth department in New Hampshire. He had acquired plenty of experience in steel before he became intrigued with the Hall process for producing aluminum. Two outstanding steel jobs on which he had inspected the materials were the Robert steel bridge across the Mississippi at Saint Paul and the Poughkeepsie bridge across the Hudson.

Capt. Hunt was what would be termed a "leading citizen" in any American community today. His engineering activities won him prominence at home as well as in national and international circles. He was a member of numerous engineering societies and a frequent contributor to technical and trade publications. In addition, he was a soldier. He helped organize Battery B of the Pennsylvania National Guard in 1884 and was elected its first Captain. When the Spanish-American War came he was among the first in his state to lead his battery into volunteer service. At an anniversary dinner in 1931, commemorating the first half century of the Engineering Society of Western Pennsylvania,

[6] *The National Cyclopedia of American Biography*, James T. White & Co., N. Y.

The home of Captain Hunt on Shady Lane in Pittsburgh. In its parlor The Pittsburgh Reduction Company was founded in 1888.

George S. Davison said, "Capt. Hunt was a fine figure of a man as he sat astride his horse when Battery B left Pittsburgh for the front."

His service to his country during the Puerto Rican campaign, when he contracted a fever, brought on the ill health which led to his untimely death in 1899. He and his battery were given an ovation on their return to Pittsburgh September 16, 1898. Artillery Armory, completed in Pittsburgh in 1920, was named Hunt Armory in memory of the military leader who endeared himself to his men during their Spanish-American War experiences. Upon his return from the war there was a well-organized movement to run the handsome, mustached hero for mayor of Pittsburgh. A news article in a leading Pittsburgh newspaper on April 29, 1899, contains two columns of favorable comment by leading citizens upon the possibility of his candidacy. Capt. Hunt did not offer himself for public office.

The other incorporators of the company and investors in the $20,000 pilot plant were all connected with the steel industry. They were willing to join Capt. Hunt with their cash even though they may have lacked the aluminum enthusiasm which actuated him from 1888 until his death eleven years later. George H. Clapp became active in the new company and served as Treasurer and Paymaster, but he devoted much of his time in those early days to the affairs of Hunt & Clapp, leaving his partner free to promote the aluminum venture. He and Hunt had become acquainted when both were employed by Park Brothers. George Clapp was to maintain through a long life a keen interest in all things aluminum. He continued on the Board of Directors of Alcoa until his death in 1949. He never sold any of his stock

29

except a meager 28 shares with which he parted in 1891 to provide a stock interest for a bright young man about whom more
will be said later.

Howard Lash was head of the Carbon Steel Company, Mil-
lard Hunsiker was general sales manager for that company,
Robert Scott was superintendent of the 33rd Street mill of the
Carnegie Steel Company, and W. S. Sample, an Annapolis graduate, was chief chemist for the Pittsburgh Testing Laboratory.
Capt. Hunt and his associates were a typical group of alert
young businessmen looking for opportunity. The oldest was
under thirty-five and Capt. Hunt was only thirty-three.

This was the group Capt. Hunt brought together to start the
project. Two other men appeared at the first and perhaps the
second meeting but dropped out of any mention thereafter. Apparently they may have thought the enterprise was entirely too
risky for them to venture any part of $20,000. People often re-
mark about what a wonderful thing it is to be in on the ground
floor of enterprise. These two men, according to their best judgment at the moment, failed to grasp what later turned out to be a
golden opportunity.

Such a pooling of limited resources to start a new venture has
been duplicated thousands of times in this land of opportunity.
America has grown into its industrial and commercial might
through this process. While Government control rather than
regulation has discouraged venture capital in recent times, the
process still functions as the very life blood of any community.
Since our system is one of profit and loss, not all ventures are
successful. The group of Pittsburgh businessmen which met at
Capt. Hunt's home on July 31, 1888, were embarking upon a

hazardous venture. They were to have many discouraging experiences before success began to emerge. Even if they had failed, it would not have been to their discredit because failures in our profit and loss system often spell progress.

A quick illustration may be found in the automobile business. Prior to and during the first ten years of the Ford Motor Company's existence, when the Ford car was receiving an amazing acceptance from the American people, 645 makes of automobiles with names ranging from Abbott to Zimmerman were built and marketed but are no longer produced. A total of 128 of these now nonexistent models which were presented to the public by their makers and hopeful backers were placed on the market even before the Ford appeared in 1903.[7] The people who invested their money in such ventures should be classed as pioneers rather than as gamblers.

The small group of enterprisers who founded The Pittsburgh Reduction Company did prove to be pioneers in the true sense of the word. They were fortunate in that they lived in an economic climate which encouraged venture capital. Much is written today about the basic concept which causes the American economy to differ from a socialistic or totalitarian brand. In 1888 these young men were able to epitomize the spirit of it—private property rights and privileges, a free market, profit and wage incentives and a fair degree of Government regulation without Government control. In short, they lived during a period which encouraged men to make, save and risk their own money.

[7] *Automotive News Almanac*, June, 1949.

CHAPTER THREE

Men, Faith, Money

☆ ☆ ☆ ☆ ☆ ☆ ☆ ☆ ☆

THE FOUNDERS of the small company were not merely investors in a new enterprise. They worked at the job. In fact, it became Capt. Hunt's major and almost sole business activity and remained so until his death just before the turn of the century. During the decade following the birth of the aluminum industry, Capt. Hunt became the enthusiastic champion and prophet for aluminum. Were he here today, it is doubtful if he would be surprised at the magnitude of the industry.

The Company can point with pride to an early price policy established by The Pittsburgh Reduction Company under Capt. Hunt's guidance. Minutes of the Board of Directors' meeting on September 17, 1895, give expression to a long-range price attitude which Alcoa has found it to be good business to follow throughout the years. These minutes include a report to stockholders, signed by Alfred E. Hunt, President. This price policy sounds much like later statements issued by Alcoa's long-time

33

President, Roy A. Hunt, son of the founder. The report in 1895 says:

> The selling price for the year has been a gradually lowering one, not on account of competition, but on account of our own voluntary wish to encourage new customers for our very much larger output for aluminum which we intend to produce.

This price policy statement came in 1895 after the Company was on its feet, so to speak, and had a reasonable prospect of success. The years prior to that were fraught with struggle and oft-times with discouragement. In the early days the Smallman Street pilot plant was a very small affair. The men who went through those early struggles included Hall, the inventor, and, for a time, Romaine C. Cole, who had played an important role as a catalyst which speeded an economic action by bringing together the inventor and a group of venturesome young businessmen.

Cole did not continue to be a major factor in the actual manufacturing operations. At the Board meeting on December 12, 1888, Hall was named as superintendent of the experimental plant.[1] Cole was apparently not the type to team up with Hall in the task of trying to prove the commercial merit of the Hall invention. Despite this, Hall evidently appreciated the previous services Cole had rendered. In a letter to his sister Julia on December 9, 1888, the inventor said, "It is to be remembered, though, that things are probably in far better shape for me for my having known Cole."

While admitting Cole's value as an entrepreneur, Hall appar-

[1] Early minutes of The Pittsburgh Reduction Company.

ently could not work with him in the trying, oft-times discouraging task of attempting to make the process a business success. Hall did far better along this line with the young man "fresh from Amherst," Arthur V. Davis, who became his fellow worker in the late summer of 1888. Romaine Cole had helped to set up the contract whereby he and Hall were to receive 47 per cent of the stock if the venture succeeded. Cole was voted a Director for one year at the Board meeting on October 22, 1889, and he later made some proposals to the Company to act in a sales capacity even though he did largely dispose of his stock during the first several years of the Company's existence.

These early minutes do mention another young man who was to have a far-reaching influence on aluminum history, a man who is today recognized as a world-wide figure. He is Arthur V. Davis, the octogenarian Board Chairman of Aluminum Company of America. On March 27, 1889, the minutes record that Hall and Davis were put on the "day turn" at the plant and a Mr. Bonger was made night superintendent. Since the aluminum process is a continuous one, with the current flowing around the clock, through the molten cryolite and alumina, this made a twelve-hour shift for each crew.

Arthur V. Davis came to Pittsburgh in 1888, immediately after his graduation from Amherst College, and entered the employ of the Pittsburgh Testing Laboratory. He was twenty-one years old. His coming to Pittsburgh was an interesting circumstance. Capt. Hunt's parents had attended a Congregational church in Hyde Park, Massachusetts, of which The Rev. Perley B. Davis was pastor. When his son was graduated from Amherst, Pastor Davis asked his former parishioner, Capt. Hunt, to secure a position

35

for young Arthur Davis in Pittsburgh. Capt. Hunt could and did. Arthur V. Davis came to Pittsburgh and had scarcely arrived when the new aluminum venture was born. Messrs. Hunt and Clapp decided he was just the young fellow to team up with Hall in the little plant on Smallman Street.

The manufacturing difficulties of that era were well illustrated by Mr. Davis in his talk in Pittsburgh on October 14, 1948, when the Historical Society of Western Pennsylvania observed the sixtieth anniversary of the founding of The Pittsburgh Reduction Company with appropriate ceremonies at the site of the first plant. Mr. Davis said, "Capt. Hunt and Mr. Clapp ran the business from the downtown office, while at the plant the personnel consisted of Mr. Hall and myself, a day and a night engineer, and a man named Bonger [2] and a man named Mike.

"I remember one day when Bonger was doing something around the two furnaces or pots as we called them, and I asked him what he was doing and he said, 'I am taking a volt out of this pot and putting it into the other one.' It was with that high grade of engineering that we started our business. Mike probably was the worst employee that ever existed. He never showed up on Monday at all, but neither Mr. Hall nor I ever thought of firing him. Neither of us had ever hired a man nor had we fired one. We just thought that Mike was a cross fastened around our necks that we had to bear. Mike used to make our aluminum fluoride of so much alumina and so much hydrofluoric acid. One day I noticed that he was just pouring in the hydrofluoric acid

[2] There is some confusion regarding the name of this man. Company minutes give it as Bonger. Arthur V. Davis has referred to him on occasion as Bucher. Charles M. Hall in a letter to his sister, Julia, said: "His name was Brugher first, then it became Budger—we call him 'Bug' for short."

Pioneer plant of The Pittsburgh Reduction Company, built on a rented lot on Smallman Street in Pittsburgh. The first ingots of aluminum were stored in the office safe.

out of a large carboy without weighing it and asked him about it, and he said that he had discovered a formula that there was one pound to every gurgle so that each gurgle was a pound."

It was truly a pioneering project. The output of fifty pounds per day was not easy to achieve. Like all laboratory successes, the Hall process developed bugs when put into commercial operation. Pots would "smoke up" and all sorts of complications arise in the little factory located in the corrugated-iron building on Smallman Street. The electric current was none too certain and was frequently becoming "unbalanced" because of almost daily engine trouble. However, the manufacturing difficulties were exceeded only by the sales problems. The daily output went into the office safe. There were so few customers that this repository was running over with the metal, which Hall and Davis were beginning to believe was not so precious after all.[3]

And there were labor problems even in those days. The early minutes tell this story:

> Meeting, June 5, 1889—Mr. Scott found Bonger (the night superintendent) asleep behind the engine and was able to awaken him only after striking him four times with his umbrella. Mr. Scott offered a resolution which was unanimously adopted and which read as follows: "Resolved, that we take immediate steps to disinfect the disgraceful state of affairs and to procure a manager to look after the plant and improve the morals of the employees."

The founders displayed sound business judgment in the selection of legal counsel, as revealed by the corporation minutes for

[3] Dramatically portrayed in "Unfinished Rainbows."

December 18, 1889. The firm chosen was Dalzell, Scott & Gordon. They were to be paid a modest annual retainer fee, commonly called a salary in those days. John Dalzell was later to become a national figure in Congress. William Scott continued as an important advisor to the Company, while George B. Gordon, a great lawyer and a fine citizen, was to loom large in a legal advisory capacity to The Pittsburgh Reduction Company and its successor, Aluminum Company of America. It is interesting to note that Alcoa's present law firm, Smith, Buchanan, Ingersoll, Rodewalt & Eckert, is the lineal successor to the firm of Dalzell, Scott & Gordon. William Watson Smith, who has headed Alcoa's cause in its various brushes with Government, became a partner of George Gordon and inherited the role of chief legal advisor to the Company.

William Watson Smith, himself a great lawyer, considers his relationship as more than that of lawyer to client. Presenting Alcoa as a law-abiding citizen and as an asset to America is little short of a religion with him. At his side in these later years have been younger men—Frank B. Ingersoll, who has represented Alcoa on many occasions, and Iowa-born, Harvard-trained Leon E. Hickman, who has been outstanding in carrying on the traditional role of legal advisor to Alcoa, a role pioneered by George Gordon and W. W. Smith. Leon Hickman became a Vice President and a member of the Board of Directors of Alcoa early in 1951.

The early manufacturing problems during the Smallman Street days were largely the headaches of Charles M. Hall, the inventor, and his associate, Arthur V. Davis. Capt. Hunt busied himself with the corporate problems and with the task of trying to find customers for the new metal. A few early sales recorded on the books included thirty pounds to one man for "experimental purposes," three pounds to the Michigan Stove Company, and 250 pounds to the Carbon Iron Company. In fact, the bulk of the early output went to steel companies who used it to prevent "blow holes," the curse of the early steelmakers. Aluminum's great affinity for oxygen made it ideal for this purpose. A few handfuls of aluminum thrown into the hot steel in an open hearth would take up the oxygen and free the resulting ingot from blow holes.[4]

Arthur V. Davis was destined to be more than a plant operating man. A fine salesman himself, he early showed the marks of genius which have made him a great industrialist. He and Hall made a splendid team, the one a research man and inventor until his death, the other a business executive of the first water. Davis became a stockholder in the aluminum enterprise on March 11, 1891, when Capt. Hunt, Mr. Clapp and Mr. Hall each disposed of some shares to their young associate. George Clapp sold him 28 shares, Capt. Hunt 14 shares and Charles M. Hall 62 shares, a total of 104 shares. The three thus expressed their faith and confidence in the man whose name was to become almost synonymous with aluminum as that metal played its part in dramatic world events during the ensuing sixty-odd years.

The sale of stock to Arthur V. Davis was not for the purpose of getting another investor into the business. Mr. Davis did not have money in those days. The young company had to look elsewhere for this support. Fortunately, the small business was located in a city where there were bankers of vision. There are

[4] Early sales records of The Pittsburgh Reduction Company.

several stories covering the circumstances which caused Andrew W. Mellon and his brother, Richard B. Mellon, to become investors in and bankers for The Pittsburgh Reduction Company. Stock-book records show January 16, 1890, as the first date on which A. W. Mellon acquired stock in the company. He became the owner of sixty shares, acquiring them from Charles M. Hall and paying $6,000, or par, for them. Undoubtedly this was for the joint account of A. W. and R. B. Mellon because they were operating the banking business known as T. Mellon & Sons and the famous expression, "My brother and I," had already become an accepted fact.

The Mellons were first exposed to the aluminum-making operations in their capacity as bankers rather than as investors. The Pittsburgh Reduction Company needed $4,000 to meet an overdue note at another bank. Neither Capt. Hunt nor Mr. Clapp knew the Mellons at that time. Mr. Clapp said in later years that a friend to whom he related the desperate situation suggested the Mellon banking firm and offered to make introductions. A. W. Mellon gave courteous attention to their story without indicating a decision. He simply told them to come back the next day for an answer. That afternoon the two Mellon brothers personally inspected the operation at Smallman Street. When The Pittsburgh Reduction Company officers returned the next day, Andrew Mellon told them they needed considerably more than $4,000. A loan was granted by T. Mellon & Sons sufficient to pay off the Company's immediate indebtedness and to provide necessary working capital. Bankers made quick decisions in those days when they were convinced of the potential merits of a proposition.

On October 2, 1889, the pilot plant had demonstrated the

40

success of the Hall process to a sufficient degree to warrant the fruition of the "million-dollar" company the organizers had envisioned a year earlier. Capital stock was increased to 10,000 shares, Hall, the inventor, and Cole, his associate, receiving 47 per cent, or 4,700 shares. Of this amount, 3,525 shares went to Hall and 1,175 shares to Cole. Capt. Hunt and his associates in the pilot-plant pioneering group received a total of 2,500 shares. This left 2,800 shares to be sold for improvements and expansions.[5]

Each stockholder had proportionate stock rights for a limited period, but if he was unable to take up his quota promptly the stock was then to be sold as the directors saw fit. Needless to say, the young men of The Pittsburgh Reduction Company and the young man from Oberlin who had invented a valuable process for making aluminum were short on one commodity—money. Doubtless the individuals in the company were just as hard up as was the company itself. It is small wonder that outside capital was eagerly sought to provide the $280,000 represented by the 2,800 shares in the treasury.

In 1891 David L. Gillespie, a substantial Pittsburgh businessman who was engaged in the lumber business, came in with a sizable purchase of stock. He is virtually one of the pioneers because of his faith in the project in those early days and his continuing investment for many years. Other early investors were Thomas L. Shields, whose father had been a woolen goods manufacturer, E. M. Ferguson, a partner of H. C. Frick in the coke business, and T. Chalmers Darsie, also in the coke business.

[5] Exhibit 1004, Alcoa anti-trust case, Agreement between Charles M. Hall, Romaine C. Cole and The Pittsburgh Reduction Company.

The Pittsburgh scene in the early Nineties furnishes us a background for the new industrial enterprise just getting underway. Pittsburgh was quite a place even in those days. A humorous editor pointed out in 1899 that his city was one of reformed habits "in that she has quit smoking." He added, however, "She still retains her bustle." Why he assumed that the smoke nuisance, now greatly removed, was lessened in those days, is hard to imagine, but the bustle was certainly there. On that date an average of 2,000 loaded freight cars entered and 1,000 departed from the city every day. The railroad and river tonnage was annually averaging 40,000,000 tons.[6] The city in 1891–92 had 20 blast furnaces with a yearly capacity of 1,000,000 tons of pig iron; 64 iron and steel mills making 1,500,000 tons yearly; 56 glass works; 20 natural-gas companies; 60 oil refineries, and 70 companies producing coal and coke.[7]

By mid-1890 money was badly needed to enlarge the aluminum works. Added equipment was placed in operation in September of that year and a daily production achieved of about 475 pounds of metal. Already it had become apparent that the Smallman Street plant was inadequate. Operations were discontinued there in March, 1891, and the business was removed to a new plant which the company had partially completed at Kensington, Pennsylvania, a place about nineteen miles from Pittsburgh on the Allegheny River. It was promptly renamed New Kensington because of confusion with a Kensington near Philadelphia.

Here again the Mellons came into the aluminum situation as

---

[6] *Pittsburgh and the Pittsburgh Spirit*, Pittsburgh Chamber of Commerce, 1928.
[7] King's *Handbook of the United States*, 1891–92.

bankers and later as investors. The Burrell Improvement Company, a real estate firm in which T. Mellon & Sons had some interest, was trying to arouse home builders over the advantages of some land it owned at a wide bend in the Allegheny River at this town of Kensington, or New Kensington. It made an offer to The Pittsburgh Reduction Company of four acres of level land on the river bank, free of charge, and the offer included a $10,000 cash bonus if the company would locate there. Again the aluminum pioneers went to the bank and borrowed the $7,000 needed to make this move.

On its net worth and its profit and loss statement, the Company was not entitled to this loan. The year ending August 31, 1890, had shown a loss of $637 and the Company was even behind in its rent on Smallman Street. However, for bankers who had faith in the venture and in the men behind it, the loan was a sound one. It enabled the Company to increase its capacity to 1,000 pounds of metal per day.

The Mellons have been among the principal bankers for Alcoa since the earliest days. It has been a mutually profitable connection of which Alcoa has always been proud. Andrew W. Mellon and his brother, Richard B. Mellon, had faith in the men as well as in the process and its possibilities. They believed in Capt. Hunt, George Clapp and their associates. They had admiration and respect for the genius of Arthur V. Davis and they were willing to stake their dollars on the integrity and ability of both Mr. Davis and Roy A. Hunt, son of Capt. Alfred E. Hunt. From 1928 until 1951, Roy Hunt was President of Aluminum Company of America and is now Chairman of the Executive Committee. Messrs. Davis and Hunt have been on the Board of

Directors of the Mellon National Bank & Trust Company for many years.

As investors, the Mellons always believed in the future of aluminum and in the ability of the Alcoa men who have made aluminum history. Although Andrew Mellon's appointment as Secretary of the Treasury and his consequent involvement in politics brought frequent charges that Alcoa was "Mellon-dominated" or "Mellon-controlled," the facts do not support this claim. By May, 1894, stock records showed that the Mellon brothers had 1,235 shares out of a total of 10,000. Later they acquired more stock, notably in 1917 when they secured 1,438 shares from David L. Gillespie. By 1920 the Mellon stock ownership had become about one third of the total and the Mellon family holdings have remained fairly constant at that percentage ever since.

The holdings of the Mellons on July 29, 1925, amounted to 35.22 per cent of the preferred and 35.22 per cent of the common. That was an important date because it was then that Alcoa common stock was reduced from $100 per share to $5 par value per share, and there were then authorized $150,000,000 of 6 per cent cumulative preferred with a par value of $100 per share, and 1,500,000 shares of common at $5 per share. Each old share of $100 stock received seven shares of the new 6 per cent cumulative preferred and six shares of the new common. Actually only half of the new preferred was issued, the balance being in the form of warrants for the preferred. The new $5-per-share common was changed to no par stock in November, 1925. While there had been prior stock dividends, this was the largest corporate reorganization in the Company's history. It gave rise later to politically inspired charges that the Mellons had made millions out of aluminum without much investment on their part. The facts are that they pioneered with their cash and took the same venture capital risk that the management group was taking.

The one-third ownership of stock has never meant Mellon control. If Alcoa stock had ever been widely scattered, it might have. The records show that the actual managers of the business also made a practice of acquiring and holding on to stock. Mr. Davis, the Hunt family, Mr. Clapp and others conceivably could have mustered enough stock ownership to outvote the Mellon holdings had there ever been a conflict of interest. However, it is scarcely conceivable that either A. W. or R. B. Mellon, sound bankers and wise investors, would have wanted to interfere with the policies of a dynamic, successful operator like Arthur V. Davis, who became the guiding genius of Alcoa upon Capt. Hunt's death in 1899. "I have depended entirely on Mr. Davis. You might say that he was practically the whole business," said Mr. Mellon on one occasion.[8]

In 1934 Andrew W. Mellon was being subjected to what his friends have considered political persecution, through the attempt of the Roosevelt administration to collect millions in alleged delinquent taxes and to sustain a charge of fraud against the taxpayer. In a letter to Attorney General Homer Cummings on March 11, 1934, Mr. Mellon indicated resentment at the Mellon-controlled charge in connection with Alcoa. In this letter, among many other things, he said, "In his statement asking for an indictment against me in connection with my tax affairs, the Attorney General has made quite irrelevant references to the Alumi-

[8] Deposition of A. W. Mellon in case of Haskell vs. Perkins et al, 1925.

45

num Company of America as a 'Mellon-controlled corporation' which is a '100 per cent monopoly in the producing field.' What this has to do with my income taxes is not apparent, but in any event, I and all the members of my family own less than a majority of the stock in the company, and certainly, the Aluminum Company, whether or not it is a '100 per cent monopoly in the producing field,' is not violating the federal laws in this respect." In conversations with this writer, Mr. Mellon went further into this charge and stated that he had always had the utmost faith in the integrity and ability of the men who guided the affairs of Alcoa. Had he not had such faith, he would have long since sold his stock, he said.

Happily for Mr. Mellon's family and for his place in history, the fifteen members of the Board of Tax Appeals voted unanimously that he had not filed a false or fraudulent tax return. They likewise failed to support the many Government charges or the innuendoes which had crept into the tax hearing. Unhappily for the peace of mind of the ex-Secretary of the Treasury, this exoneration came in a report filed three months after Mr. Mellon's death.

The Mellons kept a close eye on the aluminum project in the early days, but were always willing to see the earnings plowed back into the business. The pioneers were careful to keep their banker-investors posted. Among some yellowed papers in an old file is an interesting "draft" of a letter to A. W. Mellon to be signed by Capt. Hunt. The draft is in the handwriting of Arthur V. Davis and is dated February 9, 1897. Among other things, it says, "The cash statement of January 1, 1897, showed an excess of available assets over real liabilities of $2,014.69. In the ready assets are $70,000 worth of bonds unsold and $142,521.69 worth of metal in store."· The letter closes with some comments on current production and some predictions on probable earnings for the year just starting. Output on that date was 8,000 pounds per day. With increased production and with metal selling at $.30 per pound, the operators of the business thought they could see a profit in excess of $200,000 for the year.

Arthur V. Davis became the general manager in the Nineties and was Capt. Hunt's right-hand man. He was concerned, as were the other officers, in meeting payrolls. At times he and others borrowed money from the bank for this purpose and personally endorsed The Pittsburgh Reduction Company notes. Letters written by Mr. Hall as late as 1903 show that this practice continued at times even to that date. On December 20, 1895, a $200,000 issue of 6 per cent bonds helped the current finances. These were payable, $50,000 on February 1, 1899, $50,000 February 1, 1900, and $100,000 February 1, 1901. However, $75,000 of the proceeds were so badly needed that the Company could not wait for the bonds to be engraved. A temporary loan of $75,000 was secured from T. Mellon & Sons.

Andrew W. Mellon was never an officer in the aluminum-making company except for a brief period in 1892 when he served as Treasurer upon the resignation of George H. Clapp, who gave up the job because of the pressure of other duties. Mr. Mellon served without salary. Shortly thereafter, Charles M. Corbett became Treasurer. On September 15, 1898, Col. Robert E. Withers, Chief Clerk for The Pittsburgh Reduction Company, was named Treasurer, an office he held in the Alcoa organization until his retirement in 1948. Col. Withers, a Senior Vice Presi-

47

dent when he retired, is still a member of the Alcoa Board of Directors.

When Capt. Hunt's life was cut short in 1899, the stockholders apparently felt that Arthur V. Davis was too young to be elevated to the position of President. Richard B. Mellon, known as R. B. and the father of Richard King Mellon, present active head of the Mellon clan, was named to that position. Mr. Mellon had succeeded Horace W. Lash on the Board of Directors on September 19, 1895. Although concerned at the time with banking and other matters, R. B. Mellon took an enthusiastic interest in the aluminum enterprise and made many helpful suggestions to the active management of the Company. He served as President until February 17, 1910, when he was succeeded by Arthur V. Davis, who had been the active manager of the business for the preceding decade.

In fact, it was to Mr. Davis that young Roy A. Hunt applied for a summer job in 1902 prior to his graduation from Yale the next spring. This was history repeating itself in reverse since Arthur Davis had secured a job from Roy Hunt's father fourteen years earlier. On May 25, 1902, Roy A. Hunt wrote Arthur V. Davis as follows:

> As it is drawing toward the close of the college year and we talked over my trying to work this summer if I could get the job, I write to inquire if anything has turned up. It does not matter what it is from digging a hole to emptying paper baskets. Also the location is immaterial from the suburbs of the smallest hamlet in Canada to the center of a city.

Roy Hunt got a job at the New Kensington works that summer and began a lifetime career with Alcoa.

The Mellons did much more for the cause of aluminum than to express their faith, in dollars, in the little Pittsburgh company before the turn of the century. Members of the Mellon family continued to give evidence of this faith by remaining as substantial stockholders in Aluminum Company of America to this day. As they did in coal, steel, electricity, oil and transportation, the Mellon brothers, A. W. and R. B., contributed sound business judgment and a keen understanding of the basic importance and the great potentialities of the business. They were builders of industry and capable businessmen.

William Watson Smith, chief legal counsel for Alcoa, tells of a remark his late partner, George Gordon, once made to him. Mr. Gordon said that, in his extensive experience as a corporation attorney, there were only two men to whom he could submit a long and complicated contract or brief and then see the individual, after one quick reading, put an unerring finger on the essential points in the document, while at the same time discovering its weaknesses. These two men were Andrew W. Mellon, the banker, and Arthur V. Davis, genius of the aluminum industry.

CHAPTER FOUR

Early Patent Problems

☆ ☆ ☆ ☆ ☆ ☆ ☆ ☆ ☆

THE FRAMERS of the Constitution of the United States aimed to promote enterprise in America, for they gave Congress the power "to promote the progress of science and useful arts, by securing for limited times to authors and inventors the exclusive right to their respective writings and discoveries." Invested with this power, Congress established the United States patent system, which has been a vital factor in the growth of the Nation and a boon to inventors.

Hall could qualify as a "storybook" inventor, for he was both young and poor, and cherished great dreams. Once sure of his invention, he promptly sought the protection of a United States patent by filing an application on July 9, 1886. The first hazard was encountered in the Patent Office when an interference with the application of Héroult was declared. Hall won this round when he established his date of invention as February 23, 1886, and was awarded priority over Héroult. After the customary arguments with the Patent Office, he was issued a basic patent on April 2, 1889.[1] Theoretically, Hall and The Pittsburgh Reduction Company were then in a position to enjoy the seventeen-year exclusive use of their process guaranteed by law as a reward for disclosing the invention to the public. As too often happens, however, they had to fight for their rights.

Not all of the Company's early difficulties were confined to manufacturing and financing problems. The Pittsburgh Reduction Company, corporate name of Alcoa until 1907, was involved in patent litigation which threatened the very existence of the business and required much time and attention of the pioneering executives.

It will be recalled that Charles Martin Hall went to Pittsburgh in 1888 after an unsatisfactory attempt to interest the Cowles Electric Smelting & Aluminum Company in his process. The Cowles Company had expressed interest and had invited Hall to come to Lockport, New York. Cowles was having some success at the time in making aluminum alloys by an electrothermal process.[2] Only alloys could be produced, the most valuable being an "aluminum bronze" with 10 to 20 per cent of aluminum in it. After a time, the Cowles people told Hall they were no longer interested in his process. Hall left with a quite understandable feeling that the Cowles interest had stemmed from a desire on their part to protect their own process rather than to develop Hall's invention.

The success of the Hall process in the small plant of The Pitts-

[1] U. S. Patent 400,766, issued April 2, 1889.
[2] U. S. Patent 324,658, August 18, 1885.

burgh Reduction Company made it impossible for the Cowles Company to sell aluminum alloys made by their electrothermal method in competition with those made by alloying the pure aluminum from the Hall electrolytic pots. As a consequence, Cowles calmly appropriated the Hall process and started making pure aluminum in January, 1891. The Pittsburgh Reduction Company immediately started suit for infringement. A decision in the case by Judge William Howard Taft in 1893 upheld the validity of the Hall patent and ruled that the Cowles Company had infringed.

The decision, however, was not the end of patent litigation for the new Company. In 1883, three years before Hall had made his first aluminum, Charles S. Bradley had filed a patent application with very broad claims. Briefly, the Bradley idea was one of fusing "ores" by the use of an electric arc, then passing an electric current through the molten mass to decompose it and maintain it in a fused condition. The Patent Office rejected his original application on the basis of "prior art" as described in the writings of Sir Humphry Davy early in the Nineteenth Century. Finally, after six years, Bradley limited his broad claims to an extent which satisfied the Patent Office, and patents were issued to him on December 8, 1891, and on February 2, 1892.

Bradley had made an agreement in 1885 with the Cowles Company to assign to them any invention which would "interfere" with the Cowles process. When the Bradley patents were issued, the Cowles Company promptly laid claim to them under this agreement. The Courts eventually upheld this claim and, as soon as legal possession of the patents was obtained, the Cowles Company, now reincorporated as the Electric Smelting & Refining Company, promptly started suit for infringement against The Pittsburgh Reduction Company.

The Cowles contention was that The Pittsburgh Reduction Company could not use an electric current for both heating and electrolysis. Hall had originally heated his mixture of alumina and cryolite externally but had soon found, as he had hoped, that the electric current which separated the aluminum from the oxygen in its molten bath of cryolite would also provide the necessary heat for melting. The external heat was outmoded and costly but the Pittsburgh concern could have returned to this method and the Cowles Company would have had no case at law.[3]

However, there was no way to make the electric current stop its heating action while it was engaged in electrolysis. After much legal argument, a three-judge Court held, on October 20, 1903, that the Bradley patents had been infringed by The Pittsburgh Reduction Company. The decision created an impasse in aluminum manufacture in this country. The Pittsburgh Reduction Company could not produce aluminum by electrolysis on a commercial scale without infringing the Bradley patents. The Cowles people, holders of the Bradley patents, had already been enjoined from making aluminum by the Hall electrolytic process which separated aluminum from oxygen in a fused bath of cryolite.

A comment in a technical publication[4] on this decree by Judges Wallace, Lacombe and Coxe ended a long quotation from the decision itself with this statement:

[3] The story of the Cowles Company in its dealings with Hall and The Pittsburgh Reduction Company, including controversy over patents, is told in some detail in *The Aluminum Industry*, McGraw-Hill, 1930.
[4] *Engineering News*, November 1, 1903.

It will be noted that the above decision does not affect the validity of the Hall patent for the use of cryolite as a solvent for alumina. On the contrary, it more firmly establishes it. Nor can there be any doubt that it was the Hall invention whose successful exploitation made aluminum a commercial metal. The situation is simply one which constantly recurs in the history of inventions, in which an inventor whose work reaches commercial success finds that he must settle with the owner of some earlier pioneer patent whose claims are entitled to a broad construction.

As a consequence of this 1903 decision, the exercise of good business judgment indicated the necessity of some kind of a settlement if either of the two companies was to continue in business. The Pittsburgh Reduction Company and the Electric Smelting & Refining Company effected a settlement shortly thereafter whereby The Pittsburgh Reduction Company received a license to use the Bradley patents until they expired in 1909. This date happened to be three years later than the legal limit of the basic Hall patent which expired in 1906. The license to The Pittsburgh Reduction Company was one permitting it to manufacture aluminum by the Hall process in a "fused bath" created by heat from electricity. The Cowles Company received a small royalty for all aluminum made by The Pittsburgh Reduction Company during the remaining life of the patents, but more important to it was a commitment from The Pittsburgh Reduction Company for 146,000 pounds of aluminum annually during the life of the license at 10 per cent below list price.

The Cowles Company was thus assured of the pure aluminum

it needed for its alloying purposes. Since the Cowles concern was barred from making metallic aluminum and The Pittsburgh Reduction Company would have been seriously handicapped if prevented from using electricity for heat as well as for electrolysis, the agreement seems to have been one of mutual benefit.

In those early years there were other patent problems to plague The Pittsburgh Reduction Company. It will be recalled that at about the same time Charles Martin Hall was making his epochal invention in the woodshed laboratory at Oberlin, Ohio, another twenty-two-year-old lad, Paul L. T. Héroult, was making a similar discovery in France. As previously explained, Héroult failed to grasp quickly the commercial significance of the alumina-cryolite electrolytic process for making metallic aluminum. He spent the next few years following his discovery in pushing another process he had for making aluminum alloys. Héroult took out United States patents on his alloy-making process on August 14, 1888. Grosvenor P. Lowrey, an early associate of Thomas A. Edison, became interested in the Héroult alloy patents with the idea of making these alloys competitive in this country with the products of The Pittsburgh Reduction Company or with the output of anyone else who might engage in some form of aluminum manufacturing.

Lowrey was well acquainted with Héroult, who had made a trip to the United States in 1889 with the intention of starting operation of his alloy process. Experimental work at Bridgeport, Connecticut, on the part of Héroult did not prove successful, but Lowrey continued his interest in the possibility. He became the agent for Bradley and groomed the Bradley patent application, as yet unissued, for an assault on the Hall process. He visited The

Pittsburgh Reduction Company plant in Pittsburgh and observed the working of the alumina-cryolite process. He was the motivating force in the erection of an experimenal plant at Boonton, New Jersey. Under the name of the U. S. Aluminum Metals Company, Lowrey undertook to work the Héroult alloy process at this location.

About this time, the Cowles Company stepped into the picture and took possession of the Bradley patent under their prior agreement.[5] The Cowles people filed the already discussed lawsuit, charging The Pittsburgh Reduction Company with infringement of the Bradley patents. Since the decision in this suit resulted in the Cowles Company and The Pittsburgh Reduction Company making a mutually beneficial contract between themselves, Lowrey's dream of supplanting the Hall process with Héroult aluminum alloys came to an end. The activities of Lowrey, although a considerable headache for The Pittsburgh Reduction Company, were doubtless within the proper realm of competitive business. Lowrey was trying to cash in on some patents. The Pittsburgh Reduction Company was doing a similar thing in its efforts to build an industry based on the Hall patents.

In fact, Capt. Hunt made a trip to Europe in 1889 for the express purpose of trying to raise some badly needed money for The Pittsburgh Reduction Company through the sale, for use in England, of some of the patents granted to Hall in that country. Capt. Hunt hoped to find Britishers whom he might interest in aluminum manufacture by the Hall process. He did not have much luck. One large concern told him that they had consulted

[5] A more technical discussion of the Bradley patent will be found in *The Aluminum Industry*, McGraw-Hill, 1930.

eminent metallurgical experts who said that "a single ton of aluminum, once made, would be sufficient to supply the whole world for a year." [6]

The Pittsburgh Reduction Company ran into plenty of patent trouble with the British a bit later. The British Aluminium Company, Ltd., organized in 1894, apparently undertook to corner the United Kingdom market in aluminum the following year. In July 1895, it issued a circular reading, in part, as follows:

> Having purchased Cowles', Héroult's and other (including Neuhausen) patents for the manufacture of pure aluminium by electric and electrolytic processes, we have the sole right to the manufacture and sale of aluminium made in such a fashion within the United Kingdom.
>
> Anyone using aluminium made by the electric and electrolytic processes and not bearing the trademark of British Aluminium Company will be restrained by injunction. [7]

The British Aluminium Company, Ltd., immediately started after the American company which was making sales to Aluminium Supply Company, Ltd., of London. Faced with the probability of having to back out of the British market, The Pittsburgh Reduction Company took the matter seriously and the problem was one of considerable worry and much correspondence until April, 1897. On that date, W. S. Sample, one of the original incorporators of The Pittsburgh Reduction Company, who had moved to England to handle the sales of Aluminium

[6] Letter from Clarke Freeman to Roy A. Hunt, March 1, 1949, re trip abroad of Freeman's father and Capt. Hunt in 1889.
[7] Also printed in *The Ironmonger*, September 14, 1895.

Supply Company, Ltd., found a solution. If the Pittsburgh company would accept a firm order from him for 500 tons of aluminum to be delivered over a period of two years at a price of one shilling per pound, and would name him exclusive agent in the United Kingdom, he would see to it that British Aluminium called off its dogs.[8] To stay in the British market, The Pittsburgh Reduction Company accepted this low price proposition and the controversy was apparently settled.

The acceptance and success of the patent system in the United States is measured to some degree by the number of patents which have been issued. In 1950, the number passed the two-and-one-half-million mark. In 1940, the Patent Office celebrated the one hundred and fiftieth anniversary of the founding of the American patent system. On that occasion, seventy-five industrialists, scientists and statesmen were asked to select what, in their opinion, were the greatest American inventions patented in the United States. This is the list: cotton gin (Whitney); commercial steamboat (Fulton); reaper (McCormick); telegraph (Morse); vulcanization of rubber (Goodyear); sewing machine (Howe); typewriter (Sholes); air brake (Westinghouse); telephone (Bell); phonograph and motion-picture projector (Edison); induction motor (Tesla); production of aluminum (Charles Martin Hall); linotype (Mergenthaler); airplane (Orville and Wilbur Wright); three-electrode vacuum tube (De Forest); thermo-setting plastics, Bakelite (Baekeland); oil cracking (Burton).

Charles Martin Hall stands here among a group of illustrious inventors. The nation is indeed indebted to Hall for the contribu-

[8] Correspondence with The Pittsburgh Reduction Company now in Alcoa archives.

tion he made to its economy—a contribution the importance of which has grown with the years. It is interesting to contemplate the modest role aluminum would have played in our economy in either peace or war had no discovery been made in 1886 of an inexpensive way to separate aluminum from its ores. Even today, with our modern knowledge regarding the production of metallic sodium and aluminum chloride, it would be difficult to produce aluminum by the Sainte-Claire Deville process at a cost below fifty cents per pound.

Hall is likewise indebted to the American patent system for protecting his right to his invention. Under the patent law, The Pittsburgh Reduction Company—the owner of the patent—was given for a term of seventeen years, the "exclusive right to make, use and vend the invention." These were important rights, vital to the young business. The pioneers would never have ventured their $20,000 of capital for a pilot plant without the virtual certainty that the Hall patent, already applied for, would be issued in due course. The patent was granted, and the period until it expired gave The Pittsburgh Reduction Company a good opportunity to develop the process commercially and become established in the manufacture of aluminum.

CHAPTER FIVE

Bauxite

☆ ☆ ☆ ☆ ☆ ☆ ☆ ☆

T HE FOUNDERS of the Company were little concerned
with the rock or ore from which aluminum is extracted,
an ore usually referred to as bauxite. They *were* interested in an adequate supply of aluminum oxide (alumina), the
white powdery substance wrested from the aluminum ore by a
chemical process. For the first fourteen years of its history, The
Pittsburgh Reduction Company secured alumina from people who
were making it for various uses. Most of the purchases were
made from the Pennsylvania Salt Manufacturing Company. Some
of the earlier alumina came from Europe. Trial orders of one ton
each were ordered from a German and from an English firm,
according to the minutes of a Board meeting on October 30,
1889. In those days alumina had numerous uses in the chemical
and abrasive fields, just as it has today. The Pittsburgh Reduction Company was the only one using it directly as a source of
metallic aluminum, as a result of the important invention of
Charles M. Hall.

Capt. Hunt became very much interested in bauxite in 1897. On June 7th of that year he wrote to Charles M. Hall at the Niagara Falls works:

> If it be true, as I understand from you, that we can make as much aluminum per unit of horsepower from bauxite (of which we can obtain large quantities) as from pure alumina, then it would seem that this is the field which is now ripest for us to investigate for increasing the economy of manufacturing.

Capt. Hunt was interested in a proposal to calcine and grind high-grade bauxite and feed it directly into the electrolytic pots. This would produce a low-grade aluminum alloy from which the impurities would have to be removed. In the same letter he said, "If we can find a process by which we can purify the bauxite-made aluminum from its content of silicon, iron and titanium, there is in this the largest field for our decreasing cost for manufacturing aluminum now existing." No satisfactory method was found to remove these impurities and thus utilize the impure alumina of the calcined bauxite instead of the refined alumina the Company was purchasing. Capt. Hunt's interest can be easily understood. One half of the cost of manufacture at that time was the price paid for alumina.

Long before the Company was founded, it was an accepted fact that aluminum was one of the most plentiful metallic elements in the surface of the earth. The geochemists now estimate that it constitutes one twelfth of the solid portion of the earth to a depth of ten miles.[1] This aluminum is combined, of course, with

[1] "The Data of Geochemistry," F. W. Clarke, *Bulletin 695*, U. S. Geological Survey, 1920.

oxygen and other elements, but if it was all present as oxide (alumina), calculation shows it would amount to about 15 per cent by weight of the earth's crust. Much of this combined aluminum is found associated with silica, the oxide of silicon. Everyone is familiar, of course, with the earthy form of aluminum silicate known as clay. When Hall was experimenting to find a cheaper way of getting metallic aluminum from the oxide, he had already been intrigued by the statement of Prof. Jewett, his college teacher, that aluminum is here in abundance. The expression, "every clay bank is an aluminum mine," was common among people who talked aluminum. Up to the present time, however, bauxite has been a more economical source of aluminum than clay.

An indication of interest in aluminum-bearing ores, as well as considerable ignorance about them thirty years before Hall made his discovery of an inexpensive way to separate the metal, is found in an article in the *National Magazine* published in April, 1857. This publication, a predecessor of *Popular Science*, had a hopeful piece entitled "The New Metal, Aluminum." After bemoaning the fact that aluminum was so difficult to extract from its ores, the writer said:

The preparation of a metal begins with the finding of the ore; that of aluminum is abundant, and easily accessible. It is found in all varieties of clay, potter's clay, fire clay, and common blue clay, and even in old bricks and broken crockery! In combination with oxygen, this metal forms the earth alumina, which has been known more than a century, as constituting an essential ingredient of all clays. The other

63

constituents of clay are silica, (powdered flint), lime, and oxyd of iron, the latter giving to bricks their fine red color. Alumina is also found in alum, a substance which has been long known and used for important purposes, and which has the honor of giving name to the metal and its compounds.

The pioneers of The Pittsburgh Reduction Company were not too much concerned in the early days about producing their own supply of aluminum oxide, regardless of the ore from which it came. The Pennsylvania Salt Company seemed to have plenty of alumina to meet the needs of the little aluminum-making concern. Two pounds of alumina are needed to make one pound of aluminum, and cryolite, coke, tar and pitch in addition to alumina are required before metallic aluminum is produced. This still leaves the necessity of using other things—electricity, fuel, transportation, labor, skill, money. The Pittsburgh Reduction Company had plenty to think about in those early days other than the problem of an adequate supply of alumina.

However, the matter of ample ore reserves was to become an important one as the Company grew. Little did it realize in the Nineties that, between 1904, about the time it started making its own alumina from ores, and the year 1939, the beginning of World War II, the world production of bauxite would total 46,000,000 tons, most of it mined to obtain alumina for use in smelting metallic aluminum.[2] This bauxite output was, of course, world production, France being the leading producer with 13,000,000 tons. Finding ample bauxite reserves had not proved

[2] U. S. Geological Survey—Mineral Resources, 1904–1923.
  U. S. Bureau of Mines—Mineral Resources, 1924–1931.
  U. S. Bureau of Mines—Minerals Yearbook, 1931–1948.

Interior of the Smallman Street plant showing America's first pot line for making aluminum. Production averaged fifty pounds per day—on good days.

too difficult because the material is scattered generously around the earth. The main producing countries have been France, the United States, Hungary, Italy, Suriname (Dutch Guiana), British Guiana, Jugoslavia, Russia, Dutch East Indies and Greece.

No bauxite was mined in the United States in 1888, the year The Pittsburgh Reduction Company was started. The Merrimac Chemical Company, which used the ore to obtain aluminum salts for various purposes, was importing its bauxite from Ireland. It was a very poor grade of ore. Later, Merrimac purchased bauxite in this country but continued to import largely from France, where it could get the ore at a cheaper price.[3]

Perhaps we should take time at this point to tell something of what bauxite really is as well as to outline briefly its history. In 1821, P. Berthier, a French chemist, analyzed a hard, reddish, claylike material found near the village of Les Baux in Provence, France. His analysis showed 52 per cent alumina, 28 per cent iron oxide, and 20 per cent chemically combined water. Berthier called the new material "beauxite" after the name of the village, but he was confused over the spelling. Sainte-Claire Deville realized the error and changed it to "bauxite" in his publication of 1858. The village, in turn, had taken its name from a near-by castle which stood on a rocky escarpment. So, the word bauxite likely derived from the word "baux" which comes from the Latin "baussum," meaning a precipice. The early bauxite produced at Les Baux was used in aluminum sulfate manufacture.[4]

[3] *Charting My Life*, Henry Howard, The Merrymount Press, Boston, 1948.
[4] This information as well as other facts in this chapter about the history, occurrence, characteristics, and mining of bauxite will be found in more detail in the article, "Bauxite," by Lawrence Litchfield, Jr., *Chemical Industries*, February and March, 1941.

In 1883 a somewhat similar material was found at Hermitage, near Rome, Georgia. It was called bauxite, despite the fact that its composition was different from the French ore. American production began in Georgia in 1889, a significant date which makes the commercial history of American bauxite coincide with the beginning of the aluminum industry in this country.

Today the name bauxite is applied generally to those ores of aluminum which are composed essentially of aluminum oxide chemically combined with water. Bauxite also contains, as impurities, smaller amounts of the oxides of iron, silicon and titanium. To the chemist, this chemical combination of alumina and water is variously known as alumina hydrate or aluminum hydroxide. To the mineralogist, there are two forms of alumina hydrate important in bauxite: these are called boehmite (alumina monohydrate) and gibbsite (alumina trihydrate). The second of these minerals is the important constituent of American bauxite. Certain forms of bauxite contain both minerals. To the geologist, bauxite is the product of the decomposition of aluminum silicate rocks by weathering and is most readily formed under tropical or subtropical conditions. It is significant, therefore, that the most extensive deposits of bauxite are found in regions on both sides of the equator, extending up into lands with temperate climates.

Anyone going into the aluminum business today can find bauxite. R. J. Reynolds, Jr., President of Reynolds Metals Company, gave testimony recently that his company's Jamaican bauxite reserves had already been proved to the extent of a forty years' supply. He expressed confidence that reserves in Jamaica yet to be explored would disclose an additional forty years' supply. Mr. Reynolds, an Alcoa competitor, was a witness before Judge Knox in the United States District Court for the Southern District of New York in 1949 in an action to determine whether or not effective competition now exists in the aluminum industry. D. A. Rhodes, Vice President of the Kaiser Aluminum & Chemical Company, another competitor, said his company's reserves in Jamaica were very great.

Aluminium, Ltd., a Canadian company, is preparing to mine Jamaican bauxite in a substantial manner, yet Jamaica has only recently been added to the countries which are known bauxite producers. Jamaican bauxite is 1,100 miles from the United States, whereas Alcoa's principal bauxite reserves outside this country are in Suriname, 2,500 miles distant. In addition to the bauxite in the Guianas and in Europe now being used for aluminum manufacture, further large deposits are being readied for use in the East Indies, Africa and South America. Aluminium, Ltd., is getting substantial quantities of ore from the Los Islands, off the coast of French Guinea, and is investigating deposits on the near-by mainland of that country.

In 1887, bauxite had been found in Arkansas near Little Rock by the State Geologist, John G. Branner. Previously it had been found in Georgia and in northeastern Alabama. Bauxite has been discovered in seven States but the Arkansas deposits have proven to be the most important commercially. Here, in two Arkansas counties, lies the bulk of the known deposits of United States bauxite. For the past sixty years these deposits have been furnishing bauxite, much of it for processing into alumina for the manufacture of metallic aluminum.

Some of the aluminum pioneers had their start in the business through bauxite operations. George R. Gibbons, Senior Vice

President of Alcoa who retired in 1948 and whose death occurred in 1950, was a nationally known industrialist who came into the business via the bauxite channel. Born in Bartow County, Georgia, the son of John R. Gibbons of Virginia and Annie Felton Gibbons of Georgia, he became associated with the aluminum industry in his youth. John R. Gibbons became identified with the aluminum business in its early days when The Pittsburgh Reduction Company bought into and finally acquired full ownership of the Georgia Bauxite and Mining Company.

A close friendship and respect existed between Capt. Hunt and John R. Gibbons. A letter marked "private and personal" written by Capt. Hunt in longhand on March 1, 1898, to his friend in the South, has recently come to light. In this letter John R. Gibbons was invited to join Capt. Hunt's staff in the Spanish-American War mobilization as a noncommissioned officer should Mr. Gibbons feel free to do so. Capt. Hunt said, "I know you would be one of the men I could depend upon with a knowledge of 'how to do things.' " Mr. Gibbons was superintendent of the Company's Arkansas bauxite mining projects. His son, George R. Gibbons, came to Pittsburgh as a young man. Over the years he was to become the trusted and efficient assistant to Arthur V. Davis. Later he became Secretary of the Company, then a Vice President, and still later a Senior Vice President.

The Pittsburgh Reduction Company and its successor, Alcoa, have been pioneers in developing these Arkansas bauxite mines for alumina production for the manufacture of aluminum. Shortly after 1903 the Company started to make its own alumina from bauxite at East St. Louis and began serious mining operations in Arkansas. It found existing concerns in the South already mining bauxite for abrasives and other products. The Company's entrance into the bauxite mining business was largely through the purchase of bauxite holdings of these existing concerns. In 1904 it purchased from the General Chemical Company a mining subsidiary known as the General Bauxite Company, thereby securing 7,500 acres in fee simple and the mineral rights to an additional 7,500 acres. In 1909 it purchased the Republic Mining & Manufacturing Company from the Norton Company and thereby secured the services of Winthrop C. Neilson. Mr. Neilson was a seasoned mine operator of various minerals including iron ore. He had become interested in bauxite mining and had extended his operations from Georgia into Arkansas. Winthrop C. Neilson became a Vice President of Alcoa and had charge of its bauxite mining operations until his death in 1938.

As to The Pittsburgh Reduction Company's entrance into mining and ore-refining operations after fourteen years of buying ready-made alumina on the market, some explanation of what it was getting into is in order. Mining the ore, either from deep mines or by stripping on the surface, is only the beginning in the task of extracting alumina, a white powdery substance which looks somewhat like fine sugar. A chemical refining process is necessary to produce alumina of the quality required for the production of aluminum.

In the production of alumina from bauxite, the best-known name is that of Karl Josef Bayer. He was first granted patents in Germany for his process for producing refined alumina. A United States patent was issued to Bayer in 1894, and a plant was built in Woburn, Massachusetts. The Merrimac Chemical Company had a license in this country under the Bayer Patent, which expired in 1911. Since then anyone has been able to use the Bayer process. In 1900, Alcoa had difficulty in purchasing its full requirement of alumina and established an experimental plant at New Kensington, using an older method than that of Bayer. In 1903 an improved process was put in production at the alumina works established by Alcoa at East St. Louis, Illinois. Alcoa did not use the Bayer process then but precipitated the alumina with carbon dioxide. After the expiration of the Bayer Patent in 1911, the Bayer principle of self-precipitation by "seeding" was employed.

It is an interesting fact that the Bayer process has remained to this day the most universally used method for making alumina hydrate, which is calcined into aluminum oxide, called alumina. The Bayer process has had refinements, just as has the Hall process for making metallic aluminum, but the basic principle remains unchanged. Briefly, it consists of digesting the bauxite under pressure with hot caustic soda liquor to form sodium aluminate from the aluminum-bearing portion of the ore. This is soluble and when filtering operations are carried on it passes through as a liquid, leaving behind the impurities such as silica and iron oxide. These form a residue known as red mud. The dissolved alumina is then precipitated from the filtered liquor as alumina trihydrate. This is washed and then calcined to produce aluminum oxide (alumina).

This description will doubtless suit neither the layman nor the scientist.[5] It is too technical for the former and not sufficiently detailed for the technician. It does serve the purpose of showing

[5] Detailed description of the process is contained in an article by James A. Lee in *Chemical & Metallurgical Engineering*, October, 1940.

the chemical processes necessary to separate alumina from bauxite. It helps to explain to the layman the huge digesting cylinders
and precipitating tanks he would see if he visited one of the large
alumina works at Mobile, Alabama, Hurricane Creek, Arkansas,
or Baton Rouge, Louisiana. Although the pioneer in large-scale
alumina manufacture, Alcoa owns but two plants in the United
States today—a modern one at Mobile and an older plant at
East St. Louis, Illinois. One Alcoa competitor has the alumina
plant at Hurricane Creek, Arkansas, the largest in the world,
as well as an alumina works at Listerhill, Alabama. Another competitor has the large alumina plant at Baton Rouge, Louisiana.

The alumina-making process just described is dependent
on the quality of the bauxite used. In the beginning of this
chronicle it was said that aluminum can be made from most any
alumina-bearing clay. The deterrent in all such cases is the cost.
Bauxite from which commercial alumina, suitable for the aluminum reduction pots, is obtained should contain as much alumina as possible and a minimum of silica. The silica has a bad
habit of combining with the soda ash and alumina in the digesting operation. One pound of silica, present in the ore as clay,
thus causes a loss of about one pound of soda ash and one pound
of alumina.

That is why kaolin, the mineral of clay, which has about as
much silica as alumina, does not lend itself to the commercial
competitive manufacture of alumina under present-day conditions. Broadly speaking, the higher the grade of ore the lower is
the cost of manufacturing alumina from it. Aluminum Company
of America has regularly imported high-grade ores from South
America to supplement that mined in Arkansas. This policy has

7 1

served to conserve the so-called rich ores in Arkansas which are limited in quantity.

Such a policy proved its wisdom in the early stages of World War II when German U-boats were sinking Alcoa's ore carriers with disturbing frequency. These sinkings occurred in 1942 and during the forepart of 1943. From newspaper reports, it seemed to the public that they were occurring almost daily. Actually, a total of 26 ships were sunk out of a total of 915 sailings between Suriname and the United States. The largest number of ships sunk by the enemy in any one month was eight in May, 1942. Although Alcoa suffered a loss of only 2.9 per cent of its sailings during the period, it was a hazardous business and the Arkansas reserves of high-grade bauxite were a source of comfort to our country, which badly needed aluminum to win a global flying war.

World War II also stimulated intensive activity by Alcoa on a process it had developed to utilize the low-grade high-silica Arkansas ores for aluminum manufacture. Known as the Alcoa Combination Process,[6] this method combines the Bayer process in a novel manner with a sintering operation. It has proved so efficient that the proportion of alumina recovered from high-silica bauxite is greater and the soda loss lower than in the old Bayer process operating on high-grade bauxite. It has made possible the use of vast quantities of low-grade Arkansas ore hitherto thought unsuited for aluminum manufacture. How Alcoa brought this process into successful operation in a critical war period and later made the patents on the process available, without charge,

[6] "Alcoa Combination Process," Junius D. Edwards, *Transactions*, American Institute of Mining and Metallurgical Engineers, 1943; also "Combination Process for Aluminum," *Metals Technology*, Vol. 12, April, 1945.

to the Government to pass on to Alcoa's peacetime competitors is another story which will be told later.

To return to bauxite itself, something of its physical characteristics and its numerous uses should be of interest here. The color varies from almost pure white to a dark, liver red, with pink, buff, brown and mottled varieties quite common. European ores, because of high iron-oxide content, are usually brownish-red, while United States and South American bauxites are cream or buff or pink. Bauxite may be blocky, hard and dense; spongy and porous; pebbly; soft and chalky; or even plastic. These variations in texture add to the crushing and screening problems at the mines. The machinery must be adapted to the particular type of bauxite being made ready for the alumina works.

Uses of bauxite are many. When Berthier discovered and named the ore in France in 1821, there were uses for it even though metallic aluminum was not to become a common metal until more than sixty-five years later. The principal uses today, aside from aluminum production, are in the manufacture of abrasives, chemicals, cement, adsorption media in oil purification, refractories and insulating materials.

In the chemical field, there are many products which come from bauxite—alum, aluminum salts for water purification, etc. Calcium aluminate cement is a quick-hardening product resistant to attack by corrosive natural waters and many chemicals. Oil refiners have long been familiar with the adsorptive properties of some bauxites which, when activated by heating, can be employed to remove impurities from petroleum products.

Bauxite, an essential in alumina manufacture, has been of concern to The Pittsburgh Reduction Company and its successor,

Alcoa, since the original company began to seek its own ore supply in the late Nineties and to produce alumina in 1900. Even though it continued to buy alumina from Pennsylvania Salt Manufacturing Company for some years after the new century began, it became increasingly interested in adequate bauxite reserves as its own alumina-making progressed. The small shipment of Arkansas bauxite to the experimental alumina plant in New Kensington in 1899 was the forerunner of millions of tons of bauxite which have arrived at Alcoa alumina works since then. The Pittsburgh Reduction Company was diligent in finding an adequate supply early in the century. Alcoa has been equally diligent in subsequent years. The operations of Alcoa in Arkansas and in Suriname and the ownership of the Alcoa Steamship Company, Inc. which transports bauxite from South America are an essential part of the Company's large manufacturing business today.

CHAPTER SIX

The Consent Decree of 1912

☆ ☆ ☆ ☆ ☆ ☆ ☆ ☆ ☆

To THE HISTORIAN, it is not surprising that Alcoa, which had a legal monopoly under its basic patents until 1909, should have found itself under close scrutiny by Government shortly thereafter. This was partially due to the growth of the Company, but a more likely reason for Government intervention in 1912 was the effort of the Taft administration to "put teeth into the Sherman Act" under the vigorous and able guidance of Attorney General George W. Wickersham. The period of 1910–12 was the most active in anti-trust litigation until the late 1930 era.

The Sherman Act is almost as old as Alcoa. It became a law on July 2, 1890, two years after the birth of The Pittsburgh Reduction Company. The Act got its name from John Sherman, a Republican senator from Ohio and later Secretary of State in the cabinet of President McKinley. The author of the Sherman

Act was a brother of General William Tecumseh Sherman of Civil War fame.[1] The Law, under Section 1, makes restraints of trade illegal. Under Section 2, it declares that every person who shall monopolize trade or commerce among the several states or with foreign nations shall be guilty of a misdemeanor.

In the Congressional debates preceding its passage, the provisions of the Act as to offenders who restrain trade seemed to be of paramount importance. In these same Congressional debates, there was more uncertainty as to just what monopoly means. Both restraints of trade and monopoly were to become subjects of expanding Court interpretation over the next sixty years, an interpretation not yet clarified but one of increasing importance to the American economy.

An ideological conflict was to develop between those who believe in close Governmental control of business, regardless of wrongdoing, and those who argue that there is a happy middle ground between statism and laissez-faire. The question of whether sheer bigness of a business is good or bad, of whether the serving of a substantial portion of any given market by one company is helpful or detrimental to the American people, was to become an issue affecting not only Court decisions but Congressional discussions and politics. It will probably have to be settled ultimately before the bar of public opinion.

It is doubtful if The Pittsburgh Reduction Company gave any thought to the Sherman Act when it was passed. Certainly the men who ran the little manufacturing business could not have foreseen how important this Act was to become in the history of the venture they were starting. In the first place, the Sherman

[1] *Fortune*, July, 1948.

Act was used in its early stages to curb alleged restraints of trade by groups of business units. Even when it became a "trust-busting" tool in the era of Theodore Roosevelt, it was largely the legal machinery used to break up combinations of companies where the charge was that some powerful member of the group had "gobbled them up."

Such a charge was no concern or worry of the little aluminum-making outfit. It was so busy trying to manufacture a raw material and then to find customers for it that it had no time or inclination to think about monopolization or combinations in restraint of trade. Its management lived in a business era when restraints of trade were considered neither vicious nor illegal.

By 1912, it appeared to the Department of Justice that Alcoa had violated the Sherman Act on three counts: making restrictive covenants, engaging in alleged acts of unfair competition and participation in foreign cartels. The Government recognized the Company's legal monopoly until 1909 and, when it filed the complaint against Alcoa on May 16, 1912, it softened the charges with these words:

> It is not claimed by petitioner (that being the Government) that it was unlawful for defendant to exclude all others from the manufacture of aluminum while it was operating under the Hall and Bradley patents, and hence it is not insisted that the monopoly held by defendant (that is, Alcoa) in the manufacture of aluminum in the United States when said patents expired in 1909 was an unlawful one.

Later, in the same bill of complaint filed by the Department of Justice, there was this further concession:

77

. . . petitioner concedes that defendant's practical monopoly in both bauxite and the manufacture of aluminum in the United States which it held at the expiration of said patents was lawful . . .

There were, however, specific charges in the bill to the effect that Alcoa had made restrictive covenants in contracts covering purchases of alumina and bauxite. The Company was charged with making an agreement in 1907 with the Pennsylvania Salt Manufacturing Company whereby the Penn Salt Company promised not to engage in aluminum manufacture so long as Alcoa bought alumina from it.

When this was cited years later by the Department of Justice as an indication of Alcoa's intent to stifle potential competitors, Mr. Davis testified that when the existing contract with Penn Salt was about to expire in 1907, Alcoa wanted to drop it but Penn Salt prevailed upon the Company to continue as a customer for another five years, such continuation providing a basis for the Pennsylvania Salt Manufacturing Company to expand its alumina facilities.[2] Under these circumstances, Mr. Davis said he felt justified in inserting a clause that Penn Salt would not also go into the aluminum-making business during the life of the contract.[3]

Alcoa was charged with making a similar contract in 1909 with the Norton Company in connection with purchases of bauxite. There was a charge that the Company had made a restrictive covenant with the General Chemical Company from whom it

2 United States vs. Aluminum Company of America, et al., Equity No. 85-73, Southern District of New York, Transcript of testimony, p. 4243.
3 Id., pp. 4243-44.

had acquired the General Bauxite Company, owner of some valuable bauxite lands in Arkansas and Georgia. In connection with this purchase in 1905, The Pittsburgh Reduction Company, shortly to become Alcoa, had secured a stipulation from the General Chemical Company that none of the bauxite it would buy from the Pittsburgh concern for alum-making purposes would be used in the manufacture of aluminum.

The chemical companies, Norton and General Chemical, had entered into forty- and fifty-year contracts to buy mined bauxite from Alcoa at favorable prices. General Chemical had insisted that Alcoa stay out of the alum business and, as a quid pro quo, the aluminum-making concern had inserted a clause stipulating that the chemical company refrain from aluminum manufacture. The long-term contracts for purchase of bauxite put Alcoa in a position of competing with itself unless it inserted a clause in each contract by which the bauxite purchaser agreed not to use this material for making aluminum.

The Department of Justice devoted a substantial portion of its bill to a list of charges of unfair trade practices, complained of by competitors but never proved. In fact, in the Answer, these charges were prefaced by a statement from Alcoa that it was agreeing to future lawful conduct without implying that it had previously acted otherwise. The unproved charges had to do with unfair trade practices such as delayed shipments, price discrimination, refusal to sell and requiring purchasers not to engage in competition with Alcoa-made products.

The Department of Justice laid great stress on Alcoa's participation in European cartels, particularly the cartel of 1908, the only one in existence at the time the complaint was filed. Like

79

previous foreign cartels in which Alcoa took part, the 1908 agreement provided for the fixing of markets as well as price understandings. Alcoa had felt it was legal because it was a foreign agreement, carried out in foreign countries by a foreign subsidiary, but the Government attorneys insisted that it be canceled, thereby taking a position subsequently sustained in Court decisions. Cartels will be discussed in greater detail in a later chapter but action of the Government on this subject in 1912 erected a caution signal which Alcoa observed in the future to such an extent that it had no participation in any foreign cartel after 1915, regardless of whether the Sherman Act was involved. It did participate in one such cartel in 1912, only after advice by its attorneys that this particular cartel did not come under the purview of the anti-trust laws.

The anti-trust action by the Department of Justice against Alcoa in 1912 was not a long-drawn-out affair involving a lawsuit with testimony in the form of witnesses and exhibits. It was settled on June 7, 1912, by a Consent Decree to which officials of the Company gave their assent.[4] In this Consent Decree they agreed to discontinue doing the things charged by the Department of Justice if, indeed, they had been doing them. The contract with the Pennsylvania Salt Company, wherein that company had agreed not to engage in aluminum manufacture while Alcoa was buying alumina from it, had already been canceled. This agreement had been terminated by the two companies, voluntarily, on January 30th preceding the Consent Decree of June 7, 1912. A similar situation existed in reference to the restrictive covenants in the contracts with the two chemical companies.

4 Decrees and Judgments in Federal Anti-Trust Cases, p. 341.

These provisions had been canceled prior to the signing of the Decree. The 1908 cartel had been canceled by consent of the members on February 17, 1912.

The Government's petition in the suit which ended in the Consent Decree was signed by Attorney General Wickersham and two assistants, James A. Fowler and William T. Chantland, experienced attorneys in the anti-trust division of the Department of Justice. The petition did not charge that the Company's possession of bauxite or other raw materials was unlawful. Apparently it was the view of Government counsel that with such assets Alcoa should be scrupulously fair in its dealings with independent manufacturers of aluminum goods who competed with it. The complaint was filed on May 16, 1912; Alcoa's answer came on June 1st and the Decree, itself, was signed by the Judge on June 7. The speed of these legal proceedings would indicate that the Decree was pretty well worked out before the answer was filed and the filing of the answer was largely to permit Alcoa to make a record of its position.

The Consent Decree has been cited in later years by the Department of Justice as a demonstration of Alcoa's purpose to suppress competition, but the Courts have given little weight to this argument. Perhaps there has been a recognition of the difficulty of drawing any kind of an injunction which could apply equitably or even sensibly to a company thirty or forty years later. When Mr. Davis and his associates accepted the Decree in 1912, they doubtless recognized that they could have made a sound defense in any Court to the charges of competitors about acts of unfair competition. As to the alleged restrictive covenants, the Company could have made a good case for itself in proving

81

a lack of intent to restrain trade. Those covenants, in the mind of Company executives, were merely precautionary measures a small outfit was taking to make sure its suppliers did not overload a new business with numerous manufacturers trying to pioneer a market where virtually none had previously existed.

This type of contract was in common use at the time. Restrictive covenants imposed upon the vendor in connection with the sale of property or of a business were recognized and sustained at common law. The Sherman Act of 1890 needed numerous subsequent Court decisions to clarify the extent of the anti-trust laws in regard to this practice. Indeed, interpretation of the Sherman Act by the Courts has gone much further than a change of attitude toward restrictive covenants. Whereas in the steel case in 1919 it was held that mere size or unexerted power does not constitute monopolization and that unexerted power is not an offense, the Courts now say that power can be illegal in and of itself. In the American Tobacco case, decided in 1946,[5] it was ruled that mere power to monopolize is a violation of the law. While the Courts have not said that mere size is illegal, the doctrine of the illegality of unexerted power carries with it the factor of size.

Actually, the violations of the Sherman Act, if they were violations, were brought into the limelight in 1912 at a time when alleged offenders had been living for several decades in an economic era founded on the philosophy of the "survival of the fittest." Alcoa was engaged in a struggle to see if the infant·aluminum industry could survive in competition with steel and other older nonferrous metals. Furthermore, the restrictive covenants

[5] American Tobacco Company vs. United States, 328 U. S. 781.

Alcoa had made could not have restrained anyone from competing except in the three-year period 1909-1912. Prior to 1909 Alcoa had a legal monopoly based on its patents. No one has ever come forward to indicate that these covenants prevented him from going into the business of aluminum-making. Yet a number of companies, like Alcoa, later under sweeping indictment by the Department of Justice, have had their early actions spotlighted in an effort to prove long-range monopolistic tendencies. In the Du Pont anti-trust case now in the Courts, the ghosts of the 1912 suit against that company for consolidating several powder-making concerns are still paraded to haunt the present giant corporation. As a writer expressed it in a series of articles in *The Saturday Evening Post* in 1949, "The very active Anti-trust Division of the Department of Justice has a long and unyielding memory." [6]

The Consent Decree was doubtless a good thing for the Company in the long run. It made Alcoa conscious of the fact that Government was eying it critically. It had a decided future bearing on every action the Company took which might, in any way, be considered a violation of the Sherman Act. It caused the Company to submit to the Department of Justice, in advance, proposed acquisitions of aluminum-making facilities and to ask the Government for an opinion as to whether these acquisitions might be made under the terms of the Consent Decree of 1912.

[6] "The Du Ponts," William S. Dutton, *The Saturday Evening Post*, October 8, 1949, through November 5, 1949.

CHAPTER SEVEN

Water Power

☆ ☆ ☆ ☆ ☆ ☆ ☆ ☆ ☆

I T TAKES about ten kilowatt hours of electricity today to produce one pound of aluminum, an amount sufficient to keep
a 40-watt light burning constantly for more than ten days.
The pioneers in The Pittsburgh Reduction Company didn't know
the exact amount as they struggled to get enough steady current
from two gas-fired boilers and a 125 H.P. engine connected to
two Edison bipolar direct-current generators. However, they did
know that it took a lot. Two years before this, Charles Martin
Hall was trying to make sufficient current in homemade batteries
as he conducted his woodshed research at Oberlin, Ohio. Hall
had plenty of trouble developing enough electric energy. The
legend is that he finally had his sister Julia, his co-worker, appropriate their mother's cookie jar as the container for an additional
battery.

Hall and his later associates also knew that it required other things, but they realized that sufficient electricity was a prime essential. Aluminum oxide (alumina) is separated into metallic aluminum and oxygen by direct electric current which also provides the heat to keep molten the cryolite bath in which the alumina is dissolved. The electrolytic cell in which this occurs is usually rectangular in shape and its steel shell is lined with carbon. This carbon lining serves as the cathode, while suspended above the cell is a carbon anode. The current travels from anode to cathode and aluminum is deposited on the cathode just as in any metal electroplating operation. The oxygen is released at the carbon anode where it promptly unites with the carbon to form carbon dioxide and some carbon monoxide. The cryolite, being more resistant to electrolysis, does not break down so long as there is sufficient alumina in the bath.

Portions of this description of aluminum-making by the Hall process have been outlined elsewhere in this account, but it is necessary to picture it again to show the need for adequate electric power. There is an old custom of connecting a 50-volt light bulb across each cell or pot. The bulb lights automatically when the cell needs more alumina. When the alumina content of the bath is very low, the electrical resistance of the cell increases and so does the voltage. Thus the light glows and calls attention to the fact that the cell must be fed some alumina. This phenomenon of increased resistance with impoverished bath, provided by Nature, has for many years furnished a quick indicator to men in the pot rooms charged with responsibility of reducing alumina.

There have been many graphic presentations of the vast amount of current needed to produce the metal. Literature on aluminum is replete with these statements, of which here are a few:

One aluminum plant in a single day uses enough electricity to keep a 40-watt globe burning for 11,000 years.— June Metcalfe, *Aluminum from Mine to Sky*, Whittlesey House, 1947.

About 10 kilowatt-hours are consumed in the production of one pound of aluminum, an amount sufficient to keep a 40-watt light burning constantly for over ten days.—Stanley V. Malcuit, article on Aluminum, American Industry Series, Bellman Publishing Company, 1946.

The aluminum industry, largest single user of electrical energy in the United States, consumed an estimated 22 billion kilowatt-hours at the 1943 peak.—"Aluminum Reborn," *Fortune*, May, 1946.

To produce 2,100,000,000 pounds of aluminum will require annually more electricity than was consumed in 1940 in 27 of the 48 States. In one day the industry will draw more current than a city of 60,000 homes consumes in one year.—T. D. Jolly, Chief Engineer, Alcoa, in an address before the National Association of Purchasing Agents, New York, May, 1942—an address delivered in the war period when the industry had the capacity to produce more than two billion pounds annually.

Consumption of electric current for reducing alumina has been reported as ranging from 18,000 to 24,000 KWH per ton of aluminum. In addition there are other power demands in reduction plants for operating electric motors and other plant equipment.—Railroad Committee for the study of transportation, Sub-Committee on aluminum. American Association of Railroads, W. C. Curd, 1946.

In 1940 the aluminum industry in the United States was the largest single user of electric energy, ranking first among all industries. It is estimated that in 1943 the electric consumption of the aluminum industry was about 22 billion kilowatt hours.—Engle, Gregory and Mosse, *Aluminum— An Industrial Marketing Appraisal*, Richard D. Irwin, Inc., 1945.

The growing need for electricity had become apparent to The Pittsburgh Reduction Company even before it outgrew the little Smallman Street shop and had accepted a proposal of the Burrell Improvement Company to move its operations to New Kensington, Pennsylvania. The minutes of a Board meeting on September 18, 1888, tell of a letter from a Mr. Lyford in regard to water power near Waverly, New York. Both coal and natural gas were used after the operations removed to New Kensington. The fuel cost was low but electricity generated by steam engines did not seem to be the answer. As early as 1893 the search for cheap electricity had definitely pointed the way to the one source of electric energy which seemed best suited to aluminum production —water power.

In that year the Company made its first contract to buy hydro-electric power. This contract was with the Niagara Falls Power Company at Niagara Falls, New York. The first purchase was for direct current, but three years later, in 1896, The Pittsburgh

Reduction Company bought what is known as "mechanical power." This power from the turbine shafts of the Niagara Falls Hydraulic Power Company was converted into electrical energy by generators owned by The Pittsburgh Reduction Company. The site of the operations was an historic one. The first use of water power at Niagara had been in 1725 when the French erected a sawmill at this point.

In a paper read before the American Society of Civil Engineers in August, 1895, Capt. Hunt described the location as follows:

> The Niagara River flows as a comparatively quiet stream from the outlet of Lake Erie at Buffalo to within about a mile of Niagara Falls. From this point there is a rapid descent to the brink of the Falls, where the water suddenly descends a distance of 180 feet into the gorge below. Upon the plateau and at the point already mentioned, on the site of Old Fort Schlosser, are situated the new works of The Pittsburgh Reduction Company.

The Niagara Falls Power Company was interested in selling power and it left to The Pittsburgh Reduction Company the job of converting this power into direct current for aluminum manufacture. In a paper presented before The Electrochemical Society in 1936,[1] James W. Rickey, Chief Hydraulic Engineer for Alcoa, described the installation in these words:

> Direct current purchased from the Niagara Falls Power Company, was supplied from five 600 kw. rotary converters. This was the outstanding converter installation at that time.

[1] "Hydro Power for the Production of Aluminum," James W. Rickey, *Transactions of The Electrochemical Society*, Vol. 70, p. 185, 1936.

These converters remained in service for 25 years. The power required for the production of aluminum was increased again in 1896 by mechanical power purchased at the turbine shaft from the Niagara Falls Hydraulic Power Company. This power was converted into electrical energy by six 540 kw. generators. Additional generators, added from time to time, increased the capacity to 12,000 kw.

The powerhouse of the Niagara Falls Power Company, in which this equipment was installed, was designed by Stanford White, famous New York architect.

In placing an aluminum reduction works at Niagara Falls, the Company was inaugurating a policy Nature has imposed upon it, one of locating its aluminum reduction operations whenever possible near sources of hydroelectric energy. This custom has prevailed for a half century. It is easier to bring the raw materials to the vicinity of adequate hydro power than to send the electricity long distances to sections where raw materials are in abundance. In an advertisement in *The Saturday Evening Post* in 1937, Alcoa discussed this problem under a headline reading, "Nature Located Things Badly for Making Aluminum in America." Concerning the power problem, the Company said, "It became necessary to transport the unfinished product to distant places where great rivers run steep. In these locations, away from industrial centers, where there has been little demand for power, we must build great dams, reservoirs and powerhouses to make the essentially low-cost electricity which produces the virgin metal." [2]

[2] *The Saturday Evening Post*, July 17, 1937.

This was simply stating a fundamental of the aluminum business which needs to be elaborated at this point to explain the search for low-cost electric power which has actuated Alcoa from its earliest days. A cost of two mills per KWH means a two-cent power cost in each pound of aluminum. Current at two mills per KWH cannot be found in highly industrialized areas where electricity is in demand for all sorts of uses. It has usually been found at this figure, or slightly higher, only in out-of-the-way places where vast quantities can be made by water power.

World War II well illustrated this when, with water power insufficient to produce the aluminum needed to win the war, Government-owned plants were constructed in or near large cities which could provide only high-cost, steam-generated electricity. When the war was over, these plants were abandoned as aluminum producers because of the high cost of the power ingredient. In the aluminum business electricity is a commodity, an essential part of the cost of every pound of metal along with labor, raw materials, capital investment and the wearing out of equipment.

At the beginning of the century, another source of hydroelectric energy was pursued by Alcoa. A project was undertaken at Shawinigan Falls in the wilds of Quebec. As early as May 3, 1899, Charles M. Hall was writing J. E. Aldred stating he had discussed with Capt. Hunt, shortly before the latter's death, the possibility of aluminum manufacture in Canada. Hall said, "It is the intention of the company to start manufacturing in Canada very soon." Aldred had written Capt. Hunt on March 2, 1899, that the Shawinigan Water & Power Company would be ready to sell power by November 1st of that year. The aluminum-making company built its own power plant and purchased energy from the Shawinigan Water & Power Company in the form of water in the forebay. In 1907 additional water energy purchased from the same concern enabled Alcoa to build a second power-house. In all, Alcoa was able to obtain 46,000 KW for aluminum production at Shawinigan.

Despite the low cost of coal and gas as fuel, steam-generated electricity made in the New Kensington industrial district was too expensive for aluminum manufacturing. Niagara No. 1 Reduction Plant was placed in operation in 1895 and in 1902 was augmented by the Niagara Carbon Plant to produce carbon electrodes. On February 1, 1896, reduction of aluminum from its ores ceased at New Kensington. That plant became a fabricating works making aluminum sheet, tubing and similar semifabricated products. It has remained so to this day. Sheet, tubing, extrusions, cooking utensils, foil, bottle caps and other products have been produced at this oldest of Alcoa fabricating works.

Niagara Falls, because of available hydro-generated power, became the reduction works. Charles Martin Hall, who was interested in further experiments to produce aluminum at a lower cost as well as in developing aluminum alloys to make the metal more useful, moved to Niagara Falls. He spent years of great value to the industry at that location before his death in 1914. I. W. Wilson, now President of Alcoa, V. C. Doerschuk, present head of Alcoa's reduction works, and a number of other Company veterans, have valued and cherished memories of their years with the inventor in those early days at Niagara Falls.

But the Company was seeking more electric power and, in 1903, a reduction works was built at Massena, New York, near the St. Lawrence River. Power was purchased under a long-term contract from the St. Lawrence River Power Company, which diverted water from the St. Lawrence River through a three-mile canal to a powerhouse located on the bank of the Grasse River. In 1906 this company became financially distressed and Alcoa acquired it in order to insure a source of electric energy for the Massena plant. The St. Lawrence River Power Company is a wholly-owned subsidiary of Alcoa to this day.

Developing a satisfactory source of power by damming the St. Lawrence proved an unsurmountable task. The Company spent six or more years in trying to obtain the necessary property for a large hydroelectric plant on the Long Sault Rapids of the St. Lawrence River, but it was impossible to obtain coordinate legislation from the United States Government, New York State, Canadian Dominion Government and the Province of Ontario to permit the construction of a hydro project. Consequently, Alcoa looked elsewhere for power and located it, about 1909, in the mountains of Tennessee-North Carolina. Persistent efforts at the Massena location, however, did provide some power. In 1914 the Company purchased the Hannawa Falls Water Power to augment the current produced by the St. Lawrence River Power Company. Power developed at Massena has always been subject to seasonal fluctuation resulting from ice formations.

Spurred on by necessity, Mr. Davis and his associates started to acquire riparian properties along the Little Tennessee River and its tributaries in 1910. Studies and plans that contemplated the unified development of the entire river and its tributaries above Chilhowee, Tennessee, were undertaken. The assurance of adequate power from that swift-flowing mountain river and its tributaries, to be developed as needed, gave Mr. Davis the vision of what is today this country's largest aluminum plant, at Alcoa, Tennessee. On March 6, 1914, the first pot lines of an aluminum reduction works started operating at this location.

The Tallassee Power Company in North Carolina was acquired in 1914 and operated under that name until 1931 when it was changed to the Carolina Aluminum Company. The Nantahala Power & Light Company was organized as a public utility on July 23, 1929, to develop as needed the power sites which had been owned by the Carolina Aluminum Company on the upper reaches of the Little Tennessee and its tributaries, the Nantahala and the Tuckasegee Rivers.

The Nantahala Power & Light Company, a wholly-owned Alcoa subsidiary, is essentially a utility company serving many western North Carolina communities with electricity to light their homes and to run their motors for commercial, farm and household use. Its long-time President was the late J. E. S. Thorpe, an Alcoa veteran of thirty years' service and well-known utility operator in the Southeast. Mr. Thorpe, who had served as head of the Nantahala Power & Light Company for twenty-one years at the time of his death in 1950, was recently honored in a lasting manner by the Directors of Alcoa. The name of a mountain power development, originally known as the Glenville project, was changed to the Thorpe Development.

Although its first duty is to serve the communities in its territories, Nantahala Power & Light Company has in its domain such large hydro projects as Glenville and Nantahala, which augment the supply of power in the North Carolina mountains available for aluminum-making. The Company started operations by acquiring hydro projects at Mission, Franklin and Bryson City, as well as the distribution facilities in those localities. The installed capacity of the three hydro projects was 4,340 KW. Since then, Nantahala Power & Light Company has added other communities to its distribution system. To equip itself further for increasing service, it completed the Queens Creek project in 1949 and the Tuckasegee project in 1950.

The story of Alcoa's power projects in North Carolina would make a chapter by itself. A truism uttered by Mr. Davis some years ago still holds. He said that for every dollar the Company has invested in plant and equipment at the Alcoa, Tennessee, Works, there is another dollar invested in the mountains in dams and hydro plants. A list of these power projects is impressive. They include: Cheoah—placed in operation in April, 1919, height of dam 225 feet, 110,000 KW capacity; Santeetlah—placed in operation in June, 1928, height of dam 212 feet, 45,000 KW capacity; Calderwood—began operations in April, 1930, height of dam 232 feet, 121,500 KW capacity; Glenville—began operating in October, 1941, height of dam 150 feet, capacity 21,600 KW; Nantahala—began operating in July, 1942, height of dam 253 feet, capacity 43,200 KW.

Harnessing the swift-flowing Little Tennessee and its tributaries in their rush through the Great Smoky Mountains is a saga in which many Alcoa veterans have played a part. Surveyors, engineers, draftsmen, electricians, mechanics, transportation men and laborers were essential in numbers to build the great dams and powerhouses. These Alcoa veterans, many of them with twenty-five-year service buttons, can talk to you by the hour about the thrill of capturing the falling water which would flow through the penstocks and then into the turbines to create electricity which would travel from the giant powerhouses to the reduction pots at Alcoa, Tennessee, to make metallic aluminum.

In this Tennessee-North Carolina development of power, Alcoa came in contact with Government when the Tennessee Valley Authority came into being during the early 1930's while depression still stalked the land. TVA, one of the earliest great Governmental undertakings in power development, soil reclamation and flood control over a large area, really encompasses the whole valley of the Tennessee River and its tributaries. Of these streams, the Little Tennessee and its branches presented the most highly developed power projects. Alcoa had been working at this job for two decades. Cheoah Dam and Power House, Santeetlah Dam and lake with its impounded waters rushing through a five-mile tunnel and pipe-line conduit to Santeetlah Power House, and Calderwood Dam and Power House, were completed units of the Alcoa program of spending a dollar in the mountains for every dollar spent on aluminum facilities at the Alcoa, Tennessee, Works. Glenville and Nantahala were ready for construction and were completed within the first ten years of TVA history.

Alcoa not only had these projects in operation or ready for completion, but over the years it had purchased more than two hundred miles of riverbank land, essential to the ultimate water-power development, along the Little Tennessee and its tributaries. This included nearly all the necessary land in the Fontana basin where a great dam would someday be built high in the mountains on the Little Tennessee River. This would be the fountainhead of the power projects on the Little Tennessee. Its great storage reservoir would control the flow of water at all of the downstream dams on the Little Tennessee and would affect the flow on the big Tennessee River as well.

When a well-financed Government project undertakes a large power-development program in an area, part of which is already developed by an industry, all sorts of troubles and controversies can easily arise. This has not been the case with TVA and Alcoa. Aside from one incident, when the then Chairman of TVA exercised Governmental authority to condemn two small parcels of land in the Fontana basin, the relationship between Government and Alcoa has been pleasant. The land incident passed quickly when TVA relinquished its effort to raid Alcoa after the matter had been stirred up in Congress by members of the Tennessee congressional delegation and others. From that time forward, the Governmental agency and the private company interested in power for aluminum-making have been pointed to as a model of the way Government and industry can sometimes work in harmony for the mutual benefit of each.

Alcoa became a purchaser of TVA power to supplement its own supply as soon as TVA was ready to sell this commodity from the power plant at Norris Dam. In 1941, to the surprise of many people who could see "no good in TVA," Alcoa gave to the Governmental authority, without monetary fee, its site at Fontana, where most of the necessary land had been acquired, parcel by parcel, over many years. With the grant went roadway relocations, surveys and engineering data on which the Company had spent substantial sums. In return, TVA agreed to build Fontana, the great storage reservoir which would regulate the flow of water at Alcoa's hydro projects at Cheoah and Calderwood, as well as at TVA's own downstream projects. Alcoa was influenced in its decision by the Water Power Act of 1920, which would have required the Company to obtain from the Federal Power Commission a license to build Fontana. This license would have given the Government the right to "recapture" the project after fifty years.

A second part of the Fontana agreement gave TVA the right to control the impounding and release of water to all of Alcoa's hydroelectric developments on the Little Tennessee and to use this generating capacity as an integral part of the TVA power system. In return for this, Alcoa received from TVA approximately the number of kilowatt hours generated at Alcoa plants during a calendar year, and in addition 11,000 KW of primary power without cost. The first part of the Alcoa-TVA agreement, wherein the Fontana project regulates the flow of water at Cheoah and Calderwood, is in perpetuity. The second part, recited in this paragraph, can be canceled by either party on three years' notice after January 1, 1952.

The Fontana project, with its great dam 477 feet high and an ultimate installed capacity of 202,600 KW, is a Government-owned project. It is one of the interesting spots visited by hundreds of thousands of American tourists every year, and it was made possible through the co-operation of Alcoa with TVA. At a dramatic press conference in Washington on August 14, 1941, Alcoa executives and TVA officials gave the press an amazing demonstration of how industry and Government can work together. On this occasion Alcoa announced that it was giving up properties on the Fontana site which it had been accumulating for thirty years. Over forty separate parcels of land, aggregating nearly 15,000 acres, were in the tract. In addition, Alcoa was delivering to TVA all the engineering data it had assembled for the construction of a great dam and power project.

This agreement made possible the integrated operation of the water powers of Alcoa and TVA, including the Fontana project. Its result was the maximum production of electric energy from the available water power, not only on the Little Tennessee River but also throughout the entire Tennessee Valley, which is served by the great Tennessee River and all its tributaries.

At the press conference it was announced that the Government was prepared to go full speed ahead on the great Fontana project which it hoped to complete by mid-1942. The need for more hydroelectric power for national defense was the guiding motive with both the Company and TVA. In fact, to complete the agreement required the almost incessant work of engineers, legal counselors and executives of both parties for the six weeks preceding the announcement in 1941.

No agreement of this sort is good unless it works. This one has functioned surprisingly well considering the fact that Government accounting practices and business methods on such projects are vastly different from the system that a private utility must observe. There have been minor disagreements, but Alcoa continues to be one of TVA's largest customers. In 1943, a peak war year, Alcoa purchased from TVA 1,894,659,622 kilowatt hours of power. In commenting on the Alcoa-TVA arrangement, the Twentieth Century Fund, in its book *Electric Power and Government Policy*,[3] says:

> While the conditions under which this contract was negotiated were so unique that generalization is not justified, it

[3] *Electric Power and Government Policy*, Twentieth Century Fund, p. 677.

provided a sharp contrast to the rancor that characterized TVA's early relations with private companies. Perhaps it may not be too much to hope that once the relation of federal projects to private systems has been clearly defined and pricing policies of multiple-purpose projects have been formulated on an understandable social basis, freed from invidious comparisons based on dubious cost allocations, the scope of mutually beneficial cooperation between public and private systems will grow. Public systems must, of course, pursue those price and nonprice experiments in load building and in efficient distribution that have aroused a too complacent private management. But direct competition and duplication of facilities are uneconomical. Litigation is wasted opportunity. In their elimination, the general public has much to gain.

Alcoa came under the eye of Government on another project in the South in 1915. This was also in North Carolina, but in the Piedmont section of the state at Badin on the Yadkin River. The Government first heard of it officially when, on August 27, 1915, the law firm of Coudert Brothers in New York City applied to the Department of Justice for permission to sell the holdings of the Southern Aluminium Company to Alcoa. This company was owned by French capitalists although it was a New York corporation formed in 1912. Its assets consisted of a water-power site on the Yadkin River, together with some 19,000 acres of land, plus all of the rights and franchises of the North Carolina Electric & Power Company which it had purchased. Further assets were an incompleted dam on the Yadkin at a point known as the Narrows and a partially constructed hydroelectric plant. There were also railroad tracks and buildings.

This French-owned company had some interesting people associated with it. Paul L. T. Héroult, who had vied with Hall in the race to discover a cheap way of making aluminum, came over and was sufficiently interested in the project to remain in Badin for a considerable time in 1912 and 1913. Royal P. Lowrey, a son of Grosvenor P. Lowrey, who had promoted the Héroult alloy process in the Nineties, was also at the scene. Among the assets were a granite quarry and some miscellaneous gold-mine properties. The North Carolina Electric & Power Company had been a promotion of E. B. C. Hambley, English mining engineer, who was attracted to this section of North Carolina by gold-mining prospects.

The Southern Aluminium Company had intended to manufacture aluminum, but what it had completed could be converted to almost any large-scale manufacturing business needing power. The company lacked $7,500,000 in funds to finish the project, but everything had been halted by the outbreak of war in Europe in October, 1914. No more French money could be spared. After futile attempts to finance, the stockholders looked to Aluminum Company of America as almost the only prospective purchaser who might enable them to salvage any of their investment.

On August 15, 1915, a purchase agreement was concluded wherein Alcoa was to pay the French company $5,030,000. However, Alcoa had signed the Consent Decree of 1912 in which it had agreed to refrain from any act which might be construed as stifling competition. It was not willing to proceed with the acquisition without the blessing of the Department of Justice. It secured this approval in a letter addressed to Paul Fuller of Coudert Brothers by Assistant Attorney General J. Carroll Todd on September 3, 1915. There was no other producer of aluminum ingot in this country at that time and the French-owned corporation had few prospective customers for its dormant enterprise. The Badin Reduction Works has functioned regularly ever since as an Alcoa plant. Although a relatively small producer as such plants now go, it has been the proving ground for some successful research in the production of high-purity aluminum.

The Badin hydroelectric project has been expanded since the days when Alcoa acquired the properties of the Southern Aluminium Company. Shortly after the purchase of the French holdings, Alcoa completed the dam and powerhouse at Yadkin Narrows. This plant, which went into operation in July, 1917, has a dam 216 feet high and a capacity of 81,200 kilowatts. In July, 1919, the Company placed in operation the project at Yadkin Falls, where a dam 112 feet high was constructed to provide a capacity of 20,300 kilowatts. The High Rock power project began operating in December, 1927, with a dam 100 feet high and a capacity of 33,000 kilowatts.

The search for adequate water power to provide the electricity for aluminum manufacture, a search which continues to this day, was not confined to the United States. Indeed, the Company had not hesitated to look far afield as early as 1899 when it began negotiations for power at Shawinigan Falls. Alcoa again began looking elsewhere on the North American continent in 1922 when it began negotiating for power on the Saguenay River in Canada. This river flows southeasterly from its source, Lake St. John, a large body of water some thirty miles long and eighteen miles wide. There are two power sources, the Upper Development near the outlet of the lake at a place called Isle Maligne, and the Lower Development eighteen miles down the river at Chute-à-Caron and at Shipshaw. The lake level has been raised seventeen and one-half feet to provide greater storage and more head for the Isle Maligne and Shipshaw projects.

The tremendous water power of these two sites was owned by J. B. Duke, noted industrialist whose name is borne by some of North Carolina's present hydroelectric developments. Arthur V. Davis, as Alcoa's President, began eying this power source in the early 1920's. After two years of negotiating for power from Mr. Duke's project, Mr. Davis told W. S. Lee, Duke's chief hydraulic engineer, that he would prefer to acquire a proprietary participation in the power company itself rather than an annual contract for a specified amount of power which would need to be taken in bad, as well as good, times. Mr. Allen, a Duke associate, suggested a sale of the Duke power project at the Lower Development for a percentage of Alcoa's stock.

As a consequence, a contract was made in June, 1925, which led to a merger and the issuance of new Alcoa shares on July 29th of that year. Duke received one ninth of the securities issued by the "new" Alcoa in return for the Lower Development on the Saguenay. Since it was a stock transaction, the amount Duke received can be estimated only on the book value which was figured at $17,000,000. When one considers the vast importance of this site in providing power for aluminum production in World War II, this sum seems modest enough.

In 1926, after Mr. Duke's death, Alcoa acquired from the executors of his estate 53⅓ per cent of the stock in the Duke-Price

Power Company and a contract right to 100,000 HP annually. Both of these acquisitions were on the Upper Development at Isle Maligne. However, all the Canadian water power purchased by Alcoa with either stock or money has passed out of its hands and is now owned by Aluminium, Ltd. That Canadian corporation, about which you will hear in some detail in a later chapter, is now a vigorous competitor of Alcoa.

Alcoa power requirements led it to the great Northwest in 1939. This time it was the Bonneville Power Administration, a Governmental agency, to whom Alcoa came as a customer. Attracted by the available power at a satisfactory industrial rate which could be obtained from Bonneville, the Company built an aluminum reduction works at Vancouver, Washington. Originally designed to produce 30,000,000 pounds annually, the plant capacity was increased threefold before its completion in the fall of 1940. Alcoa was heartily welcomed by Dr. Paul J. Raver, Bonneville power administrator, when the Company announced its coming in 1939 as the first big customer of the Government-developed project. Raver needed large industrial customers at that time when a great power supply outstripped industrial and utility requirements in the Northwest. The war changed all this and postwar activity has not lessened the demand to any marked degree. In the spring of 1948 it appeared that Bonneville needed to speed up its expansion program to care for the demands in that area of the aluminum industry alone. It was estimated that Bonneville might easily dispose of 250,000 additional kilowatts annually to the aluminum-making companies in the Northwest.

The shortage of hydroelectric power to satisfy the demand for electricity for aluminum reduction pots has caused Alcoa to undertake, for the first time since its earliest days, the manufacture of peacetime aluminum with power other than hydro-generated. At Point Comfort, near Port Lavaca, Texas, Alcoa has a new reduction works producing aluminum from power generated by internal combustion engines which use natural gas as fuel. Located on Matagorda Bay in the area between Houston and Corpus Christi, the plant receives natural gas from underwater wells 11½ miles offshore on the lower Texas Gulf Coast through what is believed to be the longest underwater pipe line in the world. The generation of power from natural gas at reasonable cost was made possible by the development of an unusual radial-type engine which has a vertical axis. At the Point Comfort plant there are 120 of these engines, each having a nominal capacity of 1,000 kilowatts, which generate sufficient electricity to produce 114,000,000 pounds of aluminum annually.

Water power on the North American continent is still badly needed by the aluminum industry. Remaining undeveloped sites in the United States are fairly well pre-empted by Government. In Alaska are great water-power sites, one of which Alcoa engineers have investigated. It takes great quantities of electricity today to make aluminum in this country, with production approaching one and a half billion pounds annually. This means fifteen billion kilowatt hours per year.

It is a far cry from the homemade batteries in Hall's woodshed laboratory and the meager facilities for producing electric current in the little plant on Smallman Street to Alcoa's modern hydroelectric projects. The cost of power continues to be an important item in the making of aluminum. Hydroelectric power costs are based largely on the fixed charges in the initial expense of building dams and providing power-making equipment. The continuous pressure to reduce costs has caused Alcoa's hydroelectric engineers to pioneer many improvements. Each new installation has incorporated features never used before, thus adding contributions to the hydroelectric art.

Of interest to the engineering-minded are some features of Alcoa's hydro projects in North Carolina and Tennessee. When Cheoah was constructed, it was, at the time, the highest overfall dam in the world. Santeetlah has an operating head on the turbines of 663 feet. Calderwood is a variable-radius pure-arch dam, utilizing a cushion pool to absorb the energy of flood waters spilled over its crest. At Thorpe the head on the impulse turbines is 1,208 feet. The water is taken from the reservoir above the dam to the powerhouse through three tunnels connected by steel pipes. One of these tunnels operates under 900 feet of head. Nantahala, when it was completed in 1942, had the highest head reaction turbine in America. It is an earth- and rock-fill dam with a maximum head on the turbine of 1,008 feet.

It is also interesting to note the advances made in the electric industry which have paralleled the growth of the aluminum business. The foresight and inventive genius of the early designers in electric fields made possible the securing of sufficient power by the growing aluminum industry. In 1886 a Brush open-coil-type generator, known as the "monster," [4] had a rating of 250 kilowatts. This machine, working steadily, would be able to make about 500 pounds of aluminum per day. Within the next twenty years electric generators twenty times this size were in continu-

[4] *Men and Volts, the Story of General Electric*, John W. Hammond, Lippincott, 1941, p. 104.

ous operation. Some of them were installed in the hydroelectric aluminum operations at Niagara Falls and at Massena. Today one single generating unit in Alcoa's hydroelectric installations in the mountains of North Carolina generates 50,000 kilowatts. This is two hundred times as much electrical energy as that produced by the 1886 "monster."

Search for power from falling water has led Alcoa through a series of interesting steps. First there was a purchase of power generated by others at Niagara Falls. Then came the use of mechanical power at this location, with the Company converting into electricity the power from the turbine shafts of the Niagara Falls Hydraulic Power Company. Then Alcoa made use of the water in the forebay at Shawinigan Falls. Finally it captured the rainfall from the Little Tennessee and its tributaries and converted this water into electrical energy at powerhouses alongside its great dams. Alcoa is a large user of electricity created through hydro developments. Yet the hydroelectric industry in the United States, through both Government and private development, is so vast today that Alcoa's production of hydro power in 1948 was only about 3½ per cent of the total.

CHAPTER EIGHT

Early Markets

☆ ☆ ☆ ☆ ☆ ☆ ☆ ☆ ☆

CHARLES MARTIN HALL was right when he wrote a friend in reference to the early days, "People have said we didn't have 1,000 pounds. They were wrong, but they might have said, that so far as the users of aluminum were concerned, practically no one wanted 1,000 pounds." In a series of articles in *The Saturday Evening Post* in late 1942 and early 1943 depicting the role of American industry in its all-out war effort, Boyden Sparkes paid considerable attention to the wartime job Alcoa was doing.[1] Speaking of the great demand for aluminum today at twenty cents per pound and less, Sparkes quoted Mr. Davis as saying that the early per-pound price in dollars, not cents, "took a lot of selling to get anybody to use aluminum for anything."

---

[1] "Shoot the Works," Boyden Sparkes, *The Saturday Evening Post*, December 26, 1942, January 2 and January 9, 1943.

Price was the determining factor which made selling difficult in those days. A schedule in The Pittsburgh Reduction Company minutes for October 16, 1889, gave $2 per pound as a selling price for 1,000 pounds, with $3 per pound as the price for small lots. This price went down rapidly to $1.50 in 1891, and to $.75 per pound in 1893. This was still too high for any tonnage demand or any uses by manufacturers other than those who made novelties or surgical instruments or who needed the metal as a deoxidizing agent in steel-making.

Even as late as 1900, *The Aluminum World*, established in 1894 as a self-appointed spokesman for the aluminum industry, gave this summary of uses for aluminum at the beginning of the Twentieth Century:

1. Manufacture of utensils and in the arts, as kitchen utensils, tableware, bottles, watch hands, trimmings for books, wagon frames, etc.
2. Articles for military use, as equipment for soldiers and general warfare implements.
3. Articles for marine and aeronautical purposes.
4. Instruments and apparatus for surgical purposes and sick-room supplies, such as respirators, syringes, catheters, coffins, artificial teeth plates, etc.
5. Instruments for mathematical, physical, optical, and chemical uses.
6. In the wire industry for wire brushes, baskets, hooks and eyes, egg beaters, dog muzzles, bird cages, etc.
7. For foils, bottle caps, etc.
8. Aluminum powder and paint.

9. As a reducing agent.

10. For lithographic printing.[2]

An early use, and one which first comes to the mind of the housewife today, was for cooking utensils. There is a dramatic story so well depicted in Alcoa's documentary picture, "Unfinished Rainbows." It tells how Arthur V. Davis borrowed a molder from the Griswold Company in Erie, Pennsylvania, and brought him to New Kensington to cast an aluminum teakettle. He did this just to show Ely Griswold, a leading utensil manufacturer, why he should buy aluminum from The Pittsburgh Reduction Company and make his utensils out of the bright shiny metal.

Griswold was delighted with the teakettle, but he turned the tables on Mr. Davis by refusing to make them himself but at the same time giving the young man an order for 2,000 kettles which Griswold would sell. There was nothing left for The Pittsburgh Reduction Company but to accept this Hobson's choice and add a fabricating unit for the manufacture of cast utensils to its New Kensington works. Later the Griswold Company also engaged in the manufacture of aluminum cooking ware.

Early uses covered a wide range and many of them were experimental. In 1896 the army was using aluminum for picket and tent pins and for canteens. Teddy Roosevelt carried an aluminum canteen as he led his men up San Juan Hill two years later.[3] U. S. torpedo boats used aluminum castings, and the hatchway frames for the cruiser *Minnesota* were made of aluminum, a forerunner of the widespread use of the metal today in the super-

[2] *The Aluminum World*, Vol. 6, February, 1900.
[3] *The Aluminum World*, Vol. 4, September, 1898.

structure of ships. President Cleveland went duck hunting in 1896 in a boat whose structural work was aluminum.[4]

Cast utensils were made at the New Kensington works in the Nineties, as has been told, but the Company was primarily interested in getting other utensil manufacturers to buy its metal and make their own ware. It did what it could in those days to encourage the business. In 1895 it put out information urging the proper cleaning and polishing of cooking utensils and announced that it had developed a polish especially for aluminum which was free of the coarse grit found in other metal polishes. The early sale of aluminum utensils had been accompanied by much grief and trouble, and one of the causes, in the opinion of The Pittsburgh Reduction Company, was the fact that users did not know how to care for or how to handle the utensils.

About this time, The Pittsburgh Reduction Company had the business of making sheet-aluminum cooking utensils thrust upon it from another quarter. A concern in Waltham, Massachusetts, Hill, Whitney & Wood, to whom the Company had been selling sheet for cooking-utensil manufacture, found itself in financial difficulties. One morning the manager, C. F. Whitney, walked into the New Kensington plant office and said to Mr. Davis, "Well, you are now in the utensil business." Whitney explained that his firm could not pay for the aluminum it had bought and that The Pittsburgh Reduction Company would have to take over the business in settlement. The Pittsburgh Reduction Company did this and also acquired some know-how along with the

---

[4] Aluminum duck boats 14 feet long with 36-inch beams and weighing only 30 pounds appeared on the market early in 1896.—*The Aluminum World*, Vol. **2**, February, 1896.

machinery by employing Whitney to supervise its new cooking-utensil department. In checking over the accounts of Hill, Whitney & Wood, an unfilled order for an unbelievable quantity of 2,800 kettles, placed by one J. H. Wilson of Blue Island, Illinois, was most intriguing. The Company immediately set out to learn more about him. Meanwhile Wilson was wondering about the Pittsburgh concern which had apparently succeeded his former supplier.

J. H. Wilson, brought up on a farm near Carlisle, Pennsylvania, had a close friend, Charles E. Ziegler, who was planning to become a physician. These two young men had organized a firm in 1895 to sell the Handy Kettle Steamer and the Ideal Percolating Coffee Pot. They bought their utensils in a partially fabricated state and then assembled them in finished form. Charles Ziegler had really originated the idea because he had sold an enameled kettle to housewives to finance his education. At this juncture he had gone on to college and J. H. Wilson was operating on his own at Blue Island, Illinois, buying his partially finished utensils from Hill, Whitney & Wood.

When Wilson came to Pittsburgh in September, 1900, for an interview with Pittsburgh Reduction Company officials, Dr. Ziegler was already in Pittsburgh, an interne in the Allegheny General Hospital. Dr. Ziegler was to have a long career as a physician, his death occurring early in 1950. The two young men were promptly invited to join The Pittsburgh Reduction Company and to form a sales force to sell cooking utensils to consumers. It was not surprising that the Company liked Dr. Ziegler's canvassing idea. Charles Martin Hall had been a house-to-house book canvasser in his college days.

Although the dies and machinery of the Hill, Whitney & Wood firm were moved to New Kensington in 1900, where they formed the basis for the early manufacture of sheet-aluminum cooking utensils, Alcoa really got into the business of cooking-utensil manufacture in a substantial way in 1901 when The Aluminum Cooking Utensil Company, a wholly-owned subsidiary, was organized. One of its first problems was to improve the quality of manufacture. Hill, Whitney & Wood had failed because they would not meet the competition of manufacturers who were making very thin ware. These products were injuring the sale of aluminum cooking ware since utensils made from thin sheet proved unsatisfactory to the housewife. From the very beginning, The Pittsburgh Reduction Company made a line of thick, heavy stamped utensils. The famous Wear-Ever brand made today by The Aluminum Cooking Utensil Company provides a quality standard which has meant much to the entire aluminum-utensil business in both sheet and cast ware.

Making aluminum cooking utensils was one thing and getting the American housewife to buy them was quite another problem. Here the Company recognized the importance of that great force which goes hand in hand with production in the American economy. It is the Tree of Distribution, nourished by the four roots: marketing, merchandising, advertising and selling. To accomplish this distribution by the most direct method, the Company adopted the plan of the two young men from Carlisle, Pennsylvania.

Wilson and Ziegler were given carte blanche to employ their system of having college boys go from door to door as canvassers, demonstrating to housewives the virtues of aluminum cooking ware. These college-student salesmen were recruited at the schools each spring through what the institutions called, in those days, their "self-help" departments. This method of selling, with certain refinements, goes on to this day. There are many successful men in America who earned their first money in college days by selling Wear-Ever utensils in summer vacations. In his speech at the sixtieth anniversary celebration of the aluminum industry, held in Pittsburgh, October 14, 1948, Arthur V. Davis said, "We had from three to five thousand college students working in vacation times. It has been quite a pleasure to me to find so many men, including one of the J. P. Morgan partners, who made their way through college by selling our cooking utensils and, consequently, have become very good friends of ours and of mine."

A notable feature of the early days was the large number of manufacturers who tried to make some product out of aluminum. Even well-established firms went "aluminum crazy" in trying to make products out of the metal. As a result, aluminum was used in many applications where it was unsuitable. Capt. Hunt, who was frequently quoted in *The Aluminum World*, was constantly advising caution and experimentation before the metal was used. Despite this, it was estimated in that publication in 1894 "that if all the men employed in the aluminum trade, directly and indirectly, should form an Indian file, the line would reach from the City Hall in New York to the Connecticut State line, or from Chicago's County Court House to the Indiana line." [5]

To curb some of this and to attempt to arrive at some standards, a trade association was formed in September, 1901. As one manufacturer said, "Too many are at present trying to benefit by

[5] *The Aluminum World*, Vol. 1, October, 1894.

the few pioneers who strike out into new fields, and the new-comers, by infringing on the original makers' goods and machinery, hang like a crying kid on the apron of mother who provides the food and nourishment." The officers of the association were Joseph E. Steinmetz, President; W. F. Pflueger, Vice President; W. H. Wagner, Vice President, and Palmer H. Langdon, Secretary-Treasurer. They called their organization "The American Aluminum Association." [6]

At the second annual meeting, which was held in September, 1902, in Pittsburgh, "birth place of the commercial aluminum industry," the Association discussed the following subjects:

> The extent of the present aluminum industry, giving firm names, capital involved, and goods made by them.
>
> The future of the aluminum industry in regard to its extension and its relation to the general trend of industrial competition and combinations.
>
> What can be done to assist the present manufacturers to eliminate unreasonable competition.
>
> Should each factory establish its own designs, grades and quality of goods regardless of other manufacturers' goods.

Predictions for the future of aluminum were not lacking in those days. Some of them were ahead of their time, but they make interesting reading in the light of today's markets. The New York *Sun*, in August, 1896, had an article entitled, "Next, the Aluminum Age." [7] One of the predictions read: "Aluminum is an excellent conductor of electricity and would, at 20 cents per pound, largely replace copper for all electrical purposes." Other

[6] *The Aluminum World*, Vol. 8, October, 1901.

[7] Reprinted in full in *The Aluminum World*, Vol. 2, August, 1896.

predictions in the article forecast large uses of the metal in rail-road cars, shipbuilding, decoration, bicycles and "horseless carriages."

What advertising The Pittsburgh Reduction Company did was largely confined to price quotations in a few publications and occasional circulars. The Company received benefit from technical articles on aluminum which Capt. Hunt wrote for various publications. Occasional exhibits provided the principal publicity technique used by the Company. It exhibited at Chicago and at Buffalo, its most pretentious exhibit in those days being the one at the World's Columbian Exposition in Chicago in 1893. The Pittsburgh Reduction Company was the only commercial manufacturer present as an aluminum exhibitor at the Chicago Fair. The exhibit stressed the process rather than products, which were few in those days. It showed:

(A) Ores of the metal, bauxite, cryolite, clay, etc.

(B) Processes used in the past

(C) Model of the Hall process with a careful notation saying "protected by U. S. Patent No. 400766"

(D) Samples of the first metal made by Hall and some 99.93 per cent pure aluminum made by The Pittsburgh Reduction Company

(E) A collection of miscellaneous articles made by various manufacturers from aluminum produced by the Company

Despite this showing at Chicago, the Company was not too keen about giving details of its technical operations at world's fairs, as indicated by a letter of September 2, 1904, from Charles

M. Hall to an executive of the Louisiana Purchase Exposition in St. Louis. Hall said:

> The blanks call for considerable detailed information in regard to our business which our people are reluctant to give for general publication. If our Company were only one of a dozen Companies manufacturing aluminum in this country it would be very different but as we are alone in the business, these facts if published with reference to the industry, would give our competitors in Europe, information which we would prefer to keep from them.
>
> We have had no similar requests for information at previous Expositions, particularly in Chicago and in Buffalo, and our Company has always received the highest awards.

While early markets did not provide big tonnage, things were happening which forecast the amazing use of aluminum in transportation, architecture and other fields. In 1903 people were shaking their heads in amazement or disbelief over a report that two brothers, Orville and Wilbur Wright, at Kittyhawk, North Carolina, had actually flown a heavier-than-air craft 852 feet. The Pittsburgh Reduction Company has the proud record of having furnished the aluminum in the airplane's engine, thus inaugurating one of the major markets for the metal in this global flying age. In 1907, at the Jamestown Exposition, an all-steel Pullman was shown. It marked the shift to metal construction in railroad cars, a shift that has opened up another large market for aluminum.

Even before Hall discovered his process and aluminum was still being made by expensive chemical methods, an architectural application of the metal appeared as a forerunner of the many architectural uses for aluminum today. On December 6, 1884, a small cast aluminum pyramid, weighing 100 ounces and costing $225 for the metal and manufacture, was mounted on the tip of the Washington Monument. An inspection made after fifty years' exposure showed the aluminum cap to be in good condition; the inscriptions engraved on the cap could be easily read after cleaning the surface.[8]

Early customers also forecast the future. In 1898 Ball Brothers of Muncie, Indiana, makers of Mason jars, made a contract with The Pittsburgh Reduction Company to buy aluminum covers for their jars. Thus began the business of aluminum seals and closures for all sorts of bottles and other types of containers. This today provides the substantial manufacturing business of the Aluminum Seal Company, Inc., a wholly-owned Alcoa subsidiary located at Richmond, Indiana. An early customer who pioneered a use still in existence, although largely outmoded, was the American Washboard Company. In these days of automatic washing machines that business is somewhat like the aluminum horseshoe business. In the Nineties The Pittsburgh Reduction Company did much research to develop an alloy hard enough to shoe all the horses in America. By the time this feat was accomplished, aluminum found a bigger market in the successor to the horse, the automobile. However, aluminum horseshoes, light yet strong, are standard equipment for race horses today. The bicycle era came at a time when aluminum was coming into its early popularity. Among the many models was the "Lu-Mi-Num" bicycle manufac-

[8] "Aluminum Cap-Piece on Washington Monument," E. H. Dix, Jr., *Metal Progress*, Vol. 26, December, 1934.

tured by the St. Louis Refrigerator & Wooden Gutter Company.

The early records show that on May 17, 1901, the Company decided to employ cable supervisors. These were and are electrical engineers trained in the installation of A.C.S.R. (short for aluminum cable steel-reinforced). This is the aluminum cable for high-tension lines of which there are nearly two million miles in the United States today.

In 1899 Mr. Davis learned that the Crocker interests of San Francisco were constructing a water power in the Sierras about ninety miles from the Golden Gate. He hastened to that section and made a sale of aluminum wire as the electrical conductor. Shortly thereafter, S. K. Colby secured a larger contract from the Snoqualmie Falls Power Company in Seattle, Washington, for 140,000 pounds of aluminum wire. The two expert aluminum salesmen had convinced utility customers that aluminum could do this job as well as or better than copper. There were no aluminum-wire mills and, when copper-wire manufacturers refused to make the aluminum wire, The Pittsburgh Reduction Company had to build its own wire mill.

The early single-strand aluminum wire was drawn from a 2 per cent copper alloy but it lacked sufficient strength and was replaced by seven-strand pure aluminum cable. This minimized breakage but it soon became apparent that pure aluminum did not have the inherent strength to withstand wind and sleet loads. The problem was solved by William Hoopes, Alcoa's chief electrical engineer, who devised a composite cable in which a galvanized steel core acts as support for the aluminum wire stranded around it. Thus was born A.C.S.R., so widely used today for high-tension transmission lines.

Early Markets

Early markets in the aluminum industry meant struggles, many of them discouraging. Nobody wanted the new metal in the beginning. Instead of contenting itself with making a material nobody wanted, The Pittsburgh Reduction Company and its successor, Alcoa, had to pioneer the new uses. Oft-times it had to engage in manufacturing operations itself when it could not, at first, induce others to go into the business. The Company's basic policy remains today that of a producer of the metal and a manufacturer of its mill products rather than the maker of end-use products. However, its early market history shows why, at times, it had to help establish a place for its metal by actually making consumer goods.

CHAPTER NINE

Growth and Development

☆ ☆ ☆ ☆ ☆ ☆ ☆ ☆ ☆

T HIS CHAPTER might also be titled "Organization and Integration." Certainly the first three decades of Company history are replete with instances where the men of Alcoa had to build an integrated business, not only from mine to metal but also in the manufacture of shapes and forms which makers of end-use products could utilize. They were compelled to do all that if their business was to assume a decent place in this competitive world. In addition, they frequently had to pioneer in the making of certain products before other manufacturers would accept aluminum as a suitable material for such articles.

Men played an important part in all of this—many men throughout the Company organization as well as the directing heads. This manpower of the Alcoa organization, spearheaded by aluminum-trained veterans, is still more important than machinery and equipment. In the Alcoa family today are more than four thousand men with over twenty-five years of aluminum experience. Thinking of these men and all their associates with less years of service, President Roy A. Hunt related a few years ago the outcome of a dream in which an evil genie appeared and forced him to decide between the destruction of all the buildings and machinery of Alcoa and the loss of his organization. His answer was, "Destroy the plants but leave us the men. We will build new plants."

Pittsburgh has its rightful place in this matter of men with courage and vision. In an address in 1928, H. V. Churchill, for many years Chief of the Analytical Division of Aluminum Research Laboratories, paid this tribute to the spirit of Pittsburgh:

Aluminum is a Pittsburgh product—not because Pittsburgh has abundant supplies of bauxite ores, for she has not; and not because Pittsburgh has abundant hydroelectric power, for she has not. Aluminum is a Pittsburgh product because Pittsburgh, despite its reputation for smoke and grime, is primarily interested in men. Here in Pittsburgh, as in no other community of the United States, does creative genius get a hearing and sound backing. It was Pittsburgh that gave opportunity to Carnegie with his age of steel, it was Pittsburgh that listened to Westinghouse when he dreamed of stopping a train with air, it was Pittsburgh that listened to Brashear with his vision of astronomic achievement, and it was Pittsburgh that listened to an Ohio college boy with his vision of the possibilities of a new and light metal. Not only did it listen, but it gave substantial assistance so that today the aluminum industry, nurtured by Pittsburgh capital and fostered by Pittsburgh control, has grown to touch almost every field of endeavor.[1]

It was natural that from Pittsburgh would come the decisions to expand operations and to increase facilities. As early as 1890 the Smallman Street Works had proved to be inadequate and the move was made to New Kensington. By 1891 pig aluminum ingot was being produced there, and by 1893 a sheet-rolling mill had been installed. By 1895 Niagara Falls was the location of the re-duction works. In the decade of the Nineties and the two which followed, Alcoa spread its integrated operations from Pittsburgh into New York State at Niagara Falls and at Massena, into New Jersey at Edgewater, into Ohio at Cleveland, into Illinois at East St. Louis, into Tennessee at Alcoa, into North Carolina at Badin and in the Great Smoky Mountains, into the fluorspar mines of Kentucky, and into the bauxite fields of Arkansas, Georgia and Alabama. Today Alcoa plants, doing things which range from ore mining to the manufacture of useful consumer products, are located in sixteen states and in twenty-five different communities. With the manufacture of cooking utensils at the turn of the cen-tury, production operations for everything from the mining of bauxite to the manufacture of semifabricated aluminum shapes and forms, and even end-use products, came along as a matter of sound business.

The need for integrated operations became apparent to Capt. Hunt in the Nineties. On June 7, 1897, he wrote an important

[1] "Pittsburgh and the Pittsburgh Spirit," Pittsburgh Chamber of Commerce, 1927–28, p. 184.

policy letter to Charles Martin Hall at Niagara Falls. In the letter appeared this significant paragraph:

> In the future sale of aluminum, a development of our rolling mills, forging plant and foundry in the making of aluminum into all of the shapes in which brass is shipped and sold by the brass cutting-up mills, will be a further great aid to us in the development of the aluminum market.

All of these expansions were made with due regard to cost. The only way they were possible was through the fixed Company policy of plowing back earnings into the business. This policy gave the growing concern some reserves and a better borrowing capacity. On actual routine expenditures the Company and all of its executives, including the minor ones, were quite money-conscious. There is the amusing story of the dead horse at New Kensington which well illustrates this.

In the days before automobile trucks, horse carts were used to haul away rubbish. With considerable construction work on the way at New Kensington, the Company rented horses from the livery stables in the town. A horse pulling a two-wheel dump-cart loaded with brickbats was backed up to an old railroad tie serving as a stop bumper at the edge of the bluff overlooking the Allegheny River. It was routine practice to dump the contents of the cart into the river below. This time the driver was not careful, and over went cart, horse and all to a watery grave. The youthful Roy A. Hunt, then superintendent of the New Kensington Works, acted promptly. He sent the master mechanic, Dave McDonald, armed with $200 in cash, to buy the horse, supposedly a live one. McDonald came back shortly with a receipted bill of sale at $110 and a $90 saving. The liveryman received a fair price for his horse but nothing like what he would have asked had he known the animal was dead.

Much has already been written in this chronicle about the expansion of facilities to acquire bauxite and electric energy. Something has also been said about the entrance of the Company into cooking-utensil manufacture and into wire drawing. Not enough has been told about the securing of cryolite, a necessary material which acts as the solvent for alumina in the operation of the Hall electrolytic process. Cryolite in its natural state comes from Greenland, a colony of the Danish government. The distribution of this Greenland cryolite in the United States was handled through the Pennsylvania Salt Manufacturing Company, from whom The Pittsburgh Reduction Company purchased it. In fact, Alcoa still obtains some natural cryolite from Penn Salt, the abbreviated term by which this company is known. Shipping from Greenland in the Arctic Circle has always presented a problem since only one or two ships per year can make the round trip.[2]

The making of both aluminum fluoride and synthetic cryolite became manufacturing operations of Alcoa in due course. In 1905 a fluoride plant with twelve cast-iron stills was constructed at East St. Louis. A year later aluminum fluoride production at this plant amounted to 700,000 pounds. The process was one of producing hydrofluoric acid from fluorspar and sulphuric acid. The hydrofluoric acid was combined with alumina hydrate to form aluminum fluoride. In 1909 the records show that 1,154,000

[2] *Prologue to Tomorrow*, History of the first one hundred years of the Pennsylvania Salt Manufacturing Company, Robert Keith Leavitt, 1950.

pounds of fluorspar from the Kentucky mines were used at East St. Louis to make 625,000 pounds of aluminum fluoride and 267,000 pounds of synthetic cryolite. However, the commercial manufacture of cryolite did not begin until 1916 at the East St. Louis Works. These commercial developments were preceded by much experimentation which had started at New Kensington as early as 1898.

While The Pittsburgh Reduction Company made aluminum ingot or pig in 1890, few customers could create a business based on a supply of this commodity. Special rolling mills and other machinery had to be constructed to work the aluminum ingot into usable forms. No such mills existed and the aluminum-making concern had to expand its business to provide these facilities. There were rolling mills for brass, to be sure, but brass people were not keen about aiding a competitive material. The Company tried without success to get brass mills in Connecticut to roll aluminum sheet.

In the early Nineties two brass rollers, Harry Davis and George Doolittle, were brought from the Naugatuck Valley to New Kensington to teach the aluminum people how to roll sheet. Henry Davis, always called "Harry," was a Welshman who had migrated to New England as a lad. He had learned the art of metal rolling with Wallace & Son, silversmiths, and with the American Brass Company. Prior to joining The Pittsburgh Reduction Company he had rolled many different metals ranging from brass to gold. George Doolittle was the sheet mill superintendent at New Kensington for many years. He was most particular about the quality of his product. One of the numerous stories about him illustrates the point. If he saw a fly light on the polished rolls, he would hasten to brush off the insect before it could leave a mark on the aluminum sheet.

Coiled sheet was made first at New Kensington, and flat sheets came a bit later. The earliest aluminum rolling outside of New Kensington was done by the Scovill Company at Waterbury, Connecticut, but their operations were confined to so-called powder plates—thick aluminum slabs used in special presses by powder-making concerns. After all, Scovill was primarily interested in brass, not aluminum. Aluminum sheet, the most popular of all aluminum products today, was largely the responsibility of Alcoa in the pioneering days.

Neither brass nor steel manufacturers considered it wise or desirable to go into the rolling of aluminum sheet. Steel manufacturers would probably have installed special equipment before attempting to roll aluminum, although Harry Davis proved in the Nineties it could be done on existing equipment when he rolled for the United States Navy some aluminum sheets ninety-four inches wide on a steel mill at Hapsburg, Pennsylvania. This particular order was too large for the aluminum mill at New Kensington to handle. Brass rolling mills could have made aluminum sheet although it might not have been perfect because of surface contamination from fine particles of brass.

A similar attitude made it necessary for Alcoa to build a mill to make aluminum wire. The experiences of Messrs. Davis and Colby when they sold the first aluminum electric high-tension lines and could get no wire manufacturer to make the aluminum wire is told elsewhere. Alcoa had no choice other than to make this wire, which it did by buying a small seven-strand machine and a large twenty-six-strand job imported from England and known in the Company for many years as the "Johnny Bull" cabling machine. Wire drawing and cable making were carried on at New Kensington for several years but this operation was moved to Massena, New York, in 1904.

The practice of extruding aluminum into useful shapes was introduced early in the century. Here again Alcoa had to pioneer by buying an extrusion press in 1905 and hiring Louis de Cazenove, a relative of the Du Ponts, to operate the machine. After some years of painful experimentation, aluminum shapes produced by the extrusion method with hydraulic presses became a commercial product of the New Kensington mills.

While one or two small manufacturers made a limited amount of aluminum tubing in the Nineties, no one felt this field had sufficient promise until Alcoa tackled the job seriously by installing a modest tube-drawing plant at New Kensington. From this it was but a step to the drawing of aluminum tubing in larger sizes. Making satisfactory tubing at a reasonable cost proved to be a long and tedious process. A market acceptance had to be created at the same time. It appeared a slim chance, but since it afforded an outlet for aluminum, the Company was willing to expend the capital and effort necessary to develop this technique.

The fabrication of shapes or large sections such as channels came along in substantial fashion in 1930 when the Company built a large mill for this purpose. A description of this venture is really part of a later chapter on competition, but enough should be told here to illustrate this effort toward further integration. Nobody made these large shapes, essential in railroad-car building. Without an order on the books, Alcoa gambled on a three-million-dollar expenditure for a mill at Massena on which channels, angles and other sections could be rolled. It was a long shot which has paid off in the use of aluminum in transportation and in the building of bridges and other structures.

In all of these expansion programs personnel was important. Decisions of top management were necessary, but experienced men with aluminum know-how, or the willingness to acquire it patiently, were also essential. Much of this building of an integrated business was forced upon Alcoa in an effort to create markets for its aluminum ingot. Had aluminum been accepted promptly for all of its present uses by responsible manufacturers, it is doubtful if Alcoa would have gone further than the first three steps in integration—mining and refining the ore, making alumina, and then producing aluminum.

The Company had to go into the manufacture of sheet, cable, extruded and forged shapes, wire, rod, bar, castings, foil, powder and paste, and screw machine products. It had to go even further into the manufacture of cooking utensils, bottle caps and aluminum furniture. Alcoa stated in an advertisement recently, "We make pigs, not potato mashers," [3] thereby reiterating the Company's traditional policy of making end-use products only when someone else refused to do the pioneering. Some of these end-use products Alcoa no longer makes because other manufacturers have done the job thoroughly. In some cases, for good business reasons, it has continued to make these items. Despite its traditional policy, Alcoa on occasion has felt it necessary to carry its integration into the consumer field to add to the public's aluminum-mindedness.

[3] *Time*, May 5, 1947; *Newsweek*, May 12, 1947; *Nation's Business* and *Science Illustrated*, June, 1947.

In this development period the late Edwin S. Fickes, Alcoa's Chief Engineer and a Vice President until his retirement, was responsible for the construction of the Company's extensive reduction works and manufacturing establishments. Mr. Fickes also took great interest in the Company's research work and encouraged the professional activities of its men in technical societies.

The period of growth during the early years of the Company's history was not without some attention from Government, which has kept a watchful eye on the aluminum business throughout the years. In this expansion era, when the Company was trying to find outlets for its metal, it ran afoul of the Federal agencies whenever they thought its actions bordered on suppression of competition. Such an incident was the Cleveland Metal Products case, cited in later years by the Department of Justice as an example of Alcoa's alleged attitude.

Cleveland Metal Products Company was a concern engaged prior to 1913 in making enameled steel utensils, oil stoves and heaters. In that year it entered the aluminum-utensil field. In 1915 it completed a rolling mill, buying its ingot from abroad. During World War I it made good money selling its rolled sheet at higher prices than those at which Alcoa promised the Government it would sell. Reduced sheet prices came along at the end of the war and the Cleveland concern found itself operating at a loss. Its President, Mr. Ramsey, appealed to Alcoa, an important creditor, for help. Alcoa responded by forming the Aluminum Rolling Mill Company to take over the assets. Alcoa took two thirds of the $600,000 stock issue, with the balance going to the old company. The Federal Trade Commission attacked this transaction on the grounds that it was a deliberate attempt to suppress a competitor. The Courts upheld this contention and Alcoa sold its stock.[4]

Meanwhile, however, the new company had again become a heavy debtor to Alcoa, which was compelled to foreclose and take the property at sheriff's sale. When the Federal Trade Commission attacked this sale, the Court ruled in favor of Alcoa. The Company in this matter had gone no further than to "avail itself of the provisions of the law open to every creditor for the collection of what was justly owing it." [5]

Some of the compelling reasons for Alcoa's policy of integration were outlined in a memorandum in 1937 by George J. Stanley, Vice President and General Sales Manager. Mr. Stanley retired in 1948 after a long and successful career in the Company. He continues to be a member of the Alcoa Board of Directors. The Stanley memorandum listed these points: (1) Alcoa had to integrate in the early days because there were no markets unless the Company developed them, (2) the cost of such development and the risks involved could only be undertaken by an integrated company, (3) variations in the quality and form of any product can best be studied by an integrated setup before the product is marketed, (4) an integrated organization is able to do some of the customer's research for him, (5) accumulated knowledge of a company engaged in all phases of aluminum manufacture provides essential information on the behavior of alloying elements and thus makes it easier to perfect a product, (6) better

[4] Aluminum Company of America vs. Federal Trade Commission, 284F401.
[5] Opinion of Judge Francis G. Caffey, United States vs. Aluminum Company of America, 44 F. Supp. 97. This footnote will also serve for future references to the Caffey decision.

management efficiency comes through integration in production, sales, advertising, purchasing, transportation and standardization, (7) interchange of information in an integrated concern makes for better products at lower prices, (8) research groups large enough to include specialists in all fields who can exchange information with each other can best be financed by an integrated company.

At any rate, the growth of Alcoa during its first thirty years was all in the direction of integrated operation. This policy has continued throughout the entire history of the Company. Its corporate setup, with numerous subsidiaries, functions as a unified whole aimed at the twin objectives of making aluminum more useful and more attractive in price to those who appreciate its virtues.

CHAPTER TEN

Research

☆ ☆ ☆ ☆ ☆ ☆ ☆ ☆ ☆

Two expressions concerning aluminum and Alcoa are much more than trite sayings. One of them is "Alcoa was born of research." The other is "Nature made aluminum light but research has made it strong." Alcoa was literally founded on Charles Martin Hall's pioneering researches which culminated in his discovery of the Hall process for making aluminum.[1] Hall and the research men of Alcoa who followed him devoted themselves to the never-ending task of making aluminum and aluminum products of greater service to mankind.

The zest for experimentation animated Hall as long as he lived. In the earliest days at Smallman Street and at New Kensington, he worked early and late to increase the efficiency of operation of his process. In a letter to his sister Julia, written from Pittsburgh two months after the first aluminum was made at Smallman Street, he told how he was dispensing with external heat

[1] See page 11 for description.

and using thick linings for the pots so that the heat generated by the electrolytic current would be sufficient to maintain the fused bath in a molten state. Subsequent letters from Pittsburgh and New Kensington contain frequent references to other research projects he was planning. A notebook of the inventor has data and suggestions for experimentation on twenty projects on which he had worked between February 14, 1888, and November 15, 1889.

At Niagara Falls, Hall had further opportunity to pursue his researches. On November 16, 1900, he wrote Julia, "My new scheme for making alumina, I think, is working out finely. On our present output it will save us $200,000 and more per year, but it will take a year to install it in a large way, and, besides, we have contracts for high-priced alumina for our consumption for a year and a half." Although, as described elsewhere, Alcoa finally came to adopt the Bayer process as the most satisfactory method for producing alumina from bauxite, Hall experimented for several years with a "dry process" which uses carbon in an electric furnace to reduce the impurities, iron, silicon and titanium, to the metallic state and then separates them from the molten pure alumina. His efforts were unsuccessful, but a quarter of a century later Dr. Francis C. Frary, Director of Alcoa's Aluminum Research Laboratories, and his associates solved the problem and put the process into brief commercial operation.

Despite his earnest endeavors to improve the aluminum-making business, Hall did not confine his research activities to that field. He worked intermittently from 1884 until well after the turn of the century in an attempt to make a practical electric battery which would convert a gaseous fuel, such as hydrogen or carbon monoxide, directly into electricity by electrochemical re-action at the battery electrodes. Hall's novel idea was to employ porous electrodes, of carbon or of metal, through which the gases could be introduced and brought to the electrolyte in con-tact with the electrode. While such a battery has intrigued in-ventors before and after Hall, no one has yet made it practical.

The decade 1910 to 1920 was marked by events of world im-portance. It was also an important period in the development of Alcoa. Hall died in 1914. World War I soon brought a greatly increased demand for aluminum, and with this demand came new problems in production, fabrication and utilization. For ex-ample, a critical need for strong aluminum sheet able to resist corrosive conditions in the tropics led to the development, by Alcoa's Earl Blough, of the alloy known as 3S. Blough tested and proved his new alloy in the artificially created tropical climate of the Phipps Conservatory in Pittsburgh. Today, thirty-five years later, this alloy in its various wrought forms is still of major importance to the industry. Interest in alloys was further increased by the invention by Wilm, in Germany, of the alloy duralumin. This alloy could be given greatly increased strength by heat treatment. It received international publicity by its use in the structure of the Zeppelin airships.

This period also marked the beginning in America of industrial research, organized on a substantial scale. Although research was an activity well recognized by Alcoa, it was informally organized and frequently had to be put aside for more pressing production problems. The management clearly foresaw that the needs of the future could be anticipated and met only by a research depart-ment, well staffed and equipped with the instruments of modern science. In its search for a leader for this enterprise, the Company was fortunate to meet a young and vigorous scientist named Francis C. Frary. After investigation, Frary seized the offered opportunity and became Director of Research for Alcoa in December, 1918. The department, first known as the Research Bureau, soon began to make substantial contributions in its field. Before many years, the growth of the department necessitated new quarters. A laboratory in New Kensington, representing the most advanced ideas in construction and equipment, was finished and occupied in January, 1930. The organization was appropriately named Aluminum Research Laboratories.[2]

When the Research Bureau was first organized, it assumed supervision of the research activities of the castings division in Cleveland. The research work on castings and forgings grew to such an extent that a new laboratory was eventually required. This group moved into their modern quarters there in 1944.

To facilitate research on problems having to do with alumina and fluorides, a small research group was also established at the works of the Aluminum Ore Company in East St. Louis, Illinois. To accelerate research vital to defense, a Development Laboratory was finished at this location in 1944, and in 1950 a modern Research Laboratory was completed and occupied. These laboratories are continuing to play an important part in the utilization of low-grade domestic ores to provide an adequate supply of alumina in the event that foreign bauxite importations are cut off under war conditions.

The Alcoa Combination Process for recovering alumina from

---

[2] "Research in the Aluminum industry," Francis C. Frary, *Journal of Industrial and Engineering Chemistry*, Vol. 31, January, 1939.

low-grade high-silica bauxites was born at East St. Louis. The conventional Bayer process is uneconomical for treating bauxites of this type because of the loss of both alumina and soda in the residual red mud. Research found a way of recovering a substantial part of this alumina and soda by sintering the red mud with limestone and soda ash, leeching the sinter with water, and returning the recovered sodium-aluminate solution to the Bayer-process digesters.

Several pieces of "unfinished business" were given attention in the first years of the Research Bureau. The Alcoa Dry Process for making pure alumina has already been referred to. Although the successful development of this process was achieved by Frary and his co-workers, the stimulus of competition within the Company resulted in improvements in the Bayer process which kept it from being displaced.

Getting a high-purity aluminum from the electrolytic reduction cells intrigued Hall and his associates from the very beginning. The best they could do in production was still not pure enough to establish the properties of the "pure" metal. It was not until 1919 that William Hoopes, with the co-operation of Dr. Frary, Junius D. Edwards, and others in the new Alcoa research organization, developed a novel commercial cell and process for the electrolytic refining of aluminum to a high state of purity. Aluminum with a purity of 99.99 per cent can be produced by this process.

However, aluminum, regardless of its degree of purity, would not have gone very far in meeting the needs of industry even in the early days. Alloys were needed just as they are today. Alloying can make aluminum stronger and give to it other useful properties. In the Smallman Street days, little thought was given to aluminum alloys, the primary job being the making of commercially pure aluminum. Before many years, however, Capt. Hunt and his associates were becoming greatly interested in alloying ingredients to make their aluminum stronger and more useful. The alloys of aluminum have remained, to this day, a fertile field for investigation.

The ingenious experiments of Merica and his co-workers [3] at the National Bureau of Standards provided a working theory for the remarkable increase in strength resulting from the heat treatment of the alloy duralumin. This was a great stimulus to research in aluminum alloys. In the early Twenties, for example, Alcoa research produced 25S. Alcoa 25S was the first strong, heat-treatable aluminum alloy that proved practical for forging, an art which made the aluminum propeller standard equipment for aircraft.[4] Other alloys suitable for forging have followed in the race for greater speed and strength in the air. In addition to alloys 25S and 51S, research men Zay Jeffries and R. S. Archer discovered the secret of producing strong aluminum alloy castings by heat treatment. One of their most important inventions in this field was Alcoa alloy 195. Duralumin, a notable foreign contribution in World War I, will have its place in another chapter, but Alcoa research men have created improved heat-treatable alloys which have superseded it.

Strength is not the only requirement in aluminum alloys. Re-

[3] "Heat-Treatment of Duralumin," Merica, Waltenberg and Scott, U. S. Bureau of Standards Scientific Paper No. 347, 1919.
[4] "New Developments in High Strength Aluminum Alloys," R. S. Archer and Zay Jeffries, *American Institute of Mining and Metallurgical Engineers*, Vol. 71, p. 828, 1925.

sistance to corrosion is important. Edgar H. Dix, Jr., of Aluminum Research Laboratories, developed Alclad 17S sheet which has a strong alloy core with thin surface layers of pure aluminum integrally bonded to the core. This was followed by Alclad 24S sheet, a stronger and still more serviceable material in aircraft. With these and other clad products such as Alclad 75S developed by Alcoa research, the thin cladding electrolytically protects the strength-giving core against corrosive attack. The alclad products were first introduced in 1928. The passage of time and commercial experience have confirmed the first tests of their durability and reliability. New clad alloy products are being introduced year by year. The alclad products have, without a doubt, been a major contribution to aluminum metallurgy and indispensable in the development of military and civil aircraft.

The alloys of aluminum commonly contain, in addition to aluminum, small amounts of other metals such as copper, magnesium, zinc, manganese, silicon, iron, nickel and chromium. The metals are selected and the amounts chosen, after extensive investigation, to give as nearly as possible the desired properties. The alloy is formed by melting the metals together with the aluminum and casting the product into suitable form. Certain of the alloys can be given additional strength and other desirable properties by heat treatment of the alloy product in wrought or cast form. Certain alloy compositions are best adapted to working, such as rolling, forging and drawing. Other alloys are developed for making castings and, in general, have compositions which are significantly different from the wrought alloys.

In the year 1915, the aluminum industry operated with about three wrought alloys and several more for cast products. Today the standard wrought alloys made by Alcoa are twenty-seven in number, with a somewhat larger number of casting alloys. At the present time, Alcoa makes available to customers a series of wrought aluminum products ranging in tensile strength from about 12,000 pounds per square inch for annealed aluminum to 90,000 pounds per square inch for 75S-T6 extrusions. The objective has been to provide the widest range of useful properties with the minimum number of alloys. In the past thirty years, many alloys which once saw satisfactory service have been replaced with even better alloys.[5] Certain of the alloys have been developed for use in special applications, such as making screw machine products, reflectors, gift ware and beer barrels, to mention only a few.

While alloys have been one field of investigation singled out for special mention, the activities of Alcoa research have extended from bauxite to beer barrels, from metal production to metal fabrication, with both process and product research. The production of refined alumina has been under continued investigation to lower costs and find ways of utilizing lower-grade ores. Lower prices for aluminum lead to bigger markets—the goal of the industry from its start. Many applications of aluminum have followed the development of new methods of fabrication such as welding, brazing and soldering. Aluminum is an adaptable metal and research has developed methods of finishing, such as electrolytic oxidation (Alumilite Process), which have broadened markets.[6] Years of fundamental research on the mechanical properties of aluminum and its alloys, carried out under the super-

[5] "Aluminum Alloys—1940 to 1950," E. H. Dix, Jr.; *Metal Progress*, Vol. 58, October, 1950.
[6] "Performance and Structure of Anodic Coatings on Aluminum," F. Keller and Junius D. Edwards, *Iron Age*, Vol. 156, November, 1945.

vision of R. L. Templin, have developed the data for the efficient design of aluminum structures.[7] This information has been made available to everyone in Alcoa's *Structural Aluminum Handbook* —the first manual of its kind.

In the field of process development, Alcoa's achievements, in the production of cast ingots for making aluminum alloys in wrought form, have been outstanding. In the early days of the industry, sheet was rolled from 100-pound ingots and the size of sheet was limited accordingly. As markets developed, demands came for larger and larger ingots, sheet and plate, and particularly for large rolled sections such as angles, channels and I-beams. Many technical difficulties were experienced, however, in producing large and metallurgically sound ingots of the strong alloys. Fundamental study of the problem culminated in the invention, in the middle Thirties, by Alcoa's W. T. Ennor, of the well-known DC ingot-casting process. Molten metal is poured into a short mold and a continuous ingot drawn out at the bottom. The name DC or Direct Chill comes from the fact that the ingot is chilled and solidified by water flowing down the outside of the casting as soon as it emerges from the short mold in which the initial outside shell of the ingot is formed. Now, in Alcoa's newest mill at Davenport, Iowa, 7,000-pound ingots are regularly being cast and rolled into sheet and plate.

In the past thirty years, Alcoa research men have contributed over nine hundred articles to the technical and scientific press, carrying to the user and prospective user of aluminum authentic information about aluminum and the newest developments in the field. Books by Alcoa authors include *The Aluminum Industry*

[7] "The Fatigue Properties of Light Metals and Alloys," R. L. Templin; *Proceedings*, American Society for Testing Materials, *33*, Part II, 1933.

(Edwards, Frary and Jeffries); *The Science of Metals* (Jeffries and Archer); *Aluminum Paint and Powder* (Edwards); *The Alloys of Iron and Aluminum* (Kent R. Van Horn, Associate Director of Aluminum Research Laboratories, and S. L. Case, Battelle Institute). Alcoa's men have been active in technical societies and the Company has been generous with their time and with financial assistance. A notable example is the support given the American Society for Testing Materials. The Company has cooperated with the Army, Navy and Air Force in supplying information which might be helpful in their use of light metals. Alcoa research men have given freely of their time and technical information to promote the work of such Governmental agencies as the National Advisory Committee for Aeronautics, the Research and Development Board of the National Defense Department, and others.

Achievements by Alcoa research men have been recognized many times by scientific societies. A list of these honors would take substantial space. The famous Perkin Medal has been awarded to two Alcoa men—Charles Martin Hall in 1911 and Francis C. Frary in 1944.

The alert and efficient performances of Alcoa's research organization have received wide acclaim not only in the scientific field but in the realms of business and Government.[8] In a speech in 1944 at the dedication of the Laboratory at East St. Louis, Philip B. Wilson of the War Production Board said:

I must take this opportunity to pay, on behalf of the War Production Board, a sincere and well-earned tribute to the

[8] Many quotations could be given but one will suffice.

144

research engineers of the Aluminum Company and to the Company itself for their outstanding contribution to the war effort. Without the splendid co-operation of the Company's technical staff and the unselfish willingness of the management to take on problems and tasks, no matter how onerous, the splendid record of rapid and efficient expansion of aluminum supply to the full amount required for 125,000 airplanes per year would never have been achieved.

CHAPTER ELEVEN

World War I

☆ ☆ ☆ ☆ ☆ ☆ ☆ ☆ ☆

WHILE THE DEMAND for aluminum in the First World War was only a fraction of the requirements for the metal in the global flying struggle of the 1940's, the war which lasted from 1914 to 1918 placed great responsibilities on Aluminum Company of America, then the only producer of pig aluminum on the North American continent. The Company had to produce aluminum to meet the war demands of America and its allies and to care for, as best it could, the requests from civilian users.

Just as in the late war, the domestic customer had to do without in many instances, but Alcoa's role of patriotic service in World War I is a matter of proud record. Perhaps the best description of the Company's participation in the war is contained in a book by Grosvenor B. Clarkson published in 1923 and entitled *Industrial America in the World War*. He says:

147

The sole producer of aluminum metal in the United States and Canada is the Aluminum Company of America; consequently Arthur Davis, the president of that company, could speak and act for the whole industry in dealing with the War Industries Board. He virtually placed the industry at the disposition of the Government and acted at all times on the highest plane of service and patriotism. On April 25, 1917, he offered to the Government, through Mr. Baruch, all the aluminum it might require at that time at its own price, despite the fact that the outside price was 60 cents.

Two million pounds were immediately accepted at 27½ cents, and later six million pounds were added, delivery to be made before August. In September, Mr. Davis agreed with the War Industries Board through Mr. Meyer to fill all war industry requirements, direct or indirect, at the current 38-cent base price and to refund the difference should the Government later name a lower price. Owing to the shortage that began to develop at a later period, the Federal Trade Commission was asked to investigate the costs of aluminum manufacture. With the Commission's report before it, the Price-Fixing Committee in agreement with the Aluminum Company fixed the base price at 32 cents for aluminum ingots in fifty-ton lots, f.o.b. the producing plants. This price prevailed until June 1, 1918, when it was raised one cent, and the price remained at 33 cents until it expired by agreement March 1, 1919.

There is a considerable quantity of aluminum brought to the market each year through the resmelting of scrap aluminum, but no particular difficulty was encountered in dealing with this secondary product.

With the United States in the war, the demand for aluminum for military purposes rose to ninety per cent of the production, and control of distribution was necessary. This was effected by the application of priority principles, the Aluminum Company being allowed considerable latitude of judgment in determining the relative priority of the orders, which consumers were authorized to place with it directly. When the Company was doubtful of the validity of its own judgment in this matter, it referred the question to the Non-Ferrous Metals Section. Secondary or resmelted aluminum was also purchased by consumers directly from the smelters, but only on the approval of priority application by the section.

In the first part of the war the European demand for aluminum was chiefly for use in the form of dust to make an explosive in combination with ammonium nitrate. Other military uses of aluminum were found in the manufacture of mess, personal, and horse equipment, drop bombs, fuses, flares, fillers, hand grenades, heavy ammunition, rifle cartridges, and for airplanes, aeronautical engines, castings, and all kinds of engines. In normal times the chief industries using aluminum are the automotive industry, which consumes 15,500 tons; the steel industry, which uses 5000 tons as a deoxidizing agent; and the manufacture of utensils, which takes 12,000 tons.

During 1918 the production of primary aluminum in the United States fell from the 100,000 tons of 1917 to 67,000 tons, because of a shortage of water power during the winter, and the situation became somewhat delicate. The Aluminum Company undertook to enlarge its capacity, but this was not accomplished before the end of the war.

The control of aluminum was the perfect model of the War Industries Board's principle of concentration, because, outside of the secondary metal producers, the industry was in the hands of a single well-intentioned man, and did not necessitate even the friction that arises in a small committee. Even when it developed that the French importers were making a profit on aluminum obtained through the War Industries Board at the Government price, Mr. Davis, though protesting and asking for a rectification of this injustice, was never obstructive.[1]

The impact of the war was felt by Alcoa long before President Wilson declared that a state of hostility existed between the United States and Germany. The British took 72,000,000 pounds from the American producer between 1915 and 1917. The French and Italian governments came along later but did purchase 17,000,000 pounds in 1917 and 1918. The British, French and Italian Commissions maintained headquarters in Washington from which point purchases of aluminum were made for the various governments. Well might the Allies look to America for aluminum. Owing to a severe shortage of copper, Germany was building up her aluminum production at a rapid rate. From a total consumption of 4,000,000 pounds in 1904, Germany had increased this fivefold by 1913. At the end of the war she was con-

[1] *Industrial America in the World War*, Grosvenor B. Clarkson, pp. 355, 356, 357, Houghton Mifflin Co., 1923.

suming aluminum, largely for military purposes, at a rate in excess of 75,000,000 pounds per annum.

Germany was the leader in aluminum applications for war purposes during the First World War. Necessity, due to shortage of other materials, spurred her to prepare aluminum alloys for use in the manufacture of motor cars, trucks, tanks, machinery, utensils, aircraft and aircraft explosives, as well as scores of other military uses. A German, Alfred Wilm, contributed duralumin, a strong aluminum alloy, to aluminum metallurgy in time for it to be of real service to Germany during the war. Wilm did more than to create the alloy physically; he opened a new field of metallurgy in the heat treatment of aluminum. Wilm deserves the credit for his discovery although his name is not identified with his alloy. It was called duralumin because Wilm gave an exclusive commercial license for its manufacture to Dürener Metallwerke, a German concern. Duralumin was coined from "Dürener" and "aluminium."

Armed with this knowledge of heat treatment, C. F. Nagel, Jr., supervised the commercial development of a similar alloy known as 17S. Over the years, Alcoa's Chief Metallurgist Nagel and his associates in the many fabricating plants of Alcoa made products from a great range of tough alloys from which American aircraft manufacturers were to make the fighters and bombers which played an efficient role in World War II.

With 90 per cent of its World War I production going into war uses, Alcoa found itself at the peak with a physical plant composed of the following units: Bauxite mines, Bauxite, Arkansas; Bauxippi terminal, Bauxippi, Arkansas (near Memphis, Tennessee); fluorspar mine, Mexico, Kentucky; ore refineries,

East St. Louis, Illinois; smelting, fabricating and power plants, Niagara Falls, New York; fabricating plants, New Kensington, Arnold and Logans Ferry, Pennsylvania; smelting, fabricating, carbon and power plants, Massena, New York; fabricating plant, Edgewater, New Jersey; smelting, carbon and fabricating plants, Alcoa, Tennessee; smelting, carbon and power plants, Badin, North Carolina; power plant and transmission system, Calderwood, Tennessee; bauxite mine, Hermitage, Georgia; ore refinery, Baltimore, Maryland (under construction); ocean fleet connecting Baltimore, Maryland, to South American mines; smelting and fabricating plants, Shawinigan Falls, Quebec, Canada; fabricating plant, Toronto, Ontario, Canada.

The Company's already existing plants were expanded to meet war needs for aluminum and some facilities were created which can be classed as pure "war babies," useless to Alcoa at the end of hostilities. To increase production of alumina, the Company not only constructed an additional works at East St. Louis but began, on April 17, 1917, the building of an alumina plant at Baltimore, Maryland. The intent was to use bauxite from South America at the Baltimore alumina works. The job was rushed forward, but inability to secure machinery and other materials for two plants of like character caused the Company to hasten the completion of No. 2 Works at East St. Louis which had already been started. It had an assured supply of domestic bauxite whereas the Baltimore operation was dependent upon an adequate ocean-going fleet to transfer bauxite from South America through U-boat infested Caribbean waters.

Although at Baltimore dock and shore bulkheads were completed, trackage, sewer and water lines laid, foundations installed, much steel framework finished, and precipitation tanks and other equipment delivered, the job was not completed. At the war's close, structural iron, knocked-down tanks, bricks and machinery parts, were lying about the partially completed structures. A few of the buildings had brick walls. Even had it been finished, the plant would have been useless without the necessary fleet of ore-carrying boats.

As the war progressed, considerable anxiety was felt over the ability of the Arkansas bauxite fields to supply enough high-grade ore. In December, 1916, the officials of Aluminum Company of America entered into a contract with the Riter-Conley Company for the fabrication of two steel schooners to transport ore from South America. In May, 1918, the Company moved further in this program by contracting with the Union Shipbuilding Company (formerly Riter-Conley) to build two steel steamers and one steel tug and to convert the two schooners already under construction into ocean-going barges to be towed by the steamers. It was out of the question to charter ships as every available large craft was being operated to carry troops, food and munitions to Europe.

Although the U. S. Shipping Board gave its prompt approval to this program, the Armistice was signed before the ships and barges were finished. While the ships had some salvage value to Alcoa at the close of the war, they were of questionable market value since they were hastily constructed during a hectic war period in the shipbuilding industry.

To increase the facilities for bauxite shipment from Arkansas to East St. Louis during the war, when rail transportation was congested, Alcoa built a terminal plant on the Mississippi River near Memphis, Tennessee. This plant was at Bauxippi, Arkansas. The terminal eliminated the long delays of rail transfers in the 365-mile haul from the mines to East St. Louis. The terminal was on a direct line of the Rock Island Railroad so that the Company's 155 steel hopper cars could come directly from the mines to Bauxippi and then be sent by river barge to the alumina plant at East St. Louis without further delay. When the war ended, this bauxite terminal became definitely a war casualty and was later sold.

This wartime need for river transportation was responsible for Alcoa ownership of the famous tugboat Sprague, largest of her type ever built in the world. Originally constructed in 1902 as a conveyor of enormous fleets of coal barges from Ohio river points to New Orleans, the boat, affectionately called "Big Mama" on the rivers, was acquired by the Aluminum Ore Company, Alcoa subsidiary, in 1917. She was purchased from her original owner, Monongahela River Consolidated Coal & Coke Company. Alcoa sold the craft in 1925 to Esso Standard Oil. When that company decided recently to retire her, the citizens of Vicksburg, Mississippi, asked that she be parked on their water front as a tourist attraction.

To meet the aluminum demand during World War I, Alcoa boosted its production from 109,000,000 pounds in 1915 to a peak of 152,000,000 pounds in 1917. Actual output declined to 148,000,000 pounds in 1918 because of a severe water shortage at the hydroelectric plants. However, the Company was making every effort to increase production capacity in 1918 on the theory that the war might continue for another year or more. On August 29, 1918, Mr. Davis appeared before the Joint Inter-

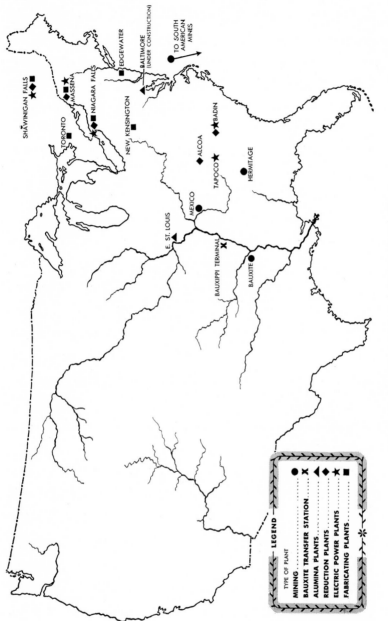

SHAWINIGAN FALLS

TORONTO

MASSENA

NIAGARA FALLS

EDGEWATER

BALTIMORE
(UNDER CONSTRUCTION)

TO SOUTH
AMERICAN
MINES

NEW KENSINGTON

BADIN

ALCOA

TAPOCO

HERMITAGE

MEXICO

E. ST. LOUIS

BAUXIPPI TERMINAL

BAUXITE

LEGEND

TYPE OF PLANT	
MINING.............	●
BAUXITE TRANSFER STATION	✕
ALUMINA PLANTS........	◀
REDUCTION PLANTS......	◆
ELECTRIC POWER PLANTS..	★
FABRICATING PLANTS....	■

Alcoa plant locations in 1918 following World War 1.

national Commission in reference to the need for a weir on the St. Lawrence River to assure a more uniform flow of water during the coming winter months and thereby increase the output of aluminum at the Massena, New York, reduction works in 1919. After discussing the great demand for aluminum from America by the Allied Governments during 1917 and particularly in 1918, Mr. Davis said:

The present situation, however, bad as it is, is not the main cause of the anxiety on our part and on the part of the interested officials at Washington. It is the future over which we are most apprehensive.

The United States is just now embarking on, as we all know, a very radical enlargement in the number of men it will send overseas. We have now about one and one-half million men, which means that within the next year an equipment equal to three times the equipment already provided must be obtained, and if it is to be done and placed in the hands of these men next year the materials must leave our hands within the next few months, as this material, as we turn it out, is to a very large extent the raw material, and has to be still further fabricated.

But perhaps the most important and crucial situation with which we are confronted is the aircraft program. Up to date, the United States has not made, as we all know, a very large number of airplanes, but fortunately this situation is just now being remedied. While I am not familiar with the production of finished planes, and have no authority to speak for the aircraft department, I take it that I can say something about the production of these parts of aircraft motors which are made from aluminum. There has been a very sincere effort on the part of all the manufacturers in the United States to bring the aircraft program up to what we term a manufacturing proposition, and we know that in the last six weeks, and with the very hearty co-operation of the manufacturers in the Detroit district, we have been enabled to produce the aluminum parts for approximately 200 motors a day as compared with eight, or nine, or ten motors a day prior to that time.

Each motor requires over 300 pounds of aluminum, but in addition to the weight of aluminum in the motors themselves there is a very large amount of aluminum in tubes, rivets, and so forth in the plates, and also in other parts of the subsidiaries to the engine itself. It seems, therefore, I may say, and I am sure that this statement would be confirmed by the officials at Washington, that while the actual orders have not yet been placed for this very enlarged program, they will shortly be placed, and that it will be necessary, not only to curtail the amount of aluminum that goes into other important munition lines, in order to give the greatest amount possible to this probably most important line, but it will be, by all means, necessary for the Aluminum Company of America to use every means at its disposal to increase its output.

The views of Mr. Davis about the need to prepare for a longer war were shared by others. The plans of the War Industries

Board were based on this assumption. Bernard M. Baruch, chairman of the board, expressed a similar attitude on August 8, 1918, in speaking on this same matter of the weir on the St. Lawrence.[2] He said: "The construction of a weir will substantially relieve the condition, and if a word can be permitted on the construction of this weir, a large increase in output for *the first three months of 1919* will be effected—the time when we most need this increase in output, especially in the production under the aircraft program."

In all these efforts and expansion programs to meet the demands of a longer war, Mr. Davis was thinking in terms of winning a war rather than of the best interests of Alcoa. He knew what a greatly expanded European aluminum industry would mean to his own company in the postwar period. Immediately following the war, his worst fears came to realization. Germany, with a producing capacity of 76,000,000 pounds, a large national debt and inflated currency, was looking for aluminum markets. Moreover, her labor rates were about eleven cents per hour as compared with the more than forty cents per hour the American workman was receiving. Switzerland came out of the war with an aluminum producing capacity twice that of 1914. Norway had over eight times her 1914 productive facilities. By 1920, imports to the United States, which had never exceeded 26,000,000 pounds and had dropped to zero during the war, rose to 40,000,000 pounds. Much of this metal was "dumped" into the United States because of lack of demand in the Euro-

---

[2] Letter of B. M. Baruch to The Chairman, International Joint Commission, "In the Matter of the Application of the St. Lawrence River Power Company—Interim Order, Opinions and Hearings," Library of Congress.

pean countries and the ease of getting quick cash here by selling below the cost of production of the American producers.

Alcoa had a productive capacity in 1919 of 152 million pounds, but it could produce more than this amount through the purchase of additional power from outside sources. The Company had an investment of roughly one dollar for each pound of aluminum produced annually. In 1919 the investment before deducting reserves was $160,000,000. Postwar conditions provided a serious threat to the American company with this investment in plant facilities and with an aluminum producing capacity far in excess of what it could sell in the face of stiff world competition.

A reasonable amortization of its war-built facilities was allowed Alcoa, which showed an increased investment for war purposes alone in excess of $27,000,000. The amortization made on these added war expenditures was 25 per cent plus some additional allowances on excess construction costs. However, the total amortization amounted to about $7,000,000, leaving a substantial plant investment to face the perilous 1920's.

Uses of aluminum during World War I were more numerous than one familiar with the vast World War II aluminum program would imagine. A list of these uses, prepared in alphabetical order shortly after the war, read as follows: airplane parts, ammonia converters, automobile parts, bimetallic tubing, auto bodies, bolts and nuts, brewery equipment, brush-guards, buoys, bus-bars, cameras, cans, canteens, cathode plates, caul plates, crank cases, deodorizing apparatus, dials, electrical supplies, explosive manufacturers' equipment, fan motor housings, electrical feeders, film-roll spindles, fireworks, funnels, fuse wire, gas-mask fittings, gasoline tanks, gasoline-pump cylinders, gear-housings, helmets, identification tags, lens housings, lightning arresters, artificial limbs, magnet wire, magneto covers, mess kits, meter bases, motor housings, nitrate fixation equipment, oil floats and pans, optical supplies, reels, reflectors, retorts, rubber molds, patterns, periscope caps, pistons, explosive powder, pump cylinders, scientific apparatus, screens, screw machine products, signals, splints, starter cables, tanks, dry battery terminals, thermit, trolley bows, tubing, U-tubes, vats, welding wire, auto wheels, windshield frames, wire cloth, yokes.

Perhaps the most significant use was in aircraft, although on a small scale compared with the role of the metal in the air in World War II. Airplanes in the First World War were largely constructed of wood jointed by gluing, fastened together by steel wire, and covered with fabric. The original changes to metal consisted of welded-steel tubular framework with many interior crossbracings but with the entire assembly being covered with fabric. Aluminum first began to be used for heavier-than-air craft during the war. The first framework was built from channels and angles formed from sheet or seamless tubing.

However, aluminum played its role in World War I aircraft in vital parts of the motor. The most notable American contribution, from an actual production standpoint, was the Liberty V-12 engine. It went into mass production before the end of the struggle. The Liberty's crank case, oil pan, pistons and rocker arm box, were Alcoa aluminum. We can rely on contemporary literature for the story of aluminum in aircraft in 1917–1918. *Engineering & Mining Journal*, in its February, 1919, issue, said:

Perhaps in no one field did aluminum play a more important part than in aeronautics. It was used in some of the most important of the component parts of aircraft, and it was found a component of some of the smallest and most delicate instruments, in the airplane. In aircraft, the most obvious and critical part played by aluminum was in the engine. Substantially one-third the weight of the Liberty motor was composed of aluminum. Though no exact figures are at hand, it is highly probable that an even higher proportion of aluminum is used in certain other engines, as, for example, the Hispano-Suiza. Aluminum has been used for many years in automobile engines, but in aircraft work great efforts were made to reduce the weight of the engine to the lowest limits, and to this end aluminum was adopted wherever possible for engine beds, crank cases, pistons, oil pumps, camshaft housings, and numerous other parts. Forty separate parts of the Liberty motor alone were made of this metal, and these parts do not include any of the auxiliary apparatus attached to the airplane. Among the other parts of the airplane where aluminum is used may be mentioned gasoline tanks, fuselage, hoods, cowling, seat backs, and aileron frames. Aluminum is used wherever possible in instruments used on airplanes, such as binocular parts, wireless telegraph and telephone, barometer cases, camera parts, and in range finders.

Although rigid dirigibles have not been adopted in the United States, aluminum is used for important purposes on observation and other types of balloons. All such aircraft has the exterior surface painted with a coat of aluminum paint, to give it a reflecting exterior, thereby obviating changes of temperature as much as possible in the interior of the balloon.

Writing in 1925, Robert J. Anderson, who had been a research metallurgist in the Bureau of Aircraft Production, discussed this same subject in his book *The Metallurgy of Aluminum and Aluminum Alloys*.[3] He said:

It is now considered impossible to build a modern aviation engine without the employment of aluminum, and in 1918 the Allied Governments put about 90,000 metric tons (200,000,000 pounds) of it into aircraft alone. Practically one-third of the weight of the Liberty 12-cylinder aviation engine was made up of light aluminum alloys, and these alloys entered largely into the construction of all the modern aviation engines during the war, notably the Hispano-Suiza, Rolls-Royce, Mercedes, Maybach, Deusenberg, Bugatti, Curtiss, and others. In aviation-engine construction, the light aluminum-copper alloys were favored in the United States for the production of crank cases, oil pans, pistons, oil pumps, carburetor bodies, camshaft housings, and other important parts. Substantially pure aluminum sheet, and some light aluminum-alloy sheet was used for the fuselage, gasoline tanks, hoods, cowling, seat backs, and aileron frames. The metal, or one of its light alloys, entered into the construction of other aircraft apparatus such as barometer cases, binoculars, camera parts, range

[3] *The Metallurgy of Aluminum and Aluminum Alloys*, Robert J. Anderson, pp. 274-5, Henry Carey Baird & Co., Inc., New York City, 1925.

finders, and wireless telephone and telegraph outfits. Aluminum paint was used during the War to cover the exterior of observation balloons, its reflecting power reducing temperature changes in the interior. Other war uses of aluminum included its employment in the high explosive ammonal, and aluminum sheet was fabricated for soldiers' field-mess equipment, parts of gas masks, water bottles, and identification tags.

Civilian uses of aluminum in America were definitely curtailed during the period when 90 per cent of Alcoa's output was being taken for war use. The Aluminum Cooking Utensil Company, an Alcoa subsidiary, engaged in manufacture for the consumer, was hard hit. However, the record shows that the makers of the famous Wear-Ever brand of cooking utensils took the situation in their stride. In 1917 The Aluminum Cooking Utensil Company joined with Armour & Company and five other concerns in conducting wartime cooking schools. As the war moved into 1918, the company was virtually out of the cooking-utensil manufacturing business in its own plant at New Kensington, Pennsylvania, because war material was being made there. Some of its manufacturing was transferred to Edgewater, New Jersey, and a considerable amount was farmed out to other concerns. During the war, the company devoted its advertising space to the slogan "Food will Win the War." Immediately the war had ended, the makers of Wear-Ever utensils were on the job. Early in 1919 the company ran advertisements in the *Stars and Stripes* offering jobs to all Wear-Ever men, specialty commission salesmen as well as salaried employees.

Government's attitude toward Alcoa during the war was one of co-operation with a producer whose help was needed in a struggle which transcended domestic affairs. In fact, the Government called upon the Company to go beyond its aluminum-producing role. After the United States entered the war, the need for nitrates became so important that the Government asked Aluminum Company of America to assist in producing this material. The Government offered to finance the project but the Company declined such aid and decided to build and operate the plant at its own expense. Actual construction was started in May, 1918, and was continued until the Armistice was signed. The aluminum-nitride plant was at Alcoa, Tennessee, and a calcining plant to treat and prepare bauxite for nitride production was under construction at Bauxite, Arkansas. The aluminum nitride was subsequently to be converted into alumina and ammonia; the nitrates were to be made from the ammonia. With the war ending in November, 1918, the nitride plant never went into actual production, but it would have been a valuable contribution to the war effort had the struggle continued.

CHAPTER TWELVE

Competition, Real and Potential–Ford Eyes Muscle Shoals

☆ ☆ ☆ ☆ ☆ ☆ ☆ ☆ ☆

T HE END of the First World War brought new and increased interest in peacetime uses for aluminum, which had proved its merit as a war material, but it also created problems of competition for the American producer. These problems were to spur Alcoa to greater research and improved manufacturing and sales techniques.

On the plus side was the greater familiarity with the metal by the engineering trade. Virtually every Government department had been a wartime purchaser of aluminum products ranging from time fuses for shrapnel to vital parts in the Liberty motor. Many of the manufacturers who made these products had gained their first experience in working with the metal and its alloys. Production of pleasure cars, which had been restricted to almost nothing in 1918, had to meet a great civilian demand after the Armistice. Improved methods and greater familiarity with aluminum as a result of war experience enabled the automotive industry to understand aluminum better. Later losses to steel for automotive bodies were more than offset by enhanced demand for electrical conductor and an ever-widening use of cast and extruded products for such diverse items as household appliances and aircraft engines. No longer did the public think of aluminum as a material suitable only for pots and pans.

The picture was not so bright from Alcoa's standpoint when all the aspects of the fight for this market were considered. Foreign producers, with capacity increased to meet war demands and an inadequate peacetime market at home, looked to America as an outlet. The imports to this country in 1920 were well above the average of the peacetime years in the previous decade. They continued at a substantial rate during nearly all of the Twenties. The Underwood-Simmons Tariff, passed in 1913, had reduced the duty on imports of aluminum ingot to two cents per pound, a barrier which the European producers could well afford to hurdle in their desire to convert surplus metal into dollars.

Manufacturers of aluminum products in this country began to increase rapidly after the war. By 1920 there were 2,169 foundries in the United States engaged in producing aluminum castings.[1] Sheet-fabricating plants, in competition with Alcoa, were in operation. United Smelting & Aluminum Company began rolling aluminum sheet at New Haven, Connecticut, in 1915. The Baush Machine Tool Company, about which more will be told later, began operations in 1919. Aluminum Products Com-

[1] Letter from *The Foundry*, Cleveland, Ohio, June 5, 1950. Data from files of this magazine.

pany, La Grange, Illinois, started its aluminum sheet rolling during April, 1921. Aluminum Goods Manufacturing Company opened its Manitowoc, Wisconsin, mill in the fall of 1924. Sheet Aluminum Corporation, Jackson, Michigan, began to roll sheet in January, 1926, and Fairmont Aluminum Company, Fairmont, West Virginia, began sheet-rolling operations in 1927. Most of these sheet fabricators secured substantial portions of their ingot supplies during the 1920's from foreign sources.

Despite this competition from foreign ingot producers and from manufacturers of aluminum mill products in this country, Alcoa found opportunity to broaden the aluminum market through its competition with older metals. Proof of the effectiveness of an aggressive policy in nonferrous competition is indicated by the figures on volumetric production of aluminum compared with zinc, copper, lead and tin in 1930 and contrasted with the production of these metals, by volume, in 1920. Aluminum showed an increase over its competitors in each instance. The greatest increase was in the ratio between tin and aluminum, with the latter showing a volume production nearly four times that of tin as compared with a less than threefold margin for aluminum ten years earlier.

Research following World War I was greatly spurred to gain for aluminum its share of the market, not only in competition with steel, the nonferrous metals and other materials, but to pioneer new uses for aluminum in products which were becoming a part of American life. Aviation and aluminum virtually grew up together. An entire chapter could be devoted to this fascinating subject.

New strong alloys, which placed aluminum on a competing

basis with steel, especially when mass in motion was involved, came into being in this period. These alloys were usually born in Alcoa's research division. Many new strong alloys were developed. Along with this came improved applications of the heat-treating process and better manufacturing methods.

To resist corrosion of the strong alloys, Aluminum Research Laboratories, under the guidance of Alcoa's E. H. Dix, Jr., developed Alclad 17S, a layer of pure aluminum grafted on to each side of the alloy sheet. The pure metal surface with an intermediate layer of alloy inside, forms a kind of metallurgical sandwich. The alloy is protected even at exposed edges since the pure metal makes a galvanic couple with the alloy. Pure aluminum was available for this coating through the perfection in 1919, by Alcoa's William Hoopes and Francis C. Frary, of an electrolytic process for further refining the product of the Hall reduction pots.

Research activities are the forerunner of industrial production and consumption. Mills and fabricating plants to handle the strong alloys were needed. Alcoa's most notable venture in this era was the construction in 1928 at Massena, New York, of a blooming mill to roll billets and form structural shapes akin in size and form to the products of a steel mill. Perhaps no single venture of the Company can excel this one as an expression of indomitable faith in the future of aluminum. Research had proved that aluminum could compete with steel in the building of streamline trains, dragline booms and bridges. Alcoa had no mill where these large shapes could be made. Without a single order on the books, Alcoa's management spent several million dollars to construct this mill. Faith in the future was justified in the early 1930's when the mill began producing shapes for such things as streamline trains.

This Alcoa attitude was well expressed by Vice President S. K. Colby in an article in *Nation's Business* in 1936. The article was by Warren Bishop and was entitled "A Fifty Year Fight for Markets."[2] Mr. Colby, who died in 1947 after spending over a half century of his life as an enthusiastic proponent of aluminum, was quoted in this article as follows:

> In the first place, we start with the assumption that the consumer does not want to buy aluminum. We were not bright enough to think this out in the beginning. We learned it by bitter experience but we now figure on it definitely.
>
> In an effort to reach into a new field, or an old field that has been incorrectly handled at one time, the first product is generally wrong in some respects. To meet this situation, some years ago a Development Division of our Sales Department was created. This division is manned by technically minded men with some commercial experience. They are rather loosely dubbed sales engineers.
>
> We have learned to keep our eyes on the buying public and not on competitors or their products. We never try to supplant another metal or material directly, but we do try to apply our metal to a given job to the best of our ability, letting the ultimate consumer decide whether aluminum is what he wanted.
>
> On the other hand, we do insist on getting a hearing in every field where we believe aluminum will give a good

[2] "A Fifty Year Fight for Markets," Warren Bishop, *Nation's Business*, January, 1936.

account of itself, and of course we have to do this against the resistance of all the older metals. However, a new field is seldom if ever exploited at the expense of an older material, that the older material is not in the long run benefited. The older material may lose an immediate market but completely new ones will be created. For instance, for every pound of aluminum put in the air tons of other materials are used on the ground.

We have discussed real competition but there yet remains unanswered the question of why no serious attempt was made by another company to enter the business of aluminum-making from mine to metal prior to World War II. There were some investigations of the possibility and one actual effort which need to be reviewed here. The actual effort was that of the Southern Aluminium Company, whose detailed story has been told elsewhere. Construction of a plant at Badin, North Carolina, by French interests, was started in 1912. In October, 1914, all work was suspended owing to the impossibility of further financing in France under war conditions.

Efforts to secure financial assistance from banking interests in this country met with no success. The French possessed their own bauxite and had enough water power at Badin for their contemplated operations. However, American bankers were not interested, even with the prospect of a rising war demand for aluminum. As elsewhere recorded, the only customer for the plant was Alcoa, which found a use for it as part of its own war expansion program. Apparently from a cold, analytical banking viewpoint the hazard of investment in a large-scale integrated aluminum business more than outweighed the prospective returns.

Other investigations, largely promotional in character, should be recorded. In December, 1918, Lloyd T. Emory, a bauxite engineer and a former employee of Alcoa, was engaged by the Uihleins, Milwaukee brewing family, to investigate deposits of the ore which might be suitable for aluminum production. The makers of Schlitz beer owned the Republic Carbon Company at Niagara Falls, New York. Since carbon electrodes are essential in aluminum manufacturing, the Uihleins apparently wished to explore the possibility of producing aluminum ingot, using Niagara Falls power. In a Federal Trade Commission hearing a few years later, Robert Uihlein explained that the project was eventually abandoned, not because of the difficulties of obtaining raw materials and power, but because the venture would entail "too much work" on himself and his brother.[3]

Emory's efforts created quite an episode in which he tangled with the Demerara Bauxite Company, then an Alcoa mining subsidiary in British Guiana, of which Emory had been general manager. Emory first visited Venezuela. Failing to find suitable deposits there, he went to British Guiana where he knew his way about. In 1919 he apparently secured from a local solicitor named Humphreys an option upon two valuable properties. This option had been obtained by the solicitor in his own name. For some time previous the Demerara Bauxite Company had been trying to obtain title to these same properties. In fact, it had a signed agreement with the owner, a Mr. Hubbard, who was adjudged insane before the transaction was completed. Later a

[3] Federal Trade Commission vs. Aluminum Company of America, 1788–90.

similar agreement, signed by two curators appointed after Hubbard's commitment, was said to be void because of the death of one of them. Emory then went direct to the widow of the former owner and secured another option despite the fact that the solicitor had proceeded to sell the property to the Demerara Bauxite Company.

Suit was brought against Emory and associates, Alcoa insisting that the ex-employee had not been diligent in following instructions to purchase the land when he was still general manager of Demerara. The litigation over the disputed tracts went through three courts. Emory won in the first court and in the West Indian Court of Appeals, but the contest was carried to the Privy Council in London which decided the lands belonged to the Demerara Bauxite Company. At any rate, the Uihleins told Emory, in 1924, that they were no longer interested in exploring bauxite deposits and that they had sold some lands they had acquired in South America. Early in 1925 they disposed of the Republic Carbon Company by selling it to Alcoa, the Carborundum Company and the Acheson Graphite Company, each of which took a one-third interest.

It is not known whether the Uihleins were actually acquiring bauxite properties with a serious intention of engaging in aluminum manufacture at that time. Such properties could usually be resold at a profit if acquired at the right price. When the Uihleins had no further job for him, Emory entered the employ of the American Cyanamid Company.

The interest of J. B. Duke in aluminum is another story which will be told in some detail in the chapter on the Baush Machine Tool litigation. It involves the activity of George D. Haskell in the possibility of domestic aluminum manufacture. Duke's interest stemmed from his desire to utilize a part of the vast amount of electrical energy he hoped to develop on the Saguenay River in Canada. Interested in hydro projects from the turn of the century because of his success in North Carolina, J. B. Duke had incorporated the Quebec Development Company with Sir William Price as his associate. Duke's interest in aluminum and his contacts with Alcoa are told in other portions of this chronicle, but none of the facts indicate any desire on the part of the noted tobacco and power magnate to do anything more than convert a great power potential into useful and profitable industrial manufacturing.

Reasons why successful aluminum fabricators did not undertake the manufacturing of alumina and aluminum may be found in the testimony in the famous anti-trust suit against Alcoa. Bohn Aluminum & Brass Corporation considered the problem on three occasions, in 1922, in 1928 and again in 1932. P. L. Markey, Vice President of that company, testified that Bohn could get power and either bauxite or alunite, an aluminum-bearing ore found in substantial quantities in Utah. The directors of the company, Mr. Markey said, decided against the venture because the possibility of gain did not seem to justify the risk.[4] Aluminum Products Company of La Grange, Illinois, considered the matter as late as 1934, but William Hastings, President of the company, testified that he did not go beyond a mere investigation because of difficulties of financing and inability to secure the requisite power he had hoped to be able to get from TVA.[5]

The most striking case history of a great industrial concern,

[4] United States vs. Aluminum Company of America et al., transcript 24,589.
[5] United States vs. Aluminum Company of America et al., transcript 11,980-12,031. Exhibit 649.

a large user of aluminum, pursuing the feasibility of going into aluminum production, is that of the Ford Motor Company in connection with Henry Ford's proposal to the United States Government to develop Muscle Shoals.[6] Aside from the Ford interest in aluminum, this incident is a fascinating bit of American history because the great industrialist proposed to do through private enterprise many of the things later achieved under social planning by the Government-owned Tennessee Valley Authority.

Muscle Shoals had become what many termed a "white elephant" after World War I. The war need for nitrate had prompted the Government to build a dam at this location on the Tennessee River and to construct a nitrate plant. When the emergency passed, Congress refused to appropriate further money. Wilson Dam, known as Dam No. 2, remained unfinished, and Dam No. 3 was only in the blueprint stage. Powerhouses, locks and other facilities were incomplete. The Government had spent $129,951,977, and engineers estimated another $40,000,000 would be needed to round out the project. The two dams and their powerhouses were the chief items in this unfinished program.

In response to an invitation from U. S. Army engineers, Henry Ford submitted his original offer on July 8, 1921.[7] Briefly, it stated that if the Government would complete the Wilson Dam and Dam No. 3, a company to be formed by Mr. Ford would lease them for one hundred years, paying 6 per cent interest on

6 *Henry Ford, His Life, His Work, His Genius*, William A. Simonds, Bobbs-Merrill Co., 1943.
7 Proposal of Henry Ford to General Lansing H. Beach, Chief of Engineers, U.S.A., July 8, 1921.

Typical Alcoa-owned hydroelectric-power installation. Started supplying power for aluminum production in 1919. Electric power is an essential "raw material" to the aluminum industry as about 10 kilowatt hours are required in the production of one pound of aluminum.

the remaining cost of the dams, locks and powerhouse facilities, estimated at $28,000,000. He would also pay an annual amortization fee into a sinking fund to amortize the cost over a hundred-year period. The Ford group would buy outright for $5,000,000 the two nitrate plants, the Waco quarry and the Gorgas steam plant on the Warrior River.

With Army engineers apparently fearful that $28,000,000 would be insufficient to finish the two dams and their appurtenances, Mr. Ford amended his offer on January 25, 1922.[8] He agreed to build with his own organization the two projects without fee or profit. He would do this at the Government's expense and then pay as annual rental 4 per cent of the cost, whatever it might be. He would also make annual payments to a sinking fund for amortization purposes. Without divulging his industrial plans, Mr. Ford made it clear that he would continue to cooperate in flood control and fertilizer manufacture, two objectives in which the proponents of Government ownership seemed most concerned. Ford would furnish free power to the Government to operate the locks. He would make fertilizer at one nitrate plant and keep the other in stand-by condition for possible wartime emergency.

While the opposition to private capital's development of Muscle Shoals had raised a hue and cry in Congress, it seems from the files on this subject that Mr. Ford must have lost interest in the opportunities for aluminum or any other large-scale manufacturing at Muscle Shoals as time dragged on. He closed the

[8] Proposal of Henry Ford to the Secretary of War and through him for appropriate action by the President and the Congress of the United States, January 25, 1922.

matter definitely in a letter to President Coolidge dated October 15, 1924, reading as follows:

> President Calvin Coolidge
> The White House
> Washington, D. C.
>
> My dear Mr. President:
>
> On July 8, 1921, there was submitted to the War Department upon their invitation to the writer, an offer for leasing the Government property at Muscle Shoals.
>
> After many conferences, hearings, etc., this proposal was amended on January 25, 1922, in which form it is still pending in Congress.
>
> Inasmuch as so much time has already elapsed, we are unable to wait and delay what plans we have any longer for action by Congress, and I am, consequently, asking that you consider this as a withdrawal of said offer.
>
> Very truly yours
(signed) HENRY FORD

That Ford was interested in aluminum manufacture is certain, without reference to the negotiations with the Government over Muscle Shoals. Had he gone ahead, aluminum manufacturing would have been almost a certainty. A former Ford executive says consideration was given to the manufacture of aluminum at Muscle Shoals to make cylinder blocks and automobile bodies. It was reported that Ford had bought some bauxite lands in Georgia in 1923. George D. Haskell, who spent considerable time trying to interest people of means in aluminum-making, approached Mr. Ford repeatedly and found him interested. We have Haskell's statement in the Baush Machine Tool case that Ford offered to back him for $20,000,000 if the Ford Motor Company could be assured of an adequate supply of aluminum. At all events, the record would seem to show that in the end aluminum-making was not sufficiently attractive to engage the genius and financial ability of a successful aluminum user such as Henry Ford after he had failed to receive the co-operation of Government in the one project which might have succeeded.

Donald H. Wallace, who in 1937 wrote *Market Control in the Aluminum Industry*, a Harvard economics study, partially answered the question of why Alcoa had no integrated competitors up to that time.[9] He says, "A complicated process requiring an investment of several million dollars, limited natural resources, vigorous expansion by the existing firm, uncertainties of obsolescence, disinclination of bankers to provide financial assistance —some or all of these elements have raised effective barriers of a sort with which the anti-trust laws as interpreted and administered were not designed to cope. From the considerations surveyed up to this point, it would not seem likely that several new firms will enter this field in America in the near future unless, indeed, some cheap process of using low grade ores is developed."

Had Mr. Wallace written his book ten years later, he undoubtedly would have added to this statement. He would have told how competitive conditions were created in the integrated aluminum industry when the Government, in its all-out war-winning effort, entered the aluminum field as a financier. The Government was not only the banker for new entrants in this

[9] *Market Control in the Aluminum Industry*, Donald H. Wallace, Harvard University Press, 1937, p. 152.

business, but it also became the owner, itself, of vast aluminum-producing facilities.

Apparently the same conditions which deterred private investors from going into the business when the Southern Aluminium Company was seeking aid in 1914 continued to prevail at least through the 1930's. Likewise, the hazards of the business were enough to discourage a well-financed concern like the Ford Motor Company from investing its own funds. The repeated charges of the Department of Justice, predicated on the fact that Alcoa had no integrated competitors during the first half century of its existence, would suggest that it might have been better for the Company if someone had gone into the business. The competitive conditions now existing as the result of war-born Government financing might be even more wholesome had these conditions been brought about through private investment.

CHAPTER THIRTEEN

The Twenties

☆ ☆ ☆ ☆ ☆ ☆ ☆ ☆ ☆

THE LIMITS of this book make it impossible to record a history of Alcoa's mill products. The detailed story of their development and acceptance would require several chapters. However, it is proper to make some mention of the part they played in the expanding American industrial scene known as the Roaring Twenties, an era marked by great commercial activity after a slow start in 1920–21 as a result of readjustments following World War I.

Demand for aluminum sheet for many uses caused the Company to expand its sheet-rolling capacity, sometimes ahead of the market. On November 8, 1920, the first sheet was shipped from Alcoa's new mill at Alcoa, Tennessee, a mill of greater size and capacity than any other the Company owned up to that time. Shortly after the first completed orders were shipped, it became necessary to close down the plant for lack of business.

While the mill was under construction, the Navy Department placed an order for a large quantity of strong alloy sheet for use in building the dirigible airship, *Shenandoah*. This material had to be made at New Kensington but it seemed to augur good business for the new mill at Alcoa. Despite this, orders for the mill in any appreciable quantity did not come until late 1921 and early 1922, when normal business conditions again prevailed.

By that time the demand for aluminum sheet, led by cooking utensils and automobile-body work, included such items as license plates, reflectors, cameras, refrigerator trays, washing-machine cylinders, drainboards, airplanes and radio parts. Coiled sheet and circles made from coiled sheet were sold in large quantities to a dozen cooking-utensil manufacturers. A still larger volume of flat sheet went to another dozen manufacturers engaged in making automobile bodies. In 1924 the Chevrolet Motor Company decided to use aluminum radiator shells and ten million pounds went into this item in the years 1925–27.

The wide use of aluminum in automobile manufacturing, in anything other than vital parts of the motor, was destined to have a short life. This was due to improved methods of deep-drawing steel body frames and radiator shells, a development most pleasing to automotive engineers because of the lower cost of steel. During the period in which aluminum enjoyed this nice volume of business, alloys 25S and 3S were used but they did not provide the cost advantage the automobile manufacturers were seeking. However, aluminum sheet found other markets as rapidly as the automobile-body business disappeared.

As early as 1900, Alcoa discovered that it would, at times, actually need to fabricate an aluminum article for a customer to pioneer a new use and to interest others in making the item. Thus was born what became known as the "Job Shop" at the New Kensington Works. In the early 1920's, the chemical industry became conscious of the merits of aluminum for equipment construction, but there was no manufacturer to whom they could go. The Alcoa specialists in the Job Shop provided the answer. Likewise, in airplane and airship development, the Job Shop produced special products not elsewhere available.

The most notable early contribution of the Job Shop was in pioneering the manufacture of aluminum furniture. In 1924 the shop produced a set of aluminum furniture for the directors' room of the Mellon National Bank. Thus began the manufacturing operation which was to carry on until it became so well established that, ten years later, the Company was able to sell the business to General Fireproofing Company, Youngstown, Ohio. After two years of Job Shop pioneering, the Company moved its furniture manufacturing to the Buffalo plant. There it continued as a full-fledged operation until the sale to General Fireproofing. After ten years and an investment of some three million dollars, Alcoa had demonstrated to furniture makers the suitability of aluminum for this purpose.

Early in the 1920's, Alcoa got into the aluminum sand-casting business on its own account rather than as a member of a group of foundry owners. In 1909, along with five other companies making castings, Alcoa had become a member of a corporation known as Aluminum Castings Company. It was formed to provide united research to improve the quality of aluminum sand castings. There were fourteen plants in the group and the officers of the corporation were chosen from the management of the different foundries. In 1916 Alcoa bought back its New Kensington foundry from the corporation and did war work at that location, mostly on canteen necks and on parts of army equipment. On December 31, 1920, the foundries still operated by Aluminum Castings Company were deeded to Aluminum Manufacturers, Inc.

As a result of stock-exchange plus later purchases, Alcoa acquired a majority interest in the new concern. Demand for sand castings was none too strong during 1921 and the first half of 1922. That, plus other operating conditions, caused Aluminum Manufacturers, Inc., to lose substantial sums. With their investment in jeopardy, stockholders took the position that Alcoa, as principal stockholder, was morally, if not legally, obligated to take over the business and make it pay. Alcoa then leased the properties of Aluminum Manufacturers, Inc., for twenty-five years, thus guaranteeing an assured return to stockholders. This action put the Company directly into the aluminum-castings business instead of indirectly through stock ownership in Aluminum Manufacturers, Inc.

Both sand and permanent-mold castings found a good market beginning in the latter half of 1922. Automotive pistons were the principal item made by the permanent-mold method. The solid-trunk and split-skirt piston design was replaced in 1926 by the T-slot and strut type of insert pistons. Aluminum pistons of this design are virtually standard equipment for automobiles today. Many new applications for permanent-mold castings came along in this period for items ranging from washing-machine agitators to aircraft and automotive cylinder heads.

A forerunner of the present wide use of aluminum cable, steel reinforced (commonly called "ACSR"), for high-tension lines, came in 1922. The electrical conductor business had started in the late Nineties, but in 1922 Southern California Edison's famous Big Creek Line, originally built in 1913, became the first line in the world to operate at 220,000 volts. Increased demand for aluminum wire caused Alcoa to expand its facilities. A new 12-inch merchant mill was built at Massena, New York, in 1926, and the first tandem-type continuous wire-drawing machine was installed at Massena in 1928. Large sizes of rod and bar, as well as structural shapes, were made available at Massena with the building of a 26-inch structural mill and the construction of the big blooming mill in 1929.

In 1922 Alcoa abandoned its earlier method of making extrusions. The basic process has always been likened to the squeezing of toothpaste from a tube. The original procedure was to fill the cylinder of a vertical press with molten aluminum, permit it to solidify, and then extrude the metal through a die at the bottom. Horizontal presses were found to be better because they prevented excessive distortion of the extrusions and allowed shearing of the butt end of the ingot after each charge was extruded. By 1923 the Company had adopted the method of inserting a preheated ingot into the cylinder so that a powerful, hydraulically operated ram could force the metal through a die at the opposite end of the cylinder. Extrusions were used in this period principally for shapes required by the growing aircraft industry, and for auto trim and molding.

Aluminum forgings, which were to become so important in aircraft construction, began to play their part as early as 1922 when the first propeller-blade forgings were developed. In 1926 forged aircraft-engine crank cases were made. Forged aircraft-engine fittings and pistons came along in the late Twenties. Press forgings, which consist of a hot formed aluminum part produced on a powerful press, did not appear until 1931.

Other Alcoa mill products, such as collapsible tubes, powder, foil, bottle caps and seals, screw machine products, die castings and cooking utensils, became increasingly important through the Company's aggressive research and development program in this period.

In 1921 Alcoa began the manufacture of collapsible tubes at Edgewater, New Jersey, thus inaugurating a pioneering operation which has grown into a business now making over 600,000 gross of tubes per year—86,400,000 tubes for toothpaste and similar items. Bottle caps and seals made by Alcoa's subsidiary, Aluminum Seal Company, were substantially developed in this period. "Rolled-on" sealing was achieved in 1924, providing a tailor-made fit and a hermetic seal for each cap. This method not only increased the use of aluminum caps but extended the market for glass bottles. Mason-jar caps of aluminum were made by the Aluminum Seal Company in 1926, and during the following year 25,000,000 were sold.

During the Twenties, aluminum die castings exceeded the sale of zinc die castings, although this ratio has not been true throughout the history of die-cast articles. Alcoa's activity in the die-casting field started in 1921 when it acquired the assets of the Acme Die Casting Corporation. Since that date Alcoa has manufactured this product and developed its usefulness through research and improved techniques at its Garwood, New Jersey, plant, now supplemented by a second die-casting plant at Chicago. In 1922 over 70 per cent of production was for parts used in the Hoover vacuum sweeper. As the Twenties progressed, sales included automotive and radio parts as well as die-cast brake shoes and hydraulic brake pistons for Bendix Aviation Corporation, and die-cast bearing caps for Packard Motor Car Company.

Screw machine products began their role as important contributions to industry when Alcoa started producing them at Edgewater, New Jersey, in 1922. The development of 17S alloy rod shortly after World War I provided the necessary raw material. Production of high-strength, heat-treated alloy tubing began in 1922, and in the following year this product was being made at the rate of 110,000 pounds per month. In 1924 octagonal-shaped tubing was introduced. Alcoa tubing found a ready market for such things as rigid conduit, vacuum cleaner handles, typewriter rolls and automobile oil lines.

Charles Martin Hall had produced some aluminum powder on an experimental basis in 1908. The business seemed to have good prospects and a plant erected at Dover, New Jersey, began production in 1910. In 1918 a new powder plant was built at Logans Ferry near New Kensington, Pennsylvania. There were two developments of major importance in this period. Aluminum paint, up to this time, had largely been used as a decorative coating for picture frames and radiators. However, research proved that aluminum paint, made with properly formulated vehicles, had excellent protective properties on wood and metal, both indoors and exposed to the weather. New and better methods for measuring the quality of aluminum powder were also originated. With improved testing methods came the production of aluminum powders of higher quality to meet the rapidly developing de mand. Thus what had been an art was rapidly being changed into a science.[1]

This rapidly expanding United States market for aluminum, requiring concentrated manufacturing and sales effort, was one of the motives which prompted Alcoa to reach an important decision regarding the Company's foreign properties which it was neglecting and not adequately developing. On June 4, 1928, these foreign holdings became a possession of Aluminium, Ltd., a Canadian corporation formed by the stockholders of Alcoa but to be independently operated as an aluminum-manufacturing and sales organization in all parts of the world. In fact, this company was to become, as the years rolled by, a vigorous competitor of Alcoa.

Although not particularly active in acquiring European property until 1922, Alcoa had been in Canada for more than a quarter-century. Following studies of water power at Shawinigan Falls, Quebec, in 1899, the Company built, shortly thereafter, a power plant and reduction works and began supplementing its aluminum production at Niagara Falls with metal made in the pot lines at the Canadian location. In 1926, through transactions with J. B. Duke, Alcoa became the owner of additional water power on the Saguenay River. The Company's acquisitions of this great water power are discussed in a previous chapter. These acquisitions made possible the building of an aluminum-producing plant at Arvida. These two aluminum plants and an alumina works at Arvida, which used the so-called dry process for refining the ore, provided Alcoa with its Canadian new metal production.

---

[1] *Aluminum Paint and Powder*, Junius D. Edwards, Reinhold Publishing Corporation, 1936.

These aluminum-producing units in Canada were the largest and most valuable of Alcoa's foreign holdings. A considerable quantity of the metal was shipped to Alcoa fabricating plants in the United States where it was turned into mill products for sale in the domestic market. The Company had a sales organization in the United States well equipped to serve the market in contrast to its rather loosely organized sales force abroad. Alcoa had built few fabricating plants in Canada. Those it had constructed were largely in response to the desire of Canadians to buy mill products made in that country. In 1927 a foil mill was started in Toronto, and during the same year a permanent mold-casting department was put into operation at the same place.

The European aluminum ventures in which Alcoa had an interest were largely the result of the Company's efforts to augment its metal-producing facilities. A list of these twenty-one companies, scattered over seven countries, shows that six were bauxite-land holdings, four were aluminum-producing plants, four were water-power rights, four were foundries, one was a plant to produce aluminum cable, one a selling organization, and one an experimental project on the use of leucite as an ore for the production of aluminum.

The bauxite lands were in France and Jugoslavia and the aluminum-producing works largely in Norway with small operations in Italy and Spain. Interests in water powers were held in Norway and France. There was a sand-castings foundry in Birmingham, England, and a die-castings plant in Germany. A small cable works was in France. The only sales organization in Europe of which Alcoa was a part was the Northern Aluminium Company, Ltd., in England. Norway aluminum production, in which the Company had a substantial interest, served to supplement Alcoa's metal requirements in this country from 1923 to 1928. Imports in substantial quantities were needed to satisfy the domestic demand during those years when consumption was outrunning the production of metal in the Company's United States plants.

This was the situation when Alcoa's management decided that it was not equipped to develop foreign markets, and that this could be done adequately only by a foreign corporation devoting its major activities to the task. With business growing in the United States, the Alcoa salesman was more interested in sizable orders at home than smaller ones abroad. Very few Alcoa people could speak foreign languages or were familiar with foreign business practices. Furthermore, a spirit of nationalism was extant which made it desirable to do business in any country in the manner of that country. Only a company geared to this type of procedure could build its manpower into a world sales organization.

In the British Empire, the slogan "Buy British" was gaining wide acceptance. A corporation of a British dominion would find a healthy economic climate under this concept. Proof of this came within a few years after the formation of Aluminium, Ltd., when its production and sales force numbered more than sixteen thousand people located in countries all over the world. The company had started with a limited personnel, trained in Alcoa's organization.

Internal conditions in Alcoa made 1928 a propitious time to create a foreign company to operate in the world aluminum market under management and policies quite independent of

Alcoa. Edward K. Davis, brother of Arthur V. Davis, was the Alcoa Vice President in charge of Sales. He had been successful in building a great sales force, but, like other Alcoa executives, he felt the Company was not equipped to make the most of the opportunity offered by the beckoning world market. Roy A. Hunt, son of the Alcoa founder, was Vice President in charge of Operations. It was a logical move to elevate Roy A. Hunt to the Alcoa presidency and to promote Edward K. Davis by making him President of the newly formed world-selling and manufacturing company, Aluminium, Ltd. Arthur V. Davis became Chairman of the Board of Alcoa.

Formation of the new company was fairly simple. Alcoa caused Aluminium, Ltd., to be incorporated and then transferred to it all of Alcoa's holdings outside the United States except the Suriname (Dutch Guiana) bauxite, Cedars Rapids Transmission Company, Ltd., Alcoa Power Company, Ltd., and Prodotti Chimici Napoli in Italy. Alcoa kept the Suriname bauxite as its source of permanent ore supply, but Aluminium, Ltd., acquired the bauxite holdings in British Guiana. The Cedars Rapids Company, still held by Alcoa, has a line over which power is brought from Canada to the plant at Massena, New York. Stock of Prodotti, owner of leucite deposits in Italy, was transferred to Aluminium, Ltd., in 1931. The Alcoa Power Company, consisting of the Shipshaw power site on the Saguenay River in Canada, plus the Chute à Caron dam and powerhouse Alcoa had constructed on the river just above Shipshaw, was purchased from Alcoa by Aluminium, Ltd., in 1938, for $35,000,000.

Aside from these properties, all the other holdings of Alcoa outside the borders of the United States became the possessions of Aluminium, Ltd., on June 4, 1928. In return, Alcoa received the common stock of Aluminium, Ltd., which it immediately distributed to its own shareholders, one share of Aluminium, Ltd., being distributed to every Alcoa stockholder for each three shares of Alcoa stock. On the day this occurred, stockholders in the two companies were identical, but this changed rapidly. Through sales or purchases by individuals within the first decade of the separation, Alcoa's stock ownership and that of Aluminium, Ltd., had become quite divergent. By 1950 stockholders identifiable with Alcoa held substantially less than one half of the outstanding stock of Aluminium, Ltd.

While the corporate changes seemed simple enough, the task of Edward K. Davis in building an organization and starting a new business was quite complex. A number of capable men in the Alcoa personnel joined the new company in key positions. With this staff, Mr. Davis proceeded to build an organization which virtually operates around the globe. Markets in Japan and China were developed as well as those in Europe and in the far-flung British Empire. For a time Aluminium, Ltd., purchased alumina from Alcoa to supplement its own supply. For a short period the new company also availed itself of Alcoa's facilities by having Canadian metal rolled into sheet on a toll basis on Alcoa's rolling mills. The severance of Aluminium, Ltd., from Alcoa made the new company dependent on the parent until adequate manufacturing facilities could be developed. In fact it required until 1935, a period of seven years, for Aluminium, Ltd., to grow into a fully integrated business which was able to manufacture not only aluminum but aluminum mill products for sale in the world-wide markets it was developing.

Today Aluminium, Ltd., because of its vast hydroelectric power resources and available raw materials, is an important factor in the world market for aluminum. Because it could develop new business more easily by an aggressive policy in Asia and in Europe than by intensive cultivation of the already well-served United States market, Aluminium, Ltd., devoted its major efforts in the first two decades of its history to these foreign fields. Its smelting and fabricating plants were located in foreign countries as was its sales organization. However, it could always compete for United States business and it has not hesitated to do so as the opportunity has presented itself.

This voluntary decision on the part of Alcoa to devote itself to the United States market was, as we have already said, inspired to some extent by the amazing acceptance aluminum received in this country in the Twenties. The wisdom of the decision was proved in the continuing increase in the United States demand for aluminum in the Thirties and by the major role Alcoa was called upon to play in World War II, when aluminum became so essential in the global air conflict. This domestic market, still growing, continues to occupy Alcoa's time and effort to a great extent, but there is nothing to preclude the Company from exploring and developing foreign markets. This it is now doing in countries which lie south of the United States.

CHAPTER FOURTEEN

Labor Relations

☆ ☆ ☆ ☆ ☆ ☆ ☆ ☆ ☆

ALCOA has had a better-than-average rating in its labor relations when its more than sixty-year history is viewed in relation to other concerns with similar widespread operations. This has been due to a policy of paying the going rate or better for comparable work in each community in which the Company has plants, along with other programs aimed at employee welfare, and to a policy of settling grievances, whenever possible, at the local level. Like many companies, Alcoa's labor problems were fairly simple until the 1930's, when the Government began to sit at the bargaining table and it became much more difficult to keep labor disputes on a plant basis to be settled as a local issue.

The Company had strikes in its earlier days but these were usually short-lived and were local affairs. During the early part of 1900, the first strike in Company history occurred at New Kensington, Pennsylvania. Thirty-seven employees of the Wire Drawing Department secured a union charter from the American Federation of Labor. During the bargaining, a strike occurred, but it proved of short duration because the Company recognized the union and signed the wage scale. Amicable relations with this union continued until 1908, when the Company found itself confronted by union dissension with four unions clamoring for recognition. These were the Aluminum Workers' Union and three other unions of the sheet rollers, metal polishers, and machinists, respectively. The Company declared for an open shop and a strike followed. It, too, proved to be a short affair and ended with the open shop.

There were scattered labor disturbances of a minor nature in the first few decades of Company history, but one, only, was serious. In 1917, after Congress had declared war on Germany, a strike was instigated at the East St. Louis Works by a German sympathizer. The proposal to the Company was the formation of a union in which this man and his associates would virtually control operations of this alumina-producing plant, so vital to wartime aluminum production. The strike lasted a month, ending in failure for the organizer. It was followed, however, by something even more serious—a race riot which caused much loss of life and a disruption of production for all industry in that location.

East St. Louis was a waypoint for southern Negroes en route to industrial centers in Chicago, Detroit and Pittsburgh during the great trek of southern farm labor to northern industrial jobs in World War I. Agitators found it easy to fill East St. Louis residents with fear and to incite them to violence by spreading stories that the seemingly abnormal black population was organizing to take over the city. A reign of terror ensued during which many people were killed. Throughout this riot, which lasted for days, the Aluminum Ore Company, Alcoa's subsidiary, gave asylum in its plant to frightened Negroes.

C. B. Fox, retired Alcoa Vice President, has vivid recollections of those exciting days. He secured a quantity of Springfield rifles from the Federal Post Office Building for possible use in the event the plant was rushed by rioters. He ordered these rifles kept under lock until such time as he and his associate executives agreed that they should be uncased. Rioters located in the Southern Railroad yards near by had been shooting at the plant. Mr. Fox advised the president of the railroad that his own people would start shooting if these rioters were not dispersed from the yards. Much to his surprise, the firing from the rioters suddenly ceased. Then he discovered that one of his own men had located one of the Springfields and was nonchalantly parading the parapet of the Ore Company building while he had been telephoning. Apparently the rioters got the message from the railroad and, at the same time, saw the armed sentry, whom they considered the forerunner of many more armed men. Evidently they decided that Mr. Fox meant what he said.

In these days of pension, hospitalization, and life-insurance programs, it is interesting to check back into the records and discover Alcoa's early attempt to give something more than wages to its employees. On March 20, 1902, the Board of Directors passed a resolution in which it created a "Permanent Employment Fund." The purpose, according to the minutes, was "to establish more permanent relations between the Company and its employees." The expressed hope was that such a fund would build up for the employee a nest egg or a pension to take care of him in his declining years.

Under the plan, the Company credited to each hourly-paid employee, at the close of each month, 2½ per cent of his previous month's earnings. The employee made no contribution whatsoever. On this credit, the Company calculated interest at 6 per cent, compounded semiannually, and credited this interest to each account. If the employee left the Company by giving thirty days' notice, he could draw out everything to his credit in the fund. If he quit without notice or was discharged, he got none of the money.

The plan was adopted first in Niagara Falls and later at New Kensington, Massena, East St. Louis and Alcoa. It lasted until 1916 when it was discontinued, largely because of defects in the plan. In the beginning, it had given little incentive to an employee to stay with his job, since he could get his accumulated money at any time on thirty days' notice. Later the plan was modified to read that an individual could withdraw his funds, except those which had accumulated during the first two years. This started a practice by employees of withdrawing the excess every six months. With the main purpose of the fund thus defeated, the Company was willing to listen to employees at Niagara Falls, in January, 1916, when they asked for higher wages in lieu of the benefits of the pension program. Similar action followed at Massena, New Kensington, East St. Louis and Alcoa.

At the time the Permanent Employment Fund was inaugurated, another social benefit operation, called "The Sick Fund," was started. This was a contributory fund. The employee paid $.25 per week and the Company matched this sum. In addition, the Company turned over to the fund all moneys forfeited by employees to the Permanent Employment Fund through quitting without notice or being discharged. Roughly, this worked out so that for each dollar in the so-called Sick Fund the employee contributed $.25 and the Company $.75. This plan survived much longer than the Permanent Employment Fund. In fact, it lasted at some locations until recent times when it was followed by the present Company-wide programs on health and life insurance.

As stated in the beginning of this chapter, Alcoa's labor relations became an important factor in operations in the 1930's. The first strike affecting a sizable group of Company plants, scattered over several states, occurred in 1934. The strike, which lasted for one month, closed the plants at New Kensington, Pennsylvania; Alcoa, Tennessee; East St. Louis, Illinois; Massena, New York; and Garwood, New Jersey. The union involved was the Aluminum Workers' Unions, affiliated with the American Federation of Labor. The strike was authorized by the union because of the refusal of the Company to meet its demands for a closed shop; check-off of union dues; universal wage rate; and acceptance of the Agreement proposed by the Union Committee. The dispute was resolved through the medium of the "Agreement Between Aluminum Company of America and All of Its Employees," dated September 6, 1934, signed by Roy A. Hunt, President, Aluminum Company of America.

The month-long 1934 strike, which completely closed the plants at New Kensington, Alcoa, East St. Louis, Massena and Garwood, was a peaceful affair. The Company made no attempt to operate and union pickets were courteous. At Alcoa, where a limited number of plant executive personnel were on duty inside the mills for maintenance purposes, food and changes of clothing were sent in by parcel post. Metallurgist John W. Hood wanted to see his three-year-old daughter. The little girl was "mailed" into the plant and out again amid the cheers of the pickets. Throughout the years, work stoppages and strikes at Company locations have been largely free from violence. Except for one instance at Alcoa, Tennessee, in 1937, when shooting occurred in an altercation between plant guards and pickets at the sheet-mill entrance, there has been an absence of the type of disturbance which has occurred in the labor problems of many industrial concerns.

A detailed history of Alcoa's relations with the various unions with which it has bargained collectively over the past twenty years would place too great a burden on this chapter. For perusal by those trained in labor relations a summary is appended on page 277. It was compiled from the records in the department of R. C. Turner, Alcoa's efficient Director of Personnel. It lists the many unions with which the Company bargains in addition to the two major organizations, the C.I.O. and the A.F. of L.

However, no mere chronology can picture the matters of import to labor relations in all industry which have been involved in discussions in Washington and elsewhere between Alcoa labor negotiators and union representatives. M. M. Anderson, Vice President in charge of Employee Relations, has represented the Company in these matters affecting policy. A recognized national figure in industrial relations, Mr. Anderson has organized and now directs all the departments and groups whose work has to do with the health and welfare of employees or with employee relations.

Starting back in the early 1930's, these departments have been organized over the years to keep pace with social, economic and statutory changes that have taken place. Trained men are in charge of each phase of this personnel work.

There is the Labor Relations Department which directs and advises on all union matters; there is the Safety Department which directs and advises on plant safety programs and compensation cases; there is the Medical Department that advises on industrial hygiene and plant medical facilities; there is the Employment Department that directs and advises on employment procedure and selection and placement of plant personnel; there is the College Recruitment Department which interviews and selects college and technical people for employment in the various divisions of the Company; there is the Salary Administration Department, which approves and advises on salary matters; there is the Retirement and Social Insurance Department that administers the provisions of the Company retirement and social-insurance programs.

The latest addition to this well-rounded personnel organization is the Training Department, which directs the "Conference Plan for Management," a medium by which all supervisory and management people are kept currently informed on facts about the Company and how the American enterprise system works. Supervisory people are given class instruction on these important facts about Alcoa and the American economy, and the program is paying dividends through an improved general knowledge on the part of all Alcoa employees.

All of these departments operate from the central office in Pittsburgh through competent managers at the various Company locations and to the individual through his immediate superior.

CHAPTER FIFTEEN

The Federal Trade Investigation

☆ ☆ ☆ ☆ ☆ ☆ ☆ ☆ ☆

BECAUSE of the watchful attitude Government has displayed toward the aluminum business for a half century, the historian finds ample source material in the record of investigations and court proceedings when he undertakes this portion of the Alcoa story. The Federal Trade Commission made an exhaustive probe into all phases of the Company's affairs beginning in 1922. This investigation, which ended eight years later with a clean bill of health for the Company, makes a record to which Alcoa can point with justifiable pride.

The Federal Trade Commission was created by Congress in 1914. It is composed of five members appointed by the President, each appointee being named for seven years. Its primary purpose is to prevent unfair methods of competition and other specific abuses which, unless nipped in their incipiency, might develop into the kind of restraints or monopolization that the Sherman Act was designed to curb. It may issue a "cease and desist" order against an offender. It may make its record in a case available to the Department of Justice with or without recommendations to that Department for further procedure under the anti-trust laws.

In 1922 the Federal Trade Commission began an investigation of the house-furnishings industry which included the aluminum cooking-utensil business. Because of the interest of the American housewife in kitchenware, the aluminum cooking-utensil phase of the investigation received copious attention from the newspapers. On October 6, 1924, the Federal Trade Commission issued a report containing some severe criticisms of Alcoa, the principal supplier of aluminum to utensil manufacturers. These charges were: cancellation of quotas, refusal to promise shipment, delays in deliveries, delays in needed sizes while less-needed metal was being shipped, dumping of large quantities of metal, discrimination in the price of sheet aluminum, discouraging potential competition, defective metal shipments.

The Federal Trade Commission followed this report by filing a complaint on July 21, 1925, charging Alcoa with unfair competition, discrimination, injury to competitors and other overt acts. Testimony on these charges started February 15, 1926. Hearings were held on forty-two days in nine different cities. The Commission closed its case on March 7, 1929, three years and eight months after the complaint was filed. Testimony for Alcoa began April 8, 1929, with hearings held on fifteen days in four different cities. The respondent closed its case on May 24, 1929, two and one-half months after the Commission had completed its testimony.

Over 5,000 pages of testimony were taken and 874 exhibits submitted. Two thirds of the exhibits were letters on the alleged cooking-utensil monopoly, which was being supported by charges of refusing to supply competitors, failure to make shipment, delivering insufficient quantities and shipping inferior material. The complaints on this score broke down when nine important cooking-utensil manufacturers wrote letters saying they had not been discriminated against. The investigation showed that from 1919 to 1924 Alcoa had received 9,600,000 letters from customers and only 644 of these voiced a total of 188 separate complaints on delayed or faulty delivery.

The facts were that Alcoa was going through the manufacturing problems common to most businesses in 1920–1923. A depression came in 1921 with orders hard to get and many cancellations. In 1922 there was sudden improvement in demand, but it was the postwar period when things were disrupted by various happenings affecting transportation, labor and ability to secure raw materials. A switchmen's strike in 1920 was followed by a railroad shopmen's strike in the last half of 1922. There were disruptions in soft-coal production, railroad embargoes and a shortage of efficient labor. Alcoa's record of delayed and defective shipments was not above the general average. From 1919 to 1924 it was under 2 per cent, although in the one year of 1926 it ran as high as 6 per cent.

The Federal Trade Commission complaint went further than the charges that cooking-utensil makers had been subjected to unfair competition. It was alleged that Alcoa had removed practically all the scrap aluminum from the market for the purpose of preventing its competitors from securing scrap; that Alcoa had sold metal to its own foundries at less than it sold to jobbing foundries; that the Company had sold aluminum sheet to various

203

manufacturers at less than to other users on condition that the buyer resell his resultant scrap back to Alcoa. The Company was also accused of a scheme to monopolize the sand-casting industry as well as a program to monopolize all raw materials including ingot, sheet, secondary aluminum and various fabricated products.

The remaining charges sound much like the ones embraced in the sweeping complaint made by the Department of Justice in the anti-trust case filed in 1937. They included: an alleged effort to monopolize bauxite; an alleged attempt to monopolize the water power of the world; alleged domination and control of the foreign market for aluminum in the United States; alleged control of Aluminum Goods Manufacturing Company; alleged price cutting injurious to Baush Machine Tool Company. It was also charged that Alcoa had violated the Consent Decree of 1912.

In the hearings it became evident that aluminum scrap enjoyed a free market at prices which fluctuated daily. Maytag Washing Machine Company, for instance, purchased great quantities of scrap from a St. Louis dealer. Alcoa scrap purchases were voluntary and were not conditioned upon contracts to purchase aluminum. Automotive manufacturers were getting the best price they could for their scrap. In some cases a buyer urged upon Alcoa a scrap contract; in other cases large buyers found they could sell their scrap to better advantage to others or on the open market. With a limited amount of new metal on hand in 1922 and 1923, Alcoa was a substantial buyer of scrap but there were plenty of competitors for this useful commodity. Scrap was used extensively by the sand-casting industry. There were over 2,000 secondary or scrap-aluminum dealers in the country. A number of them had smelting facilities and scrap prices rose or fell almost daily with the demand.

An agreement to purchase the resultant scrap from a buyer of its aluminum mill products was not a one-way proposition ending in Alcoa's advantage. Sometimes these contracts proved unsatisfactory. There was the instance of the agreement with the Edward G. Budd Manufacturing Company. Budd asked Alcoa for prices on aluminum sheet and also the price Alcoa would pay for returned scrap to enable Budd to make sound estimates on the cost of finished stampings for Ford sedan bodies. Later a controversy arose over what constituted acceptable scrap. Alcoa insisted that Budd broke the contract by holding out large pieces of scrap and selling them on the outside to others at higher than the agreed price. Budd claimed these large pieces should not be included because they could not be briquetted into small compact blocks for smelting.

The principal complainant from the business world in the Federal Trade Commission case was the Charles B. Bohn Foundry Company of Detroit. The official name of the company in 1924 became the Bohn Aluminum & Brass Corporation. It had been the Bohn Foundry Company, founded in 1918 from the General Aluminum & Brass Manufacturing Company, established in 1912.

The Bohn complaint was primarily a charge of unfair practices by Alcoa in the aluminum sand-casting industry, but the legal staff of the Federal Trade Commission went on from there to develop the widespread general charges of monopolization and suppression of competition in almost every phase of aluminum manufacture.

After extensive investigations and hearings spanning an eight-year period, the Federal Trade Commission, on April 7, 1930, closed the case with an order of dismissal reading as follows: [1]

April 7, 1930

ORDER OF DISMISSAL

The above-entitled proceeding coming on for consideration by the Commission upon the complaint of the Commission, the answer of respondent, the record, briefs and oral argument of counsel for the Commission and the respondent, and the Commission having duly considered same and being fully advised in the premises,

It is ordered that the complaint herein be and the same hereby is dismissed for the reason that the charges of the complaint are not sustained by the testimony and evidence.

The order was signed by Otis P. Johnson, Secretary. It was listed as Docket No. 1335 with the full Commission participating. The Federal Trade Commission on that date was composed of Garland S. Ferguson, Chairman, C. W. Hunt, William P. Humphrey, Charles H. March, and Edgar A. McCulloch.

This thorough probe by the Federal Trade Commission, ending in a complete exoneration for the Company, was not the only investigation growing out of these charges. Acting within the scope of its authority, the Federal Trade Commission transmitted to the Attorney General on October 17, 1924, a copy of its report listing criticisms against Alcoa. The Department of Justice promptly assigned Joseph E. Dunn, a special agent, to make a general survey of the aluminum industry to ascertain whether it was necessary to make a special investigation to see

[1] 13 F.T.C. Dec 333.

if there had been any violation of the Consent Decree of 1912 or any other violations of the anti-trust statutes. Following Mr. Dunn's report, he and William R. Benham were sent to Pittsburgh by A. F. Myers, special assistant to the Attorney General. They were joined by Albert E. Radert, an expert accountant.

These three trained investigators for the Department of Justice proceeded to take temporary residence in Pittsburgh with their headquarters at Alcoa's main offices in the Oliver Building. William R. Benham, who filed a formal 368-page report of his findings, said the Company "gave us full and free access to all files, documents, and records of every nature and description desired and extended every aid to facilitate the work in hand." This prolonged visit of the Department of Justice men gave rise to the expression at Alcoa headquarters of the "Government room." This was a well-equipped office furnished by Alcoa with suitable office furniture.

After a thorough investigation, the painstaking report to the Attorney General by William R. Benham gave Alcoa a complete exoneration.[2] In a covering memo, William J. Donovan, assistant to the Attorney General, said that there was no evidence to support a contention that the Consent Decree of 1912 had been violated. He also said that the proof submitted not only failed to establish any intent on Alcoa's part to suppress competition, "but goes far to sustain the contention of the Aluminum Company of America that the cancellation of quotas, shipment of defective metal, etc., resulted from conditions then existing in the industry and beyond the control of the Company." [3]

[2] Senate Document No. 67, 69th Congress, 1st Session.
[3] *Id.,* p. v.

The charges investigated by the Federal Trade Commission and by the Department of Justice during this period were again to be aired in the long anti-trust suit filed against Alcoa in 1937. The thoroughness of this probe in the Twenties into Alcoa's affairs and the record showing lack of misconduct gave convincing evidence of the Company's good business intentions and its desire to deal fairly with its competitors.

CHAPTER SIXTEEN

The Baush Cases
and George D. Haskell

☆ ☆ ☆ ☆ ☆ ☆ ☆ ☆ ☆

I N ADDITION to thorough investigation into its conduct by
Governmental agencies, Alcoa's relationships with competitors have been exhaustively reviewed in Court actions. Prior
to the anti-trust suit against the Company filed by the Department of Justice in 1937, the most extensive of these Court actions is found in the two trials of the case of the Baush Machine
Tool Company vs. Alcoa.

These lawsuits, with Baush as the complainant, were brought
under the anti-trust statutes. Special emphasis was given to
charges that Alcoa had been guilty of combinations or agreements
in restraint of trade and that it had cut prices for the purpose of
restraining competition, conduct prohibited by Section 1 of the
Sherman Act and Section 2 of the Clayton Act, respectively.
Both statutes provided that any competitor injured by such unlawful conduct might recover threefold the damages determined
to have been sustained by him.

Baush Machine Tool Company got into the business of rolling sheet aluminum in 1920. The year before it had acquired the Metals Production Equipment Company, a brass plant and gray iron foundry at Chicopee, a community adjacent to Springfield, Massachusetts. Baush called the plant at Chicopee its metals division and converted it into a mill to manufacture aluminum sheet. The company retained its plant in Springfield proper and continued it as a machine-tools works. Baush had been in this business since 1896 and had devoted itself largely to the manufacture of drills and multiple-spindle drills.

The aluminum-sheet-rolling mill occupied an area of 6.96 acres. It consisted of a rolling mill for aluminum sheet and some equipment for making extrusions, tube, rod, wire and forged products. Most of the forging was done by outside concerns because of the meager equipment in the plant. There was one rolling mill with three units or six pairs of rolls for breakdown, roughing and finishing. There were two melting rooms where cast ingots were made. Ingots were preheated and scalped prior to rolling.

The speed of the rolls was 78 feet per minute as compared to from 210 feet to 460 feet per minute in Alcoa mills. Flat sheet 18 inches wide was the greatest that could be produced commercially in the Baush mill. Coiled sheet could not be made except by taking the already manufactured flat sheet and using a coiler. At this time in Alcoa mills, coiled sheet was being made at great speed on equipment especially designed for this purpose. Alcoa mills were rolling flat sheet to a width of 100 inches and coiled sheet 24 to 30 inches in width. Duralumin-type flat sheet 60 inches wide was also being produced by Alcoa.

One brick building with a few other lesser structures housed the equipment at the Baush plant. Extrusion, tube and rod mills were somewhat antiquated. The Baush Company, according to testimony in the lawsuit, spent $18,000 on improvements when it changed the old brass mill and iron foundry into an aluminum rolling mill. Subsequently it spent $42,000 on improvements to its rolling mill equipment. During this same period Alcoa spent $7,500,000 to expand and improve its own fabricating facilities. Indication of the value of the Baush plant after it had ceased to operate is shown by the sale figures when it was put up for auction on March 29, 1943. It sold for $4,700.

Baush Machine Tool Company and its efforts to compete in aluminum manufacture is really the story of a man, George D. Haskell. His desire to succeed and his belief, at times, that influences and people were conspiring against him can be understood. However, as he later admitted, there were two basic causes for his failure. He was starting a new business in competition with steel and copper as well as with experienced manufacturers of aluminum products. He had to meet constant and repeated changes in demand which would involve large capital outlays. He said he realized all this in 1924 when the Harrison Radiator Company, making shells for Chevrolet radiators, declined to consider Baush as a source of supply because he could not roll sheet more than 18 inches wide.

Haskell was a law-office employee from 1909 until 1917. He became a director of the Baush Machine Tool Company in 1913 and joined the company as an officer when he left the law firm four years later. He became President of the Baush Company which made little money in its machine-tool business from that date until 1920 when it bought the defunct brass works and went into the business of aluminum manufacture. Thereafter for several years George Haskell sought backing to enable him to get into the business of making aluminum from mine to metal. The Baush Company bought its ingot from foreign sources, usually a cent or two below what it would have paid Alcoa, but Haskell charged that there was an agreement between Alcoa and the foreigners pegging the imported price at the Alcoa price.

George D. Haskell was essentially an entrepreneur rather than an industrialist, manufacturer or salesman. The modest size of his aluminum-fabricating plant was only incidental to his lack of success. A manufacturer of drills, he was diverted to larger things when he had a chance to buy an old brass mill at a bargain price. This led to manufacture of hard aluminum alloys which, in turn, led him to search for bauxite and water power. As a first-rate promoter rather than a manufacturer, he perhaps never realized how obsolete his equipment was. His mill was simply a stepping stone to what he hoped would be larger fields of operation.

Haskell engaged in litigation against Alcoa other than the suit of the Baush Machine Tool Company. In 1925, 1926 and 1927 he had filed suits in Massachusetts, New York and New Jersey, all based on the acquisition by Alcoa of the Saguenay water power in Canada from J. B. Duke. Haskell claimed he had been promised support by Duke in his (Haskell's) efforts to go into the aluminum-making business and that he was a victim of a conspiracy between Duke and Alcoa to substitute the latter for Haskell as Duke's partner in a Canadian aluminum enterprise. The Massachusetts suit was against Alcoa, James B. Duke and

George Allen, a Duke associate. It was based on an alleged conspiracy to injure Haskell. The case was never tried and was dismissed on January 2, 1930, without prejudice and without costs. Haskell also filed a suit in New Jersey against Alcoa and the Duke estate. This case was likewise dismissed on June 29, 1929. Finally a suit in New Jersey against the Duke estate, based on alleged breach of contract between Duke and Haskell, was actually tried before a jury. It resulted in a verdict for Haskell, but on appeal to the U. S. Circuit Court of Appeals by the Duke estate the verdict was set aside and remanded back to the lower court.[1] It was never tried again.

The Baush lawsuits against Alcoa grew out of the unsuccessful attempt of the Baush Machine Tool Company to manufacture and market aluminum sheet and forgings made of duralumin. Although the hard aluminum alloy, duralumin, was in use in Germany as early as 1912, its manufacture in this country did not occur until after World War I when American manufacturers obtained the patent rights from the Alien Property Custodian. Baush undertook to make it and Alcoa perfected its own 17S alloy with similar properties. Legal action by the Baush Machine Tool Company against Alcoa was filed in July, 1931, in the U. S. District Court in Connecticut. Baush claimed damages for injuries to its metal business through violation of the anti-trust laws on the part of Alcoa. Damages asked were $3,000,000 and, under the triple damage clause of the anti-trust laws, this could amount to $9,000,000.

Charges of unfair competition in the Baush case centered largely around dealings of Alcoa and Baush in the automotive

[1] Haskell vs. Perkins, 28F 2nd, 222, 31F 2nd, 53.

field. Alcoa was accused of underbidding with the intent of driving Baush out of business in contracts with the Franklin Motor Car Company, the Stutz Motor Car Company and the Hupp Motor Company. The three automobile companies were customers for forged aluminum connecting rods. Alcoa was also charged with deliberately attempting to injure the Baush Machine Tool Company by taking from Baush the sheet business that it had enjoyed with Eastman Kodak Company. The evidence showed that the inadequacy of Baush to produce forgings economically caused its loss of the connecting-rod business, and the limitations of its rolling mill, which could produce commercial sheet only 18 inches wide, was responsible for its loss of the Eastman business.

The Baush complaint went much further to include charges that Alcoa was in a conspiracy with foreign producers and with Aluminium, Ltd., the Canadian company, to permit monopoly practices in the United States. These practices, it was alleged, enabled Alcoa to fix prices and compel Baush to pay exorbitant prices for metal as well as to force Baush to sell below a fair profit figure. These charges, along with those concerning deals with domestic customers, were tried for the third time in the anti-trust action initiated by the Department of Justice in 1937. All of them were dismissed by Judge Francis G. Caffey as groundless after full opportunity for testimony and exhibits was given to both sides. The Department of Justice, in the preparation of its suit against Alcoa, used the incidents in the Baush case as source material for many of its charges.

George D. Haskell certainly used every legal effort to achieve his purpose, although in the anti-trust suit a few years later he

said his actions were purely a business matter with him and that
he "never testified that the Aluminum Company was intentionally
trying to injure the Baush Machine Tool Company or to put it
or anyone else out of business."

There were two trials of the Baush case and two appeals to
the U. S. Circuit Court of Appeals. In 1933, after a trial of eleven
weeks at New Haven, Connecticut, the jury found for the defendant, Alcoa. U. S. Circuit Court of Appeals for the Second
Circuit, a three-judge court sitting in New York, reversed this
judgment and ordered a new trial. The opinion was written by
Judge Manton. Judge Swan did not join in the opinion but
contented himself with a two-paragraph concurring opinion
limited to a single issue.[2] A second trial in March 1935, at Hart-
ford, Connecticut, resulted in a verdict for the plaintiff with
damages against Alcoa of $956,300. Threefold, this would have
amounted to $2,868,900. Alcoa appealed to the U. S. Circuit
Court of Appeals and, on September 16, 1935, this Court reversed the verdict and directed a new trial.[3]

Baush Machine Tool Company thereupon initiated steps for
a settlement. Arthur V. Davis, Alcoa's Board Chairman, insisted
that the only justification for a settlement was the avoidance of
vexation and expense of further litigation and that it must be
stipulated that Alcoa was making no admission of wrongdoing.
A major condition was that Haskell secure in writing a statement
that the Attorney General of the United States had no objection
to a settlement and would not use it as the basis for an argument

[2] Baush Machine Tool Co. vs. Aluminum Company of America, 72F 2nd, 236,
242.
[3] Baush Machine Tool Company vs. Aluminum Company of America, 79F 2nd,
217.

that Alcoa had admitted any of the charges hurled at it in the Baush cases. Haskell obtained such a letter from the Attorney General. Thereupon a settlement was reached with Alcoa paying the costs of the second trial. No restriction was placed on Baush which would prevent it from continuing in the aluminum business if it so desired. However, the Baush Machine Tool Company had ceased all aluminum fabrication as of June 1935, and it never started its mill afterward.

The Baush cases were expensive affairs for Alcoa when the time of executive personnel is taken into account. They did serve the useful purpose of enabling the Company to assemble the facts with which to refute the same charges when they again were brought forth by the Department of Justice in its preparation and presentation of the many complaints against the Company in the anti-trust case filed in 1937.

CHAPTER SEVENTEEN

The Anti-Trust Case

☆ ☆ ☆ ☆ ☆ ☆ ☆ ☆

O N APRIL 23, 1937, the Department of Justice filed a
sweeping bill of complaint against Alcoa in the Federal District Court for the Southern District of New
York and asked that Alcoa be dissolved. The Company was
charged with monopolizing interstate commerce in no less than
sixteen markets and commodities and with being a party to
comprehensive conspiracies with foreign producers. While it is
difficult to sort out all of the separate charges in the bill, the
estimate has been a total of 140. There were 103 separate paragraphs in the Government's position, but some of the paragraphs
embraced more than a single charge.

Thus was begun an unprecedented legal record which was
to last for thirteen years before the lawfulness of Alcoa's position in all phases of the aluminum industry was established.
The proceedings were to go up and down the scale of Federal

Courts—District Court, Supreme Court, Circuit Court of Appeals, and back again to District Court for the Southern District of New York.

Preparation of the charges was in the hands of the Anti-Trust Division of the Department of Justice, as was the actual trial of the case. Alcoa's history, including the records of early patent litigations and the proceedings in the two trials of the Baush Machine Tool Company versus Alcoa, was easily available to the Department of Justice. Homer L. Cummings was the Attorney General while the case was under preparation. His law firm, Cummings and Lockwood, represented Baush Machine Tool Company in the Baush-Alcoa cases; but Mr. Cummings, who had then become a Cabinet member, insisted he had withdrawn from active participation in the law firm when the cases were tried. Thurman Arnold was the Assistant Attorney General and head of the Anti-Trust Division during the long trial in the District Court, but he left the actual conduct of the Government's case to Walter L. Rice, a department trial lawyer with the title of special assistant to the Attorney General. Before the decision was rendered in the District Court, Rice had left the Department of Justice to become a Vice President of Reynolds Metals Company, a substantial competitor of Alcoa in the integrated aluminum-manufacturing business.

After preliminary legal skirmishes, the case went to trial on June 1, 1938, before Judge Francis G. Caffey. Thereafter for many weary months in the Federal Court Building at Foley Square in New York City, the taking of testimony and evidence proceeded. Alcoa's legal staff moved from Pittsburgh to New York. Experienced Alcoa personnel was assigned to them to assemble records, documents and other portions of Alcoa's long history. Company files were ransacked to assemble a truckload of papers which were carted to New York to answer sweeping Government subpoenas. Sixteen thousand of these papers were actually photostated for the Government. Qualified Company people were given the task of preparing two volumes of answers to Government interrogatories which developed statistical information as to the growth, financing and activities of Alcoa for the more than half century of its existence.

Alcoa executives and other key personnel were held in readiness to testify and many of them did so. Arthur V. Davis was on the stand continuously for six weeks. His testimony covers 2,105 pages on direct and cross-examination. His amazingly accurate memory of transactions which had occurred thirty and forty years before was verified by actual documents time and again during the ordeal which occurred in the hot summer months. Roy A. Hunt occupied the witness chair for a total of two weeks on important issues. I. W. Wilson, then Vice President in charge of Operations and now President of Alcoa, had the distinction of being the last witness in the longest court trial in history. His time on the stand was only six days since the Government paid him the compliment of not cross-examining him.

In all, 155 witnesses testified either for the prosecution or for the defense. There were more than 58,000 pages of testimony, making the trial the longest in the history of Anglo-Saxon jurisprudence. The actual trial lasted from June 1, 1938, until August 14, 1940—26 months interrupted only by brief summer recesses in 1938 and 1939. The late Alva Johnston, the author of two interesting articles on the Alcoa case in *The New Yorker* in January, 1942, did some estimating of his own on the size of the record. He commented in this colorful language:

> The transcript of the testimony weighed three hundred and twenty-five pounds, or more than three times as much as the Encyclopaedia Britannica. The record, exclusive of the Judge's decision, which has been rendered impromptu from the bench but has not yet been edited into final shape, was printed in four hundred and eighty volumes. It contained fifteen million words, or more than thirty times as many as "Gone with the Wind". . . . England's best effort in this field was the case of the Tichborne Claimant. That trial, held in 1874, lasted a hundred and eighty-eight days. Thurman Arnold outscored England by a hundred and seventy-six days. If the period of preparation is included, the Alcoa case outlasted the Civil War.[1]

The Government's complaint fell under three main headings, monopolization, illegal conduct in domestic competition, and conspiracy with the foreign producers. To support its assertion that Alcoa had intended to monopolize from the very beginning despite its legal monopoly until 1909 under its basic patents, the Department of Justice cited early patent litigations with Cowles and alleged law violations enumerated in the Consent Decree of 1912. Judge Caffey found that nothing Alcoa did in its early patent litigation lent any support to the charge that it was either monopolizing or restraining trade. It was simply a

[1] "A Reporter At Large—Thurman Arnold's Biggest Case," *The New Yorker*, January, 1942.

Alcoa executives in 1937. Seated, left to right: Senior Vice President George R. Gibbons (now deceased), Senior Vice President Edwin S. Fickes (now deceased), Board Chairman Arthur V. Davis, President Roy A. Hunt, Vice President Charles B. Fox (now retired). Standing, left to right: Vice President George J. Stanley (now retired), Vice President Paul J. Urquhart (now retired), Vice President Irving W. Wilson, Senior Vice President Robert E. Withers (now retired), Vice President Safford K. Colby (now deceased). Absent from group was Vice President Winthrop C. Neilson (now deceased).

fight for survival between the owners of competing patents. He also found that the original complaints by the Government which ended in the Consent Decree had been settled by that Decree and deserved scant consideration in any attempt to prove intent of wrongdoing on the part of the Company.

The principal commodities which Alcoa was accused of monopolizing were bauxite, water power, alumina, virgin aluminum, castings, cooking utensils, pistons, extrusions and structural shapes, foil, sheet and miscellaneous fabricated products. Since most of these commodities are discussed elsewhere in this chronicle, a brief mention here of the monopoly charges and the Court ruling will suffice.

In the long trial of the case, many days were consumed in a thorough airing of the bauxite monopoly charges and their refutation by the Company. The testimony of two experts filled some 1,900 pages of the record. In his decision on this issue, the Court decided there is no monopoly of bauxite and there never has been.

There seemed to be no question of the plentiful supply of bauxite as a world commodity. Judge Caffey therefore made a searching analysis of the testimony regarding a possible control of United States bauxite by Alcoa. He found both the Government and Alcoa admitting that it is "impossible to foretell, with any degree of accuracy, the bauxite which underlies any given acreage because of irregularities in the natural placement of the ore." The Court then relied largely on two experts who gave their separate opinions of what constitutes the bauxite lands in Saline and Pulaski Counties in Arkansas and who owns this ore, suitable for the commercial manufacture of aluminum.

The experts differed slightly, but a composite of their opinions, based on test borings, was that Alcoa owns about half of it and others own the remaining 50 per cent. Judge Caffey's conclusion was that the adequacy of bauxite for aluminum manufacture precluded any charge that this raw material was being monopolized.

On the issue of whether Alcoa has monopolized water power, the Court dismissed that contention by taking judicial notice of the facts. Statistics of the Federal Power Commission disproved the monopoly charge. Installed water-power generating capacity in the United States in 1938 was 10,700,000 kilowatts. There were 3,903 electric generating plants in this country in that year producing 114,000,000,000 kilowatt hours. The number of kilowatt hours produced from water power in 1938 was 44,000,000,000. Great Government hydroelectric projects had been developed in the Tennessee Valley and in the Northwest. Had Judge Caffey been able to review the statistics for 1948, ten years later, they would have been even more impressive. Installed capacity at hydro sites in 1948 was 15,700,000 kilowatts, and the number of kilowatt hours produced from water power in 1948 was 82,000,000,000. Alcoa produced in its own hydroelectric plants in 1948 less than 5 per cent of this nation-wide production of electricity from water power.

It became evident that it would be physically and financially impossible for any industrial concern to monopolize water power in this country. The American taxpayer who has made possible the vast Governmental projects of the past few decades would not accept such a thesis. Judge Caffey said, ". . . The amount of power developed or potential and fit to produce aluminum, owned by Alcoa, is but an insignificant portion of the total available in the United States." [2]

Judge Caffey held that the anti-trust attorneys had failed to prove any of their charges of monopolization by Alcoa of either alumina or aluminum. He started with the premise that Alcoa was, at the time the charges were filed, the sole producer of alumina for aluminum manufacture in the United States, as well as the sole manufacturer of virgin aluminum. He found nothing in the long record which sustained the Government's charge that Alcoa had excluded or sought to exclude any competitor or potential competitor from producing or selling aluminum in the United States. The Court also reviewed the history of aluminum castings in this country and concluded that no evidence showed a monopolization by Alcoa of that widely manufactured product.

The charge of the monopolization of cooking utensils centered largely around Alcoa's ownership of a minority interest in The Aluminum Goods Manufacturing Company of Manitowoc, Wisconsin. The Government contention was that Alcoa and Aluminum Goods controlled the aluminum cooking-utensil market with Alcoa as the dominant factor. Aluminum Goods Manufacturing Company was named as a defendant in the suit, largely because of its alleged connection with Alcoa. The Court found that vigorous competition has always existed between The Aluminum Goods Manufacturing Company and The Aluminum Cooking Utensil Company, Alcoa subsidiary, and that Aluminum Goods' policies are directed by the Vits, Hamilton and Koenig families, long-time majority owners of the business.

[2] United States vs. Aluminum Company of America et al., Finding of Fact 77.

Alleged charges of monopolization of aluminum pistons, produced principally by the permanent-mold method, were dismissed by Judge Caffey after careful examination of the Piston Patent Estate, a pooling of patents by various companies engaged in piston manufacture. The charge that Alcoa monopolized aluminum foil failed, in the Court's judgment, since the Reynolds Metals Company was shown to be a larger factor in that market than Alcoa.

The assertion by Government counsel that Alcoa had monopolized aluminum sheet brought forth much testimony on both sides and occupied weeks of the trial. Alcoa's entire history as a manufacturer of aluminum sheet since 1895 was reviewed, along with its relations with customers and competitors. The evidence in the Baush Machine Tool cases was gone over again. The Court found the charges of monopolization were not sustained, but did find possible injury to competitors in the narrowness of the spread between Alcoa's ingot price and the price it charged for some of its sheet during the years 1925 to 1932. The Court confined its finding to twenty out of seventy-two items of aluminum sheet which were examined. This spread, in the opinion of the Court, made it difficult for an independent aluminum-sheet roller to make a profit on the margin between the cost of raw material and the sale price of the finished product. Judge Caffey noted that Alcoa had widened the spread between ingot and sheet prices after 1932 and further observed that the Company was constantly being urged by sheet purchasers to narrow the spread between sheet and ingot prices, whereas the owners of rolling mills wanted the spread widened.

The conspiracy charges, in which Alcoa was accused of making deals with foreign producers, designed to control the price of aluminum in the United States, harked back to 1895. The Government virtually claimed that there was a continuous conspiracy from that date forward, with Alcoa the nucleus of the conspiracy. Five European cartels formed between 1895 and 1915 were cited by the Department of Justice as evidence of Alcoa's participation in the alleged conspiracy. The records showed that only one of these cartels, the first one organized in 1895, was signed by Alcoa. The others were participated in by the Aluminum Company of Canada, Alcoa's subsidiary.

The 1895 cartel did not fix prices in the United States. It specified that Alcoa was not to sell aluminum in four European countries, and the Swiss company, a member of the cartel, was not to sell in America. The 1901, 1906 and 1908 cartels provided for allocation of certain markets or the fixing of prices. The 1912 cartel applied to sales outside the United States, and Alcoa insisted it was in no way a violation of the Sherman Act.

In weighing these cartels as evidence of any continuing conspiracy, Judge Caffey observed that the 1895 cartel had ended in 1896, just forty-five years before the anti-trust suit was filed. The 1901 cartel expired in 1906, thirty-three years before the Department of Justice made its charges. The 1906 cartel was dissolved by consent of its members on October 1, 1908. The 1908 cartel was not only terminated by its members on February 17, 1912, but was also canceled by the Consent Decree Alcoa had signed on June 7, 1912. Because of World War I, the 1912 cartel soon became inactive and it was canceled by the contracting parties on January 23, 1915. The Court held that none of these cartels could be considered to have the weight the Government attempted to attach to them as indicating a long-range program of Alcoa to conspire with foreign producers and thereby fix prices in the United States market.

Cartels, or agreements between competing companies, are an accepted device for regulating quotas and even for fixing prices in Europe, although they are illegal in the United States. It was not difficult for the Government's attorneys to find numerous European aluminum cartels formed in the period subsequent to 1912 and to draw these cartels to the attention of the Court. One such cartel was formed in 1923. Arthur V. Davis testified that Alcoa was asked to join it but declined. Again in 1928 executives of the French Aluminum Company and the British Aluminium Company asked Alcoa to join a cartel limiting imports into the United States. Mr. Davis again flatly refused. No evidence was introduced at the trial in the elaborate array of testimony and exhibits to show that Alcoa or any subsidiary was a member of any cartel after 1915.

The Government attorneys, still insisting that there must have been a "tacit" understanding between Alcoa and the foreigners after 1915, sought to prove the point by witnesses who quoted alleged statements from foreign producers indicating that such a pact existed. Judge Caffey carefully reviewed twelve conversations which allegedly occurred between aluminum customers or competitors of Alcoa and foreign sources. Among the witnesses who testified were George D. Haskell and Roger D. Babson of the Baush Machine Tool Company, James L. T. Waltz of the Bremer-Waltz Company, and Laurence J. Harwood of the Fulton-Harwood Brass Works of South Bend, Indiana. Each had been seeking better prices for aluminum and on the witness stand was giving from his memory or from his own conclusions the impressions he thought he received from his conversations with foreign producers. In each instance the witness thought he detected some arrangement with Alcoa when he was unable to get a price concession. None of the foreigners and none of their agents testified about these conversations. The Court held that this hearsay testimony was entirely unreliable and unworthy of belief.

Finally the Anti-Trust Division of the Department of Justice relied upon the formation of Aluminium, Ltd., as a means of proving the conspiracy charges. The Government's contention was that Aluminium, Ltd., was created purely as a device by which Alcoa could participate freely in the European cartels and fix aluminum prices on a world-wide basis without regard to the prohibitions of the Sherman Act. The business motives which prompted the creation of Aluminium, Ltd., have been told in another chapter and need not be reviewed here. However, Government counsel sought to show that marketing agreements Aluminium, Ltd., had in 1931 and subsequent years with British and Norwegian aluminum producers, as well as Aluminium, Ltd.'s, connection with Alliance Aluminium Compagnie, represented indirect participation of Alcoa in the European cartels.

The Alliance group was composed of British, French, Swiss and German companies to fix production quotas of members in order to prevent the accumulation of large surpluses of aluminum. It did not concern itself with the United States market. Aluminium, Ltd., a Canadian corporation engaged in world trade, was a member. The Court held that there was no credible evidence to show that a conspiracy ever existed between Alcoa and Aluminium, Ltd., or that there has been, since 1915, any agreement between Alcoa and foreign producers.

Under the heading of other alleged misconduct, Judge Caffey considered the accusations that Alcoa had charged extortionate prices and had made exhorbitant profits. He found neither of these charges to be supported by the evidence.

On the issue of abnormal earnings, the Court found that, over the entire life of Alcoa, the average earnings had been at a rate of slightly less than 10 per cent. This he held to be a not unreasonable rate of return. Alcoa stockholders have fared well in equity values through the Company's long-established policy of plowing back earnings into the business, but their cash yield in the form of dividends has been at a far lower rate than have been the returns to stockholders of many high-dividend-paying companies.

A parade of witnesses had appeared before the Court in reference to Alcoa's conduct. Near the end of his decision, Judge Caffey said:[3]

> The astonishing thing is the great number of witnesses who appeared on the stand, competitors as well as customers of Alcoa, who have completely exculpated Alcoa from blame and have praised its fairness as well as its helpfulness to the aluminum industry. I think I should add that such conduct of those witnesses, nearly all of whom were entirely independent, is in great part a tribute to Mr. Arthur V. Davis.

Judge Caffey, Alabama-born jurist in his mid-seventies at the time he made his decision, performed an amazing feat in

[3] United States vs. Aluminum Company of America et al., 44 F Supp. 97, 308-9.

rendering an oral opinion from the bench. For nine days, he spoke in logical sequence from his notes. When his written opinion in the monumental case appeared some months later, it contained no different conclusions and few changes in phraseology.[4] He found Alcoa innocent of all the charges of monopolization and conspiracy which the Department of Justice had marshaled against it.

Near the end of his long opinion, Judge Caffey said:[5]

> I think it clear that, with the access to the two raw materials of ore and power named which is and, save when prevented by a patent, always has been open to everybody in the United States, anyone possessing the four cardinal tangible elements of intelligence, industry, courage and money or credit is and has been able, with confidence, to go into the production of virgin aluminum. Anyone in the United States outfitted with the four prerequisites I have mentioned is now free, and since the expiration of the Bradley patent in 1909 has been free, to produce virgin aluminum.

On July 23, 1942, the District Court entered its judgment, dismissing the 103-paragraph petition of the Government. Sweeping as the decision was in reference to all the charges which had been hurled at Alcoa, it was not the end of this litigation. The Department of Justice appealed the case to the Supreme Court. There was an absence of quorum in that body because four Supreme Court justices had previously participated in anti-

[4] United States vs. Aluminum Company of America, 44 F Supp. 97.
[5] U. S. vs. Aluminum Company of America et al., 44 F Supp. 97, 306.

trust action against Alcoa when they were connected with the Department of Justice. Discussion of this stalemate reached Congress and resulted in the passage of an act on June 9, 1944, which made it possible for the U. S. Circuit Court of Appeals for the Second Circuit to act in the Alcoa case in lieu of the Supreme Court. The act did not mention Alcoa by name but did provide that when there was a lack of quorum in the Supreme Court a civil anti-trust case which had been appealed to that body should immediately be certified to the Circuit Court of Appeals in which was located the district where the suit was originally tried. The Alcoa case is the only application of the statute to date. Upon passage of the law, the Supreme Court entered an order certifying the case to the U. S. Court of Appeals for the Second Circuit. This Appeals court was composed of Judges Learned Hand, Augustus Hand and Thomas W. Swan, the three judges who rendered the decision in the Associated Press anti-trust case. Judge Learned Hand wrote the opinion after the judges had heard arguments from counsel on both sides.[6]

The decision upheld Judge Caffey on all counts except one, the alleged monopolization of the aluminum ingot market. The Court of Appeals held that Alcoa had monopolized this market up to August 14, 1940, when the testimony in the original trial was closed. The Court found the monopoly to have existed simply in the act of growth by the Company over the preceding twenty-five years with the result that Alcoa was supplying 90 per cent of the United States market for aluminum ingot on the closing date of the trial. In the opinion of the Court, this proportion of the aluminum ingot market was alone sufficient

[6] United States vs. Aluminum Company of America et al., 148F 2nd, 416.

to show violation of the Sherman Act without any evidence of Alcoa's intent to monopolize. The Court held that Alcoa monopolized the ingot market simply because it held too large a proportion of it. The District Court was affirmed in its ruling that there was no monopoly of any raw material or any fabricated article of aluminum. The lower Court was also affirmed in its holding that there was no conspiracy with foreign producers.

The Circuit Court of Appeals was careful to limit its ruling with respect to the aluminum-ingot market to the period ending August 14, 1940. It recognized that the war had followed this date, that aluminum-ingot plants with capacities greater than Alcoa's had been built and that these plants would have to be disposed of under a program to be set up by Congress. The Court specifically said that, because Alcoa had a monopoly in 1940, there was no reason to assume that it would have one after the war.[7]

On the one issue of monopolizing the aluminum-ingot market in which the Circuit Court of Appeals had failed to agree with the District Court, the higher Court specifically forbade the District Court to rule until disposition had been made of the Government's aluminum plants. The Court of Appeals said:[8]

> It is idle for the plaintiff to assume that dissolution will be proper, as it is for Alcoa to assume that it will not be; and it would be particularly fatuous to prepare a plan now, even if we could be sure that eventually some

[7] United States vs. Aluminum Company of America, 148F 2nd, 416.
[8] United States vs. Aluminum Company of America et al., 148F 2nd, 416, 446.

form of dissolution will be proper. Dissolution is not a penalty, but a remedy; if the industry will not need it for its protection, it will be a disservice to break up an aggregation which has for so long demonstrated its efficiency.

This put the case back in the lap of the U. S. District Court. On April 23, 1946, ninth anniversary of the case, this Court entered a final judgment making disposition of the issues but giving the Attorney General the right to institute further proceedings on the one ground of possible monopolization of the aluminum-ingot market. The Government was privileged to do this if it appeared that disposition of Government-owned aluminum-producing plants in the postwar period had not brought about competition. Alcoa was also privileged to apply to the Court for determination of this issue if it appeared that competition had come about.

On March 31, 1947, Alcoa did petition the Court, asking for a judgment that it no longer had a monopoly in the ingot market in the United States because competitive conditions existed in the industry. The case was set for trial on October 15, 1947, but, a month before the trial date, the Department of Justice petitioned the Court of Appeals for a writ of mandamus ordering the lower Court to stop the scheduled trial and to dismiss Alcoa's petition. It was the Government's contention that, until such time as it chose to apply for a remedy, the case should remain indefinitely suspended.

The Department of Justice failed in this action but it had the effect of postponing the trial in the District Court. The Circuit Court of Appeals ruled that it did not have jurisdiction to decide the issue raised by the Government.[9] A ruling was sought in the Supreme Court. The highest Court decided[10] that the U. S. Circuit Court did have jurisdiction and returned the matter to that body, which then proceeded to rule against the Government's request that Alcoa's petition be dismissed. It also ruled that a petition of the Government of September 25, 1948, asking that Alcoa be divested of some of its properties, could be heard by the District Court at the same time the Alcoa petition was being decided.[11]

All this resulted in a delay of the actual trial, which did not begin until March 28, 1949. Judge John C. Knox presided in the District Court room in Foley Square, New York City, in place of Judge Caffey who had retired from the bench on October 31, 1947. Two petitions were at issue. One was Alcoa's request that the ingot monopoly charge be dismissed. The other was the Government's petition asking that Alcoa be directed to divest itself of some of its properties. The trial lasted from March 28, 1949, until November 9, 1949, including a summer recess and a further interruption because of the illness of Judge Knox.

Alcoa contended that the well-planned disposal of surplus aluminum war plants to two domestic competitors, Reynolds Metals Company and Kaiser Aluminum and Chemical Corporation, had terminated Alcoa's prewar ingot production advantage on which Judge Hand had based his decision. In short, Alcoa pointed to competitive conditions in the aluminum-ingot

[9] United States vs. District Court, 171F 2nd, 285, 286.
[10] United States vs. District Court, 334 U.S., 258.
[11] United States vs. District Court for Southern District of New York, 171F 2nd, 285.

market in 1949 which were far different from those in 1940.

Judge Knox filed his opinion on June 2, 1950.[12] In it, he prefaced his specific rulings by a discussion of the changes in court interpretation of the Sherman Act which had come about in recent years. Now, it is no longer necessary to prove wrong intent or overt acts to find a company guilty of violating the law. The Courts have said that mere power to monopolize amounts to monopolization regardless of whether the power is exercised. The unexercised powers to control prices or to put competitors out of business have been held as evidence of monopolization. Mere size or efficiency, under the present concept of the higher Courts, carries with it an opportunity for abuse that cannot be ignored.

In Alcoa's case, Judge Knox found that price domination had not been established and, while Alcoa's resources are greater than those of its competitors, there is no reason to believe that Reynolds and Kaiser will not continue to thrive and prosper. In the opinion of the Court, Alcoa is not guilty of monopolization so long as there is effective competition from these or other sources. The Court, therefore, denied the Government's request that Alcoa be required to sell some of its plants and facilities. It did retain jurisdiction in the case for five years to provide opportunity for the Department of Justice to petition for further relief in the event it thought it could prove that effective competition did not exist in the industry.

Judge Knox mentioned the constructive role that Alcoa has played in the postwar aluminum industry and stated that no instance of unfair competition by the Company appeared on the record. He said that Alcoa had served the public well and effi-

[12] United States vs. Aluminum Company of America, 91 F Supp. 333.

ciently. He recognized Alcoa's contributions to the disposal program wherein the Company co-operated with the War Assets Administration in the sale or lease of Government-owned war-built aluminum plants to Alcoa competitors. In this, he was referring largely to Alcoa's grant of royalty-free licenses under certain patents to competitors who had acquired Government-owned aluminum plants which Alcoa had built for the Government and which the Company had operated during the war.

The Court found in Alcoa's favor in connection with the vigorous attack the Department of Justice had made on the Company's patent structure. The Government had argued that Alcoa's patent position dominated the industry and that it should not be allowed to collect royalties from its competitors. The Court denied both these contentions but did direct that a so-called "grant back" to Alcoa of a license on any improvements, contained in the royalty-free alumina licenses which Alcoa had given to Reynolds and Kaiser, should be unenforceable.

Judge Knox upheld Alcoa's purchase of the Government-owned St. Lawrence aluminum reduction plant, located adjacent to the Company's Massena Works. The Department of Justice had objected to this sale because it made a slight increase in Alcoa's aluminum-producing facilities.

While finding no illegal relationship between Alcoa and Aluminium, Ltd., or between the stockholders of the two companies, the Court did stipulate that those who owned substantial stock in both companies should sell their stock in one or the other company. The Court's position on this matter was that such stock divestiture would remove any appearance of collusive action in the future. Since Alcoa and Aluminium, Ltd., have been competing with each other in vigorous manner, the ruling does not change existing policies.

On January 16, 1951, Judge Knox accepted with slight modifications a stock-disposal plan submitted by major shareholders of Alcoa and Aluminium, Limited, of Canada. Under the plan Alcoa's major stockholders will dispose of their common-stock holdings in Aluminium, Ltd., over a ten-year period, during which time voting power of such stock will be exercised by three Court-appointed trustees. All but one of the major stockholders of Alcoa elected to sell their holdings in Aluminium, Ltd., the exception being Edward K. Davis, retired President of Aluminium, Ltd., who will dispose of his Alcoa stock.

Addressing the attorneys for Alcoa at the close of the stock-disposal acceptance by the Court, Judge Knox said, "This is the end of a long period of litigation and I should think that you would sing the Doxology."

Thus, after thirteen years, during which Alcoa's corporate life was thoroughly probed, the anti-trust case reached what may well be termed a state of stabilization. The Government and Alcoa had sixty days from July 6, 1950, in which to appeal from the decision of Judge Knox. Neither side did so. The accusations and rebuttals hark back to the long trial before Judge Caffey and his exhaustive opinion exonerating Alcoa of all the charges by the Department of Justice. The Company came out of it as a law-abiding concern and as an asset to the life we know as the "American Way." Legal battles are expensive and time consuming, but Alcoa can point to this one as proof of its good citizenship, after being investigated perhaps more thoroughly than any other company in America.

CHAPTER EIGHTEEN

Magnesium

☆ ☆ ☆ ☆ ☆ ☆ ☆ ☆

N O STORY of Alcoa would be complete without telling of
the part the Company plays in the development of
magnesium as a useful light metal. Alcoa's active interest in magnesium began at the close of World War I when
great impetus was being given to the development of strong
alloys of aluminum. Magnesium is an important alloying ingredient in many of these alloys.

While Magnesium's principal use in the first World War was
for flares and explosives, it showed possibilities of becoming a
structural material. Magnesium prices were high. As a large consumer of the metal in aluminum alloys, Alcoa saw interesting
prospects for other uses in the very lightness of the material as
well as opportunities for reducing the cost of manufacture. American Magnesium Corporation owned what seemed to be a prom-
ising production process. However, the concern was hampered
by limited capital and was quite willing to sell a controlling in-

terest to Alcoa in 1919. Within the next five years, Alcoa had purchased virtually all of the stock in American Magnesium Corporation.

Alcoa became a producer of magnesium at Niagara Falls, New York, as well as a manufacturer of magnesium castings, extruded rods, tubing, wire and sheet. The fluoride or Seward process for producing magnesium was the method used. This is an electrolytic process in which magnesium oxide is added to a molten salt bath of mixed fluorides and subjected to an electric current. Intensive research was instituted for improved methods of production—metal of high purity, stronger alloys, better casting and fabricating techniques. Much information was accumulated on the characteristics of the metal. This pioneering by Alcoa helped industry to begin to use magnesium to a limited extent.[1]

While this was occurring, Dow Chemical Company of Midland, Michigan, began to produce magnesium from magnesium chloride, until then a useless by-product of other chemical processes. The magnesium chloride, which has been dehydrated, is electrolyzed in the molten state, producing magnesium and chlorine gas. The magnesium chloride is obtained from salt brines found in Michigan and also in sea water. Dow continued to use this process at Midland until 1946. Since then it has utilized magnesium chloride recovered from sea water at its Freeport, Texas, plant.

By 1927, although Alcoa had become the largest customer for magnesium (for use in alloying aluminum), it found it could buy

[1] "Production of Metallic Magnesium from Fused Salts," W. G. Harvey, *Transactions* of American Electrochemical Society, Vol. 47, p. 327, 1925; "High Purity Magnesium Produced by Sublimation," H. E. Bakken, *Chemical and Metallurgical Engineering*, Vol. 36, June, 1929.

the metal from Dow cheaper than it could produce it by its own process. Consequently, American Magnesium Corporation, Alcoa subsidiary, stopped manufacture of the metal and began purchasing its requirements from Dow. American Magnesium Corporation continued as an important manufacturer of magnesium mill products.

Briefly, this is the history of Alcoa's magnesium activities, but it is not all of the story. Development of magnesium in Europe, particularly in Germany, went on at a rapid pace in the era following World War I. The U. S. Bureau of Mines estimated that prior to 1933 German production was four times that in this country. The reasons for this are easy to understand. Germany had within her borders everything with which to produce magnesium. She had vast quantities of dolomite and other magnesium ores close at hand, but she had no copper and it was necessary to import bauxite for aluminum production. Germany was preparing for war and magnesium is used in considerable amount in aircraft and other appurtenances of war. Lack of raw materials also caused the Germans to use magnesium for many applications for which American engineers would select other metals because of their better performance and lower cost.

On this side of the Atlantic Ocean the availability of other materials made the acceptance of magnesium a slow process. In 1939 the Dow Chemical Company, then sole producer of magnesium metal in the United States, made only 6,700,000 pounds. American Magnesium Corporation, largest fabricator of the metal in this country in that year, sold only 3,411,374 pounds of mill products. Not only was American industry slow to realize the merits of magnesium, but the Government was also cautious.

It was not until 1938 that the Bureau of Aeronautics began to urge aircraft manufacturers to consider the use of magnesium in unstressed parts. American Magnesium Corporation was finding that the magnesium business was an unprofitable venture. From its inception until December 31, 1940, this Alcoa subsidiary showed a net loss of over a million dollars.

Meanwhile, better understanding of magnesium by the Germans was making itself felt in this country. United States patents on their processes had been obtained by the foreigners. Some of these patents, particularly on casting methods, protected improved practices which American Magnesium Corporation wished to employ. To overcome this handicap and to promote a greater use of magnesium in America, Alcoa entered into an agreement in 1931 with the I. G. Farbenindustrie, the noted German chemical corporation, to create a company called the Magnesium Development Corporation to be owned 50 per cent by each company. The Germans were friendly with America on that date, which was two years before Hitler appeared on the European scene.

I. G. Farbenindustrie was the owner of more magnesium processes and patents than anyone else in the world. From a standpoint of developing magnesium for both civilian use and for later essential war applications in this country, the Americans got all the best of this deal. The Germans contributed to the Magnesium Development Corporation all their American patents and an obligation to turn over all future patents they might be granted in the United States. They also agreed to turn over their techniques and superior know-how on magnesium production and fabrication. Neither Alcoa nor its subsidiary, American Mag-

240

nesium Corporation, was obligated to furnish any future patents or techniques to I. G. Farbenindustrie. About all the Germans received was a 50 per cent interest in a patent-holding company.

Upon its creation, Magnesium Development Corporation endeavored to license other concerns to use its patents. The Germans were quite willing to license others to use their fabricating patents, but they did insist upon a limitation of production by their patented reduction method. In the agreement with American Magnesium Corporation, they specified that production under this one patent would be limited to 4,000 tons per annum unless the German company consented to an increase over this amount. Since 4,000 tons was much more than had been produced in any one year by any company anywhere, and Dow already had a successful production process in this country, Alcoa readily accepted this condition as a quid pro quo for the great benefit it was receiving through securing the German processes on casting and other fabricating techniques.

Further to transmit this magnesium know-how to industry in this country, Alcoa in 1933 sold half of its stock in American Magnesium Corporation to I. G. Farbenindustrie, which later turned this interest over to the General Aniline & Film Corporation. Early in 1941, this half ownership was reacquired by Alcoa, and American Magnesium Corporation again became a wholly-owned Alcoa subsidiary.

The Dow Chemical Company came into this patent-licensing picture in 1934 when it joined with American Magnesium Corporation and Magnesium Development Corporation in an important agreement whereby fabricating patent licenses of the three companies were exchanged and agreement was made to grant free licenses to any manufacturer in the United States. Dow, as the metal producer in this country, did all the sub-licensing and issued royalty-free licenses to some thirty companies. This stimulated activity as well as competition in the magnesium-fabricating business. Prior to this, sales of magnesium mill products had been modest. Shortly after 1934 they jumped into a bracket where total tonnage was reported in amounts of several million pounds, although acceptance of magnesium did not create a large market until World War II.

These patent arrangements gave opportunity to the Department of Justice to engage in some of the activities through which it achieved newspaper headlines about the time World War II was getting well started. In line with its attack on the General Electric Company—because that company had dealt with the Krupp munitions firm in Germany to obtain a license to manufacture in this country a hard metal alloy known as carboloy— the Department of Justice secured a grand-jury indictment in 1941 against Alcoa, Dow and representatives in this country of the I. G. Farbenindustrie. The charges were that these companies had engaged in a conspiracy to vest monopoly production of magnesium in the United States in the Dow Chemical Company; that there was a pooling and a cross-licensing between all of the parties and an agreement between American Magnesium Corporation and I. G. Farbenindustrie to limit production in this country; that an obligation to pay royalties was imposed upon all licensees except Dow and American Magnesium Corporation unless the metal fabricated was purchased from said companies.

From the facts outlined earlier in this chapter, it is reasonable to assume that none of these charges could have been sustained in a lawsuit. However, Alcoa had just been through a time-consuming legal battle with the Department of Justice. Both Alcoa and Dow were faced with serious demands upon them as the war tempo increased. Furthermore, the inflamed feelings of wartime would have provided a fertile climate for injuring the companies before the bar of public opinion even with the successful refutation of conspiracy charges in a court trial.

Despite the publicity the Department of Justice had given to the unproved charges, the defendants felt they should accept a proposal from the governmental agency. This proposal was that the case should be settled by the signing of a decree of nolo contendere without any admission of guilt, payment of fines and the taking of a consent decree which imposed no penalties on the companies. From Attorney General Thurman Arnold the defendants gained the impression that this would also be the end of what Alcoa and Dow felt had been a smear campaign in the press through releases and statements from Department of Justice sources.

Even though the statements to the press did not entirely cease, the decree itself made it clear that there was no admission or indication of wrongdoing on the part of the companies. This decree in its preface read:

> . . . and each of said defendants consents to the entry of this decree, without any findings in fact, upon conditions that neither said consent nor this decree shall be evidence, admission or adjudication that they have violated any statute of the United States, and that this decree shall relate solely to future conduct; and the United States of America,

by its counsel, having consented to the entry of this decree and to each and every provision thereof . . .[2]

World War II saw an amazing increase in demands for magnesium. Manufacturers of mill products produced three to four times their previous annual output. In 1943 American Magnesium Corporation sold 18,623,245 pounds of fabricated products compared to slightly less than 3,500,000 pounds in 1939. Dow, sole producer of magnesium metal from 1927 to 1941, had raised its capacity to 18,000,000 pounds by April of 1941. In that same year came the first commercial production of magnesium from sea water in a plant built by Dow at Freeport, Texas. This brought the 1941 production capacity of the Dow Chemical Company to 36,000,000 pounds.

During the war period Permanente Metals Corporation, organized by Henry Kaiser, constructed a plant at Permanente, California, using the Hansgirg process. The Government stepped into the situation to help meet the ever-increasing military demands for magnesium and developed a capacity for 222,000,000 pounds per annum in five plants. Magnesium producing facilities, which had been slightly less than 7,000,000 pounds in 1939, reached a total annual capacity of nearly 600,000,000 pounds in 1943. All of this capacity was not needed and the largest annual production was 370,000,000 pounds in the peak year of the war.[3]

Peacetime production of magnesium ingot reached 23,000,000

[2] United States of America vs. Aluminum Company of America, Dow Chemical Company, American Magnesium Corporation and Magnesium Development Corporation in the District Court of the United States for the Southern District of New York Civil Action No. 18-13.
[3] "Wartime Aluminum and Magnesium Production," Hans A. Klagsbrunn, *Industrial and Engineering Chemistry*, July, 1945.

pounds in 1949 as compared with 6,700,000 pounds ten years earlier. With increased production, the price of the metal has shown a downward trend since prewar days. In July, 1950, magnesium metal was selling at $.225 per pound as compared with $.27 per pound in midyear of 1939. A large factor in the increase in postwar demand for magnesium mill products was the greater amount going into aircraft. Over 10,000 pounds of magnesium sheet are used in a B-26 while 2,000 pounds of magnesium extrusions are used in the Douglas C-124 Globemaster. Principal fields of use for magnesium in 1948 were in aircraft, portable and pneumatic tools, household appliances, yard tools and textile machinery. Substantial amounts of magnesium sheet are used by the printing industry for photoengraving.[4]

Postwar uses of magnesium continue to show an increase over prewar although they do not approach the astronomical amounts used in 1943 for war purposes.[5] American Magnesium Corporation no longer exists as a corporate entity. That subsidiary has been dissolved but manufacture of magnesium mill products by Alcoa still continues with Alcoa's sales force selling these light metal products wherever magnesium seems to be the material to use. Alcoa salesmen consider themselves to be in the light-metals business, whether the product be aluminum or magnesium.

[4] "The Economic Status of Magnesium," J. D. Hanawalt, Dow Chemical Company, *Modern Metals*, January, 1948.
[5] "The Magnesium Casting Industry—Its Problems and Outlook," R. T. Wood, *Modern Metals*, Vol. 5, May, 1949.

CHAPTER NINETEEN

World War II

☆ ☆ ☆ ☆ ☆ ☆ ☆ ☆ ☆

U NLIKE many companies, Alcoa did not publish a book on its war record at the close of the great struggle in 1945, although such a volume might well have been produced with justifiable pride. This chapter will cover a few of the highlights in that story. The only published record of wartime performance over the Alcoa signature was a "Timetable of Aluminum for Victory" issued in the spring of 1943. It appears as an illustration of this text.[1]

The figure of $250,000,000 mentioned in the "Timetable" as the amount of Alcoa's own money or credit invested in expansions became $300,000,000 by V-J Day. In addition to this, the Company built for the Government, without fee or profit, aluminum plants representing an investment in excess of $450,000,000.

Then the Company stretched its capacity for management to a point where it operated twenty-two plants for the Government. Eight of them were aluminum-producing works and ten were

[1] *Time,* April 12, 1943, *Newsweek,* April 19, 1943.

plants making aluminum mill products essential for wartime use. Two were large alumina works and two more were plants for processing low-grade bauxite. Technical, engineering and management personnel were gathered from the entire Alcoa organization to accomplish this task. Since Alcoa's salesmen are frequently trained in technical schools, sales executives became plant managers and salesmen became personnel directors at plant locations. Still other salesmen came from various offices to Pittsburgh to form what was known as the "co-ordinating group." These men, nicknamed the "exiles" since they were away from their homes and families for months at a time, performed an amazing job of getting scarce materials routed to the new aluminum plants under construction.

Since it became Alcoa's responsibility to carry out the major portion of the vast wartime aluminum program, I. W. Wilson, then Senior Vice President of the Company, virtually commuted between Pittsburgh and Washington during the war years. There was need for co-operation and co-ordination with the War Production Board and other departments of the Government as well as with all branches of the armed services. At his side to counsel and advise, as well as to participate actively in decisions, was the veteran Chairman of the Board, Arthur V. Davis, who was again going all out to win the war, just as he had done in World War I. Mr. Davis spent as much time in Washington as he did at his New York office during the war period. Trained Alcoa men were moved to Washington to assist Government agencies in the aluminum phase of the war struggle.

With its new aluminum reduction plant in operation at Vancouver, Washington, in September, 1940, Alcoa was on its way

248

in its own expansion program when World War II began. Following this came expansions in metal-producing facilities at Alcoa, Tennessee, further expansion of alumina facilities at Mobile, Alabama, and additions to existing Company plants engaged in manufacturing mill products. All this proved helpful when the war emergency came, but the expansions started prior to the war were based on long-range future prospects rather than immediate markets. The Company had an inventory of more than a year's supply of metal at the beginning of 1939 and it started 1940 with 215,000,000 pounds. The total production in 1939 had been 327,000,000 pounds.

Aluminum reduction works built by Alcoa for the Government and operated by the Company during the war were located at Burlington, near Philadelphia; Jones Mills in Arkansas near Hot Springs; Los Angeles, California; Meade, near Spokane, Washington; Queens on Long Island; Riverbank, near Sacramento, California; Troutdale, near Portland, Oregon, and the St. Lawrence plant adjacent to Alcoa's works at Massena, New York.

The Government-owned Alcoa-operated plants to manufacture aluminum mill products were located at Chicago (McCook sheet mill); Spokane, Washington (Trentwood sheet mill); Newark, Ohio (rod and bar mill); Kansas City, Missouri (cast cylinder head plant); Cressona, Pennsylvania (extrusion plant); Phoenix, Arizona (extrusion and tubing plant); Monroe, Michigan (forging plant); Newcastle, Pennsylvania (forging plant); Canonsburg, Pennsylvania (forging plant); Glassmere, Pennsylvania (aluminum powder plant).[2]

2 "Aluminum Plants and Facilities"—First Supplementary Report of the War Assets Administration to the Congress, February 12, 1947.

The alumina works were at Hurricane Creek, Arkansas, and at Baton Rouge, Louisiana. The Alcoa Combination Process plants to process low-grade bauxite were located at Hurricane Creek, Arkansas, and at East St. Louis, Illinois. Alcoa also built for the Government two more of these plants, located at Mobile, Alabama, and at Baton Rouge, Louisiana, respectively, but they did not get into actual operation.

The slowness of the entire country to recognize the great demand World War II would make on the American economy was evidenced by Congressional action which did not get around to the matter of possible Government aluminum plants until mid-year of 1941. In January of that year the National Defense Advisory Committee had estimated aluminum supply adequate to meet the requirements up to October. In February, 1941, aluminum was placed on priorities with virtually all capacity going to defense. By July, 1941, the authorities in Washington recognized the probable scope of the air war and approved the first Government aluminum program.

Expansion of aluminum production for war was provided in three steps: (a) Private industry expanded as rapidly as possible. Alcoa was already well under way with its $300,000,000 expansion program. Reynolds Metals Company, a long-time manufacturer of aluminum foil, went into the business of producing alumina and aluminum at Listerhill, Alabama. A loan from the Reconstruction Finance Corporation assisted the Reynolds Company in its desire to enter the aluminum business from mine to metal. (b) The Defense Plant Corporation let contracts for the construction of aluminum plants, placed as advantageously as possible so as to be of value as producers after the war. (c) The

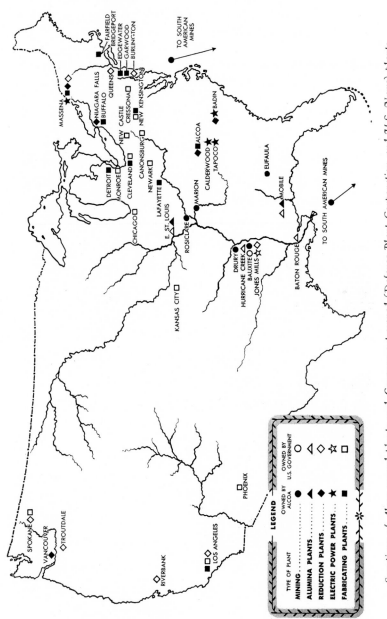

Locations of Alcoa-owned plants and Government-owned (Defense Plant Corporation and U.S. Navy) plants operated by Alcoa in World War II.

Defense Plant Corporation provided for the building of emergency smelter plants to produce aluminum, using power available in large industrial centers even though this high-cost electric energy would make these plants uneconomical to operate after the war.

The first phase of the Government program started in October, 1941. The second phase came in February, 1942. The first phase added 512,000,000 pounds annually to the nation's productive capacity and the emergency program of early 1942 added 640,000,000 pounds more per annum. These private and Government increases in aluminum-producing capacity, plus metal from Canada which the Metals Reserve Corporation had purchased, brought the total aluminum ingot available to America to more than 2,500,000,000 pounds of metal annually at the peak of the war.[3]

This amount, far greater than the Nazis could produce, can be easily dramatized. It would replace every passenger car on America's railroads threefold. It would put a 30-piece high-quality-aluminum cooking-utensil set in every one of America's 34,000,000 homes with enough metal left over to build 5,000,000 miles of aluminum high-tension electrical transmission lines. To make the vast amount which could be produced in aluminum plants in the United States would require more electrical power than was consumed in 1940 in twenty-seven of the forty-eight States. Actually, at peak production in 1943, the number of kilowatt hours consumed in producing aluminum pig at Alcoa-operated plants reached the staggering total of 6,500,000,000.

[3] "Wartime Aluminum and Magnesium Production," Hans A. Klagsbrunn, Defense Plant Corporation, *Industrial and Engineering Chemistry*, July, 1945.

Some idea of Alcoa's production, not only of aluminum but aluminum mill products during the war, may be gathered from an article which appeared in *Fortune* in 1946 entitled "Aluminum Reborn." [4] The article discussed war and postwar conditions in the industry. On this point it said:

> Altogether, between the start of the defense program in May, 1940 and V-J Day, Alcoa produced 11.4 billion pounds of alumina, smelted 5.5 billion pounds of aluminum, and fabricated 2.7 billion pounds of sheet, 450 million pounds of extruded shapes, 500 million pounds of forgings, and 400 million pounds of castings.

In the same paragraph of the article was this significant sentence:

> Aluminum and Alcoa may not be quite so synonymous as they once were, but if U. S. air power won the war, they, too, may be said to have won it.

Building of Government plants gave Alcoa's engineering staff a great responsibility. Operating closely with Governmental agencies, yet maintaining an objective viewpoint to get the job done speedily and efficiently, taxed this important Alcoa department to the utmost. Thomas D. Jolly, Vice President and Chief Engineer for Alcoa, who had never traveled more than a short distance by air in peacetime, flew over 100,000 miles in the years 1942 and 1943. The Government plants are a monument to the efficiency of Mr. Jolly and his staff. In the article already mentioned, *Fortune* said:

4 "Aluminum Reborn," *Fortune*, May, 1946.

Alcoa has been criticized—with not much justice—for its part in determining the location and size of the government plants. It is argued that, suspiciously, some of the plants are located where extra power, transportation, and other costs would make them uneconomical for competitive peacetime operation; also that they are too large to invite Alcoa competitors. The fact is that, while Alcoa engineers helped select the sites, Army engineers had the final word—which was based on military security, available labor and power regardless of cost, proximity to aircraft plants, and other strictly wartime considerations. As for the size of the plants, it was necessary to economize on limited technical and supervisory personnel and on critical construction and operating materials—which could be done only by concentrating production under the fewest possible roofs. And it is generally conceded that Alcoa did an amazing construction job. The Truman Committee—which had once accused the company of underestimating aluminum requirements in order to avoid any competitive challenge to its monopoly—found that the Alcoa-built government plants were "equally or more efficient than those owned by Alcoa itself."

Not only in the building of plants for the Government, but in their operation, Alcoa can claim credit for an achievement typical of the job American industry did to win the war. The actual cost of the Government construction program entrusted to Alcoa amounted to $462,000,000 against an estimate of $473,000,000. Savings were made by Alcoa's Purchasing Department through mass buying and wise engineering practices. For instance, each of the pot rooms in the Government-owned aluminum plants was equipped with two 6-ton electric traveling cranes. By synchronizing the requirements of these cranes, it was possible to order 175 identical jobs from the builder without the necessity of separate drawings for each.

The operation by Alcoa of Government aluminum-producing and fabricating works was likewise an accomplishment in business efficiency and economy. Alcoa operated all but one of the Government aluminum smelting plants under a contract which gave the Government 85 per cent of the profits. From this the Government received nearly $30,000,000 during the Alcoa lease period. Government fabricating plants built by Alcoa were operated by the Company during the war under lease agreements which yielded a profit of more than $20,000,000 to the Government. Alcoa had to do considerable financing on its own account to operate under these leases. It had to provide $225,000,000 of working capital to operate the Government-owned facilities and at the same time carry on its own plant operations on a greatly expanded basis. Anticipating the fact that it would likely be called upon to build aluminum-producing facilities for the Government, the Company, early in 1941, contracted for more than $16,-000,000 worth of construction materials even before it had an order from the Government to proceed.

At no time during the war was there ever an actual shortage of aluminum for military purposes. There were great needs for more war material in which aluminum was an essential part, but the metal was available as rapidly as manufacturers could use it. Such temporary bottlenecks in the aircraft program as did occur were not due to any shortage of the metal but to sudden changes in design which necessitated new shapes and forms of aluminum. Alcoa's own expenditures for privately financed expansion were greater by 50 per cent than the total worth of all the aircraft plants in the country at the start of the war. The aircraft manufacturers expanded their facilities by leaps and bounds once the real emergency was recognized, but aluminum was on hand when they needed it.

One of the most effective methods of keeping aircraft manufacturers supplied promptly with the right sizes of aluminum sheet was an Alcoa-devised plan in co-operation with Wright Field to standardize strong alloy sheet needed for aircraft and to keep it boxed and ready for shipment from the Company's Alcoa, Tennessee, Works. This stockpile of aircraft sheet grew from 5,000,000 pounds in 1941 to 25,000,000 pounds in 1943.

There were criticisms and charges of shortages during the war, with two investigations of the aluminum situation by the Truman Committee, ending in praise of Alcoa's role after the final hearing. There were charges by Harold Ickes, Secretary of the Interior, which were unsupported by the facts, and there were some comments by columnists and news writers. However, the actual record of aluminum production for all-out war is one of which Alcoa can be proud. The Truman Committee in its Third Annual Report said:

> The committee believes that Alcoa should be commended for the prompt and effective manner in which it expanded at its own expense its annual production from 350,000,000 pounds to more than 830,000,000 pounds per annum as well as the expedition with which it constructed the Government-owned aluminum and alumina facilities.

On another occasion in a letter to Arthur V. Davis on January 14, 1946, W. Stuart Symington, then head of the National Resources Board, said: "The Aluminum Company of America made an outstanding contribution to the winning of the war, for which this Nation should be forever grateful."

No one realized what was happening on the American aluminum front any better than Adolf Hitler. In 1942, eight trained Nazi saboteurs were landed from U-boats on bleak stretches of the American coast. Four of them came ashore on Long Island and four were quietly beached at a point below Jacksonville, Florida. Fortunately they were all captured by our F.B.I. Papers found on their persons and subsequent testimony by one of them showed their specific mission to be the destruction of Alcoa plants at Alcoa, Tennessee, Massena, New York, and East St. Louis, Illinois.

A perusal of the testimony of Ernest Peter Burger before Judge William J. Campbell in the United States District Court for Northern Illinois in Chicago in October, 1942, makes interesting reading. Burger, one of the saboteurs, was testifying in an action by the Government accusing certain relatives and friends of the group of giving aid to the enemy by harboring funds and otherwise abetting their nefarious purpose. None of the evidence in the military proceedings in which the actual saboteurs were tried was ever made public, but Burger's statements in the Chicago court action reveal their determination to injure America's aluminum production.

Under Lieut. Walter Knappe, two groups were trained in sabotage on an old estate near Brandenburg, Germany, in April, 1942. The training included a visit to a near-by aluminum plant to familiarize the saboteurs with the layout in Alcoa plants in this country. Burger said their specific assignment was "to harm as much as possible aluminum production of the United States." Training was given the men in the use of explosives which they could carry about inconspicuously and in the best method of damaging railroad lines "connecting the aluminum plants with the manufacturing plants that were manufacturing products for airplanes."

Hitler's great worry about the amazing production of aluminum in America was because of its essential role in the Allied aircraft program which was spelling defeat for the Nazis. Production of military aircraft had increased from 6,000 planes in 1929 to 86,000 in 1943. A grand total of 304,000 military airplanes were turned out in the United States in the five and one-half years of defense preparation and of the war itself. It required 3,500,-000,000 pounds of aluminum to produce them. The average aircraft of 1943, exclusive of engine, propeller and landing gear, weighed approximately three times as much as the 1939 airplane. Three fourths of this weight was aluminum. At the war peak, it was estimated that more than 85 per cent of Alcoa's output was going into the aircraft program.

Aircraft designers did not have to start from scratch when World War II came. They had been making real progress since World War I. Alcoa research and engineering had co-operated. In 1930 Alcoa offered a new duralumin type alloy to the aircraft industry. It was called 24S-T and it was to replace, to a large extent, the alloy 17S-T. Getting the new alloy, with its tensile strength of 68,000 pounds per square inch, ready for commercial use, entailed manufacturing problems, but it was in the hands of the aircraft manufacturers and ready for practical application eight years before Hitler began his effort to conquer Europe. Other new alloys came along—14S for airplane structural fittings and 76S for use in propeller blades. The very high-strength alloy, 75S, had been through the experimental stage when war began and was being produced for use in combat planes before the struggle was over. A product of Alcoa research, this alloy has a tensile strength in excess of 82,000 pounds per square inch, enabling it to resist terrific stresses.

The value of 75S in that great air weapon, the Boeing B-29, was well illustrated in its use in the upper wing skin. Both the sheet covering and the extruded hat-shaped sections which stiffen it were made of the new alloy, thus reducing material thickness enough to save 400 pounds per airplane. This gave rise to the story of the "phantom B-17." It was pointed out that translating this weight saving into bomb-load would enable each group of ten Super Fortresses to carry an additional bomb-load equal to that carried by a B-17.

Aircraft performs other tasks in war besides the work done by bombers and fighter planes. Transport aircraft, besides moving material and men to combat areas, also evacuates wounded from battlefields. During the height of the battles in Europe casualties were being removed to the rear at the rate of 2,000 per day. Aluminum alloys were an essential in the Douglas C-54's which did most of this evacuating, including oversea transport of wounded to hospitals in the United States.

Despite the need for all-out aluminum production to win the war, Alcoa personnel in large numbers found their way into the armed services. Alcoa men from mills and offices left their jobs to join the Army, the Navy, the Air Corps, the Marine Corps,

Coast Guard and the Seabees. Alcoa women from Company offices became Wacs and Waves. Qualified Alcoa men in the executive group rendered special services.

An outstanding example was James P. Growdon, Chief Hydraulic Engineer, whose services were requested by the Government to design some method for safely storing fuel oil at Honolulu. Growdon, who served as a Lieutenant Colonel of Engineers in World War I and was to be called back to duty as a full Colonel in World War II, was asked as a civilian to work out the oil-storage problem at Honolulu prior to the war in the Pacific theater. The Government asked Alcoa for his services and the request was promptly granted. He solved the problem by planning the construction of 20 vertical vaults, 100 feet in diameter and 250 feet high, hewn out of solid rock in the interior of a mountain overlooking the city and harbor. When the Japanese sneak attack on Pearl Harbor came, our planes and ships were damaged or destroyed but our vital oil supply was saved.

Alcoa charged the sum of one dollar for Engineer Growdon's services. In 1946 Admiral Ben Moreell, noting that payment had been overlooked, wrote a letter of commendation to Board Chairman Arthur V. Davis in which he referred to a conversation between James P. Forrestal, then Undersecretary of the Navy, and the Admiral, on the occasion of their tour to the Pacific area in 1944. Admiral Moreell said:

During the inspection, Mr. Forrestal expressed great astonishment at the enormity and complexity of the project and complimented me on its accomplishment. I told the Secretary that the project had only one objectionable feature.

We were forced to call upon the "economic royalists" for assistance and they made us pay "through the nose." The Secretary pricked up his ears and said, "Who were they and how much did they charge you," and I replied, "That great octopus, the Aluminum Company of America, and they held me up for one dollar."

Admiral Moreell enclosed a dollar bill with his letter. The bill is now framed under glass as part of the Alcoa historical exhibit in its New York office.

Civilian manufacture of aluminum products was either drastically curtailed or was nonexistent during the war. Many manufacturers of end-use products converted their plants into factories making war items. A large number of them, including automobile makers, ran their plants day and night making tanks, army trucks and airplane parts. They continued to demand aluminum but it was for war rather than peacetime use. Alcoa's one job was to do its part in winning the war. On one occasion Mr. Davis said, "The Company's faith in the ultimate triumph of the Allied cause never wavered and at no time did it slacken its efforts in anticipation of defeat."

Alcoa's efforts were in due course recognized by many Governmental authorities. Providing ample aluminum for war demands was a challenge to Alcoa and likewise a responsibility. Since the Company was producing in its own or Government-owned plants about 90 per cent of the aluminum requirement, it was gratified by the statement made by J. A. Krug, Chairman of the War Production Board, in his report of October 9, 1945, when he said:

THE TIMETABLE OF ALUMINUM FOR VICTORY

1938 Sept. *Munich.*
Oct. *Czechoslovakia invaded.*
Nov. Alcoa inaugurated an expansion program which by 1943 cost $250,000,000.
Dec. Alcoa 1938 production, 287 million pounds; started 1939 with more than a year's supply on hand.

1939 Jan. Alcoa begins operation of new extrusion and tube mill.
Feb. Alcoa starts building excess stock pile of airplane sheet.
Apr. *Congress authorizes Army to acquire 6,000 planes in 2 years; and Navy 3,000 in 5 years: Approximately one month's 1943 goals.*
Sept. *Poland invaded.*
Alcoa authorizes new metal-producing capacity.
Nov. *Finland invaded; Cash-and-Carry Act signed.*
Dec. Alcoa authorizes another huge metal-producing plant, although it begins new year with 215 million pounds on hand.

1940 Jan. *First Request for defense appropriation in Budget Message.*
Mar. Alcoa reduces price of ingot from 20c to 19c.
Apr. *Denmark, Norway invaded.*
May *Low countries invaded.*
First of new Alcoa metal-producing plants starts production.
June *Dunkerque; France capitulates.*
Alcoa authorizes still another metal-producing unit.
July *Congress gives first go-ahead on faster plane production.*
Aug. Alcoa reduces ingot price from 19c to 18c; adds large alumina capacity.
Sept. *Egypt invaded; Selective Service Bill passed.*
Another new plant starts operating; still more units authorized.
Oct. *Rumania invaded.*
Nov. Alcoa reduces ingot from 18c to 17c; authorizes still more metal-producing capacity.
Dec. Alcoa faces new year with 154 million pounds on hand.

1941 Jan. *NDAC says aluminum supply adequate to meet October, 1940, estimates of requirements.*
Feb. *Aluminum put on priorities to give all capacity to defense.*
Mar. *Lend-lease.*
Apr. *Yugoslavia invaded; U. S. occupies Greenland.*
May Very large new Alcoa metal-producing units start operation.
June *Crete lost; Russia invaded.*
Alcoa authorizes further expansion at own expense.
July *Government authorizes first of its own plants to supplement the enormous expansion of Alcoa.*
Aug. *Government announces Alcoa will build and operate 3 of these plants. (All Alcoa designing and building of Government plants done without profit.)*
Sept. *Government decides on more plants; instructs Alcoa to build them.*
Oct. *Government decides to build more plants; instructs Alcoa to build them.*
Alcoa reduces ingot from 17c to 15c.
Nov. *Government reviews detailed plans for own large sheet mills.*
Dec. *Pearl Harbor; Churchill-Roosevelt strategy conference.*
First metal rolled on Alcoa's own 50-times-faster sheet mill, largest in the world. Alcoa receives further new plant instructions from Government.

1942 Jan. *Pan-American Conference.*
Another Alcoa metal-producing plant in operation; additional instructions from Government to build new plants.
Feb. *Government authorizes large alumina plant, several aluminum plants and large sheet mills. Alcoa to design and build.*
Mar. *Government authorizes Alcoa to build more casting capacity, extrusion capacity, and forging capacity.*
Apr. *Government authorizes blooming mill, and enlarged tubing capacity.*
May *Government-owned plants, built and operated by Alcoa, start operation.*
June *Special authorization for airplane cylinder-head capacity.*
July *As instructed by Government, Alcoa starts additional plants for*
to   *various types of fabrication, as special needs of war produc-*
Dec. *tion are made apparent by changing emphasis on war equipment.*

1943 The aluminum industry will have a metal capacity of over two billion pounds, seven times prewar. Alcoa has more than doubled its metal producing and fabricating capacity through a self-financed expansion program. The expansion by private industry has been augmented by a vast Government program where the kind, amount and time of expansion has been at the direction of the Government. In addition to operating its own twenty plants, Alcoa has been honored with the responsibility for constructing and operating 40 Government projects in 25 different locations.

ALCOA ALUMINUM

This "Timetable of Aluminum for Victory" was published by Alcoa in April, 1943. Note that Alcoa's expansion program started in 1938, almost a year prior to the Nazi invasion of Poland and start of World War II.

The war history of aluminum is the record of a successful race to expand facilities fast enough to meet the multiple increases in military requirements, principally for aircraft. From the beginning of the defense program in 1940 through 1942, requirements estimates were repeatedly lifted to new high levels, and plans for increasing capacity had to be constantly revised. In 1943, basic metal supply caught up with and exceeded requirements, and by 1944, the surplus of primary production was large enough to force cutbacks in output and plant closings.

CHAPTER TWENTY

Postwar Competition

☆ ☆ ☆ ☆ ☆ ☆ ☆ ☆ ☆

At the end of World War II ownership of aluminum-producing facilities in the United States presented a vastly different picture from that which existed before the war. The Government emerged in the immediate postwar period as the largest owner of such facilities. It had $672,000,000 invested in 50 wholly-owned aluminum plants for either aluminum production or aluminum fabrication as compared to Alcoa's net investment of $474,000,000, a portion of which was borrowed money. Not all of the Government investment was useful for peacetime production, but a substantial part of it was. The capacity of Government-owned aluminum-producing plants capable of competitive operation was 552,000,000 pounds as compared to 650,000,000 pounds for Alcoa and 162,000,000 pounds for Reynolds Metals Company.

It will be recalled that the Government program for building aluminum-producing plants was divided into two phases. The first phase included the building of plants which were located with an eye to their possible peacetime use. The second phase provided for the construction of aluminum producers in large industrial centers where the use of high-cost electrical energy made these particular plants definitely war-emergency projects.

It was the disposition of Government-owned facilities erected under the first part of the Government program which brought about much controversy and the activities of a number of nationally known persons. Alcoa was involved in these discussions. Although the Company had no opportunity to purchase any of the important Government-owned plants it had built and operated during the war, the Company's fight against subsidies and other socialistic suggestions, plus its liberal attitude toward competitors who acquired the plants, did much to bring about the present competitive conditions in the industry.

The Surplus Property Act, which provided the machinery for a disposal program, was a compromise of two sharply divergent views in Congress. The House favored a bill which would result in speedy disposal of surplus property with the highest possible cash return to the Government. The Senate favored a bill which would emphasize the fostering of competition. The compromise included both sets of objectives, with emphasis, however, on the Senate provisions. Objectives included in the Act were: encourage free enterprise; facilitate transition from wartime to peacetime production; discourage monopolistic practices; provide for no sale of a plant costing more than five million dollars until thirty days after the Surplus Property Board had filed with Congress a report describing the industry; require the advice of the Attorney General with respect to any possible violation of the anti-trust laws prior to the disposal of any plant costing more than a million dollars. The policy-making end of the Act was entrusted to a three-man board which was organized and ready for business in January, 1945.

President Roosevelt appointed former Senator Guy M. Gillette from Iowa as Chairman of the Board. When the ex-Senator announced that he wished to retire from the position in May, 1945, President Truman sent the name of W. Stuart Symington of St. Louis to the Senate as Gillette's successor. Symington was President of the Emerson Electric Company and a friend and supporter of President Truman in Missouri. When the new appointee took office on July 16th, President Truman recommended that the three-man board be abolished and that surplus property matters be placed under the direction of a single administrator. Mr. Symington then began to function as the policy maker for the board although the Surplus Property Act was not amended and the Board abolished until September. Mr. Symington was sworn in as Administrator on October 2nd.

The aluminum-disposal program became a matter of major concern to the Surplus Property Board early in its administration.[1] The total cost value of all domestic surplus eventually reached the staggering total of forty billion dollars, while all Government-owned aluminum plants exceeded a little over a half billion of this total, and the key aluminum plants presently useful for peacetime production of metal represented an investment of only $140,000,000. However, the aluminum problem was one of the most spectacular with which the Board had to deal. Two special

[1] "The Disposal of the Aluminum Plants"—Committee on Public Administration Cases, Library of Congress, Washington, D. C., 1948.

advisers on aluminum had been secured by the Board before Symington took charge of surplus property disposal. One of these was Samuel Moment, an economist, formerly with the Department of Agriculture and the TNEC and more recently with the Bonneville Power Administration. The other was Gordon W. Reed, a businessman who had been an official of the Aluminum Division of the War Production Board during the war.

A conflict in ideology quickly developed between Moment and Reed. The former proposed a program to establish competition with Alcoa even to the point of substantial Government aid to newcomers. Reed took a different approach by recognizing Alcoa's leases of the Government-owned plants until 1947 and 1948 and by recommending a program of disposal in which Alcoa would participate. Judge Hand, in his decision in the Alcoa antitrust case, had said that control of aluminum ingot output of 90 per cent by any one company was contrary to the intent of the Sherman Act. Reed felt that Alcoa might easily comply with Judge Hand's "rule" if the Company had up to 60 per cent of the United States capacity, a figure mentioned by the Court as being probably below monopoly proportions.

Meanwhile, various offers for Government-owned facilities were being made to the Surplus Property Board. On July 24, 1945, Alcoa offered to buy the Jones Mills, Arkansas, aluminum plant and the near-by Hurricane Creek alumina plant or to buy Jones Mills and to lease Hurricane Creek, selling alumina to others at a price to be set by the Government. Henry J. Kaiser was indicating an interest in acquiring some of the plants. Columbia Metals, which had operated an experimental alumina-from-clay plant in the Northwest, also began to negotiate. On August

1st Reynolds Metals Company made a preliminary offer for some of the properties.

In the opinion of the Surplus Property Board, two matters stood in the way of any conclusive disposition of the key plants if they were to be sold or leased without consultation or negotiation with Alcoa. One was the fact that Alcoa had continuing leases on alumina and aluminum reduction plants expiring two and three years hence. The other was Alcoa's strong patent position and its knowledge of the techniques of manufacture. Various Government officials, in conjunction with Department of Justice representatives, cut the Gordian knot of the first dilemma, if it was one, by summarily canceling Alcoa's leases on Government-owned alumina and aluminum smelting plants in a letter to the Company dated August 30, 1945.

Alcoa was told by the Reconstruction Finance Corporation, title holder of the Government plants, that effective October 31, 1945, it must vacate the properties and remove its own effects from the premises. Cancellation was based on a clause in the leases making it possible for either side to terminate them if production fell below 40 per cent of capacity. The Government claimed that production was below this percentage on the date of cancellation. In arriving at this figure, the Government attorneys conveniently overlooked the fact that they were including the unused capacity of the aluminum plants at Queens, New York, Burlington, New Jersey, Riverbank, California, and Los Angeles— plants which had long since been closed by order of the War Production Board.

Alcoa made no formal protest to this order, although it considered the procedure unfair. It closed the plants in accordance with the order. It also agreed to a request from R.F.C. to sell to the Government at cost the store supplies and spare parts as well as raw and in-process materials at these plants. To an offer from the Governmental agency, made a few days after the closing order, to permit Alcoa to continue as the operator of these plants on a sixty-day basis, the Company said "No." The reason was the obvious one that it could not ship raw materials and schedule production on such a program. It was difficult enough to close the plants under a sixty-day notice, let alone operate them on any such temporary schedule.

Shortly thereafter it became apparent that none of the key plants would be sold to Alcoa. The Surplus Property Board was then faced with the necessity of making them sufficiently attractive to other potential customers. This led to what was termed the "Government subsidy" program embraced in three separate reports quite similar in their import. One was an interim report of the War Property Committee of the Senate Small Business Committee. Another was a report of the Attorney General on the aluminum situation. The third report was that of the Surplus Property Board filed September 21, 1945. All three embraced the general idea of every possible aid to potential competitors of Alcoa, but the report of the Surplus Property Board spelled it out. This report embodied all the features of Samuel Moment's original suggestions plus outright Government subsidy.

Joint hearings on the various reports were held before the Senate Small Business Committee in October. At the hearings it became evident that some of the Senators were opposed to the "subsidy" implications. Alcoa appeared at these hearings through presentation of a document dated October 15, 1945, answering

Typical modern pot line designed, built and operated by Alcoa for the U.S. Government in World War II. These lines were installed in eight Defense Plant Corporation plants (see World War II map, facing page 250) and, during 1942 to 1945, inclusive, produced 1,873,865,014 pounds of aluminum for victory.

the subsidy phases of the report made by the Surplus Property Board. By this time the Board no longer existed and its authority was invested in the Surplus Property Administrator. In its presentation, Alcoa protested more as a citizen and taxpayer than as a pleader for the Company's just rights in any disposal program. In its protest to the Surplus Property Administrator, Alcoa said:

> The report proposes the following six-point subsidy program which applies to every phase of aluminum manufacture and sale—a cradle to the grave program which, once started, can never be terminated:
>
> Subsidy No. 1: Government guarantee against losses.
>
> Subsidy No. 2: Purchase options based on earnings' record under the subsidized leases.
>
> Subsidy No. 3: Government procurement of bauxite.
>
> Subsidy No. 4: The subsidized manufacture of alumina for sale at prices equal to or lower than Alcoa's cost of manufacture.
>
> Subsidy No. 5: Reduced power rates on government-owned power to operators of government plants.
>
> Subsidy No. 6: Government stock-piling of aluminum ingot purchased from operators of the government plants.

After the hearing, the subsidy proposal was apparently abandoned. It did not appear that Congress would favor it. Indeed, on the last day of the hearings, President Truman, at a press conference, said he thought the aluminum plants could and would be disposed of without subsidy. However, with business steadily improving in the postwar period, there seemed to be other ways in which the disposal of surplus aluminum facilities might be accomplished. Active negotiations for plant sales continued, particularly with the Reynolds Metals Company. A lease proposal for the Hurricane Creek alumina plant was worked out with Reynolds, but this did not suit Congressional leaders in the Northwest who feared the aluminum plants in that area might remain closed. They introduced a bill in Congress to open the Northwest plants and stockpile aluminum in an amount of one and one-half billion pounds in excess of normal civilian demand. This would have meant actual Government operation of the plants. The bill did not meet with favor in Congress and was not reported out of committee.

The apparent stumbling block in the plans of the Surplus Property Administrator to dispose of the big Hurricane Creek alumina plant was the matter of patents. While there were no patent obstacles facing any prospective competitor of Alcoa in the manufacture of alumina under the well-established Bayer process, there was a difficulty at Hurricane Creek because of the patented process designed to utilize low-grade bauxite found in substantial quantity in Arkansas. The method, known as the Alcoa Combination Process, has been described elsewhere in this book. There were two or three other Alcoa patents in use at Hurricane Creek which were important in the production of alumina.

When Reynolds Metals Company asked the Government to indemnify it against any infringement of these patents in case it acquired Hurricane Creek or other Government-owned facilities, the Surplus Property Administrator seemed to be facing a dilemma. Alcoa solved the matter for the Government and all concerned by giving royalty-free licenses on its valuable patents in use at Hurricane Creek. It gave these royalty-free grants to the Government to pass on to any competitor who might acquire the plant. Surplus Property Administrator Symington was highly pleased and said so at a special press conference which he called. At his request, both Attorney General Clark and Senator O'Mahoney, who had been active in the disposal program, sent expressions of commendation. In making the offer, Mr. Davis said:

> Except for the public considerations which you have presented to us so effectively, we could not consider a royalty-free license under such a valuable asset. However, we are glad to accede to these considerations and, if by so doing we have contributed in any substantial way to the solution of the complex problems of surplus property disposal confronting the Congress, the Surplus Property Administration and other governmental agencies, we are well repaid.

In reply, the Surplus Property Administrator stated:

> If in the past I have had occasion to be critical of the Aluminum Company of America, today's action on your part demonstrates to my complete satisfaction that your company, no less than the Government agencies concerned, is moving constructively toward the solution of the problems which confront the Surplus Property Administration, the aluminum industry, and the country as a whole.

Attorney General Tom C. Clark, when informed of the agreement, wrote a commendatory letter to Administrator Symington in which he said in part:

I want to express my gratification at the outcome of these negotiations. The consummation of this lease and the granting of this license on the terms above stated should contribute substantially to the establishment of real competition in the aluminum industry. It is entirely in line with the objective of this Department in the pending anti-trust suit.

It is this teamwork of Government and business—evidenced by the public spirited action of Alcoa in granting a royalty free license and in the cooperative spirit of the Reconstruction Finance Corporation and Surplus Property Administration—that will get the reconversion job done. My hearty congratulations to all of you.

This understanding made possible the disposal of Government-owned alumina plants as well as aluminum plants which were dependent upon alumina. Reynolds Metals Company acquired through lease and subsequent purchase the Hurricane Creek alumina plant as well as the Jones Mills, Arkansas, and Troutdale, Oregon, aluminum plants. Kaiser Aluminum & Chemical Corporation obtained the Baton Rouge, Louisiana, alumina plant along with the aluminum-producing plants at Spokane and at Tacoma, Washington. This divided the aluminum annual capacity in the United States among three primary producers, Alcoa having 50.6 per cent, Reynolds 29.4 per cent, and Kaiser 20 per cent.

This percentage was to change slightly after 1945. At that time Alcoa's percentage included the Niagara Falls plant with an annual capacity of forty million pounds and the Reynolds percentage took into consideration only half of the pot lines at

Jones Mills. Since then Alcoa has closed the Niagara Falls plant and has built a new aluminum reduction works at Point Comfort, Texas. Reynolds is now operating all the lines at Jones Mills. Kaiser has stepped up capacity at both Spokane and Tacoma. Judge Knox set the capacities of the three producers as of June 2, 1950, as follows: Alcoa 50.86 per cent, Reynolds 30.94 per cent and Kaiser 18.2 per cent. Minor changes in these percentages continue to occur as time goes on.

Alcoa was permitted to acquire only one Government-owned aluminum-producing plant, the St. Lawrence Reduction Works adjacent to the Company's Massena, New York, operations. The manner of this acquisition has been described in another chapter. Objections of the Department of Justice intervened to prevent Alcoa from purchasing Government-owned fabricating plants it had built and operated during the war. The Company did purchase the extrusion plant at Cressona, Pennsylvania, when it seemed to be the only customer. Reynolds Metals Company acquired two major plants making mill products, the large Chicago sheet mill and the extrusion plant at Phoenix, Arizona. Reynolds also obtained a sheet mill at Listerhill, Alabama, a forging plant at Louisville, Kentucky, and an extrusion works at Grand Rapids, Michigan. Kaiser Aluminum & Chemical Corporation owns the Trentwood (Spokane) sheet mill and the Newark, Ohio, blooming mill.

Gradually during the five years following World War II, disposal of Government-owned aluminum facilities has been increasing the number and strength of Alcoa's competitors. As recently as 1950, the aluminum plant at Riverbank, California, was being dismantled and its aluminum reduction facilities sold.

Idle equipment from the wartime aluminum plant at Burlington, near Philadelphia, was also sold to aluminum producers by the General Services Administration. Apex Smelting Company of Chicago, a prospective new producer, was the purchaser of one pot line and the necessary rectifier equipment for an installation near the Grand River Dam in Oklahoma. Harvey Machine Company of Torrance, California, a manufacturer of aluminum extrusions, obtained some of the material for three aluminum pot lines probably to be located near Hungry Horse Dam in Montana. Reynolds Metals Company and Kaiser Aluminum & Chemical Corporation also obtained additional equipment for use in existing aluminum-producing plants owned by them.

Production of aluminum mill products for war created many new manufacturers and peacetime demand has added more. The number of aluminum foundries is at an all-time high; new manufacturers of aluminum extrusions, stranded aluminum cable and other products have entered the field.

Recently in one section of a southern state a rural electrification system negotiated with an electric utility company to supply it with power. To do so, the utility had to construct a 100-mile high-tension line from its powerhouses to the REA system. The Alcoa salesman in that territory was on the job early. In his calls on the engineering staff of the utility, he met stiff competition from copper companies. This was routine since Alcoa salesmen, selling aluminum cable steel-reinforced (ACSR), usually meet competition from copper. When the job was finally specified for aluminum, the Alcoa salesman had to compete not only with other aluminum companies but also with the same copper company which had originally sought to have the line built of copper.

There are no less than ten manufacturers of ACSR and the copper company happened to be one of them.

This little story is typical of what happens almost daily in the sale of aluminum mill products. In this case it was a success story since the Alcoa salesman got the order. However, if anyone should tell him or any other Alcoa man in the sales force that the Company has little competition, the answer would be an amazed, "What's that?"

Not only does Alcoa meet a genuine challenge from other aluminum producers for the United States market, it also has to meet competition from Aluminium, Ltd., which has a capacity to produce over one billion pounds of aluminum annually. Aluminum Company of Canada, the operating subsidiary, known as Alcan, finds no great difficulty in hurdling the two-cent tariff wall in selling metal at a profit in this country. Alcan is also alert to the possibilities of aluminum markets in Central and South America.

All this competition is in addition to the bids for consideration from steel, other nonferrous metals and plastics. It is a wholesome situation in which Alcoa plays its part. The Company has reason to take pride in the co-operative role it played in bringing about a solution of the disposal of Government-owned aluminum facilities suitable for peacetime operations. The Company can feel some satisfaction in this despite the fact that it received scant consideration in the disposal of these properties which it had built for the Government and operated so efficiently during the war.

The existence of highly competitive conditions in the aluminum industry is now taken as a matter of course. Plans by both private industry and Government for expansion of aluminum production following the outbreak of hostilities in Korea are a concern of the three major producers and of others [2] who are entering the business of making aluminum. This account ends just prior to further aluminum expansion occasioned by war clouds since the Korean incident. In outlining Alcoa's expansion programs in February of this year, I. W. Wilson, then Senior Vice President and now President of Alcoa, said: "I can, of course, speak only for the Aluminum Company of America, but, given the opportunity, Alcoa stands ready and willing to assume its share of the burden and responsibility of adequately serving the aluminum requirements of our country in war and in peace."

[2] *Business Week*, August 26, 1950.

Chronological Record
of Alcoa's Labor Negotiations
1935–1950

☆ ☆ ☆ ☆ ☆ ☆ ☆ ★

OLLOWING the Agreement which ended the strike in 1934, as described on page 197 of Chapter XIV, a second Agreement, also signed by Mr. Hunt, was executed on October 14, 1935. This, again, was an Agreement "between the Aluminum Company of America and all its employees." While this Agreement was between the Company and all of its employees, it in no way implied lack of recognition of the Aluminum Workers' Unions, A. F. of L., at the Company's plants at Alcoa, Tennessee; Badin, North Carolina; East St. Louis, Illinois; Massena, New York; and New Kensington, Pennsylvania.

On December 2, 1936, an Agreement including recognition of the unions as bargaining representatives, as well as working rules and procedure, was signed by both the Company and the Aluminum Workers' Unions, A. F. of L., covering the Company plants at Alcoa, Tennessee; Badin, North Carolina; East St. Louis, Illinois; Logans Ferry, Pennsylvania; Massena, New York; and New Kensington, Pennsylvania. This Agreement was signed by Mr. I. W. Wilson, Vice President, and remained in effect until April 13, 1939. During this period, dissension arose between the A. F. of L. and some of their local unions mentioned above with the result that during 1937 the local unions at Alcoa, Badin,

277

Logans Ferry, and New Kensington transferred their affiliation from the A. F. of L. to the International Union, Aluminum Workers of America, C.I.O. Thus, the Aluminum Workers' Unions, A. F. of L., were left for a time with representation rights at just two of the Company's plants— Massena, New York, and East St. Louis, Illinois. During the spring and summer of 1938, the Aluminum Workers' Unions, A. F. of L., sought and won certification through the National Labor Relations Board as bargaining representatives, at both of these locations. Subsequently on April 13, 1939, and again on April 24, 1940, the Aluminum Workers' Unions, A. F. of L., on behalf of the workers in those two plants, entered into new working Agreements with the Company.

On April 19, 1941, several years after the completion of the Company's new ore-refining plant at Mobile, Alabama, the N.L.R.B. certified the Aluminum Workers' Union, A. F. of L., as bargaining representative, for the employees at that location. The Agreement between the Aluminum Workers' Union, A. F. of L., and the Company was extended to cover the employees at that plant.

Thereafter, on March 24, 1942, and again on March 24, 1943, new Agreements were executed between the Company and the Aluminum Workers' Unions, A. F. of L., on behalf of the employees at the Massena, New York; East St. Louis, Illinois; and Mobile, Alabama plants. Early in 1943, employees at the Company's fabricating plant at Lafayette, Indiana, had petitioned the N.L.R.B. for a collective-bargaining representation election. As a result, on May 13, 1943, the Aluminum Workers' Union, A. F. of L., was certified as bargaining agent. The parties at this location, however, chose to have their own separate working Agreement which they signed July 20, 1943.

During 1943, the Aluminum Workers' Unions, A. F. of L., won bargaining rights at three Defense Plant Corporation plants which had been built and were being operated for the Government by Alcoa. This included the plants at Baton Rouge, Louisiana; Maspeth, New York; and Burlington, New Jersey. The terms of the general Agreement with the Aluminum Workers' Unions, A. F. of L., were made applicable at Baton Rouge and Maspeth, but the local union at Burlington insisted on a separate Agreement.

Appendix

On May 20, 1944, the Company and the Aluminum Workers' Unions, A. F. of L., again signed a general working Agreement which covered the Company's plants at Massena, New York; East St. Louis, Illinois; Baton Rouge, Louisiana; and Maspeth, New York. The Mobile, Alabama, employees, who since 1941 had been represented by the Aluminum Workers' Union, A. F. of L., and had been a party to the previous general Agreement by that union, had become embroiled in a jurisdictional conflict between the Aluminum Workers' Unions, A. F. of L., and the United Steelworkers, C.I.O., which resulted in an N.L.R.B. election and certification of the United Steelworkers as bargaining representative for the employees at that plant in July, 1944.

Another general working Agreement was signed between the Company and the Aluminum Workers' Unions, A. F. of L., on behalf of the Massena, New York; East St. Louis, Illinois; Baton Rouge, Louisiana; and the Lafayette, Indiana Works on May 20, 1945. This was the first time the parties at Lafayette elected to participate in the general Agreement in preference to a separate contract. The Maspeth, New York, plant was not covered in this general Agreement inasmuch as it, along with the Defense Plant Corporation plant at Burlington, New Jersey, had ceased operations by that time. When the next general working Agreement, which is the current one, was entered into between the Company and the Aluminum Workers' Unions, A. F. of L., on April 9, 1947, the Baton Rouge, Louisiana, Defense Plant Corporation plant had also ceased operations.

In 1947, the Company purchased the former Defense Plant Corporation plant at Cressona, Pennsylvania, from the Reconstruction Finance Corporation. The Aluminum Workers' Union, A. F. of L., won bargaining rights at that plant on June 26, 1947, and the general Agreement applicable at the other Aluminum Workers' Unions, A. F. of L., plants was applied to the Cressona Works.

A short time after the completion of the plant of The Aluminum Cooking Utensil Company, a subsidiary of the Aluminum Company of America, at Chillicothe, Ohio, the Aluminum Workers' Union, A. F. of L., sought and won bargaining rights covering the workers at that plant. The N.L.R.B. certification was issued June 26, 1947, and a separate Agreement was entered into between the parties covering that location on August 15, 1949.

On November 9, 1950, as the result of an N.L.R.B. election, the Aluminum Workers' Union, A. F. of L., was certified by the N.L.R.B. as collective bargaining representative for employees at the Company's new Davenport, Iowa, fabricating plant, and the general working Agreement effective at other plants represented by the Aluminum Workers' Unions, A. F. of L., was adopted for the Davenport Works.

It will be noted in the beginning of this Appendix to Chapter XIV that during 1937 the unions at the Company's plants at Alcoa, Tennessee; Badin, North Carolina; and New Kensington, Pennsylvania, transferred their affiliation from the Aluminum Workers' Unions, A. F. of L., to the International Union, Aluminum Workers of America, C.I.O. The terms of the A. F. of L. Agreement were extended to apply to the Aluminum Workers of America, C.I.O., in the plants where this change of affiliation had taken place. This also was extended to the plant at Detroit, Michigan, where the Aluminum Workers of America, C.I.O., was certified as the bargaining agency in an N.L.R.B. election on August 30, 1938. Similarly, it was extended to cover the Company's plant at Edgewater, New Jersey, where the Aluminum Workers of America, C.I.O., was certified as the bargaining agency in an N.L.R.B. election on June 15, 1939.

On November 11, 1939, an Agreement was entered into between the Company and the International Union, Aluminum Workers of America, C.I.O.—which had been recognized as the result of N.L.R.B. certification as the exclusive bargaining agency for employees at the Company's plants at Alcoa, Tennessee; Detroit, Michigan; Edgewater, New Jersey; and New Kensington, Pennsylvania—and Local No. 2 of the National Association of Die Casting Workers, which the Company agreed represented its employees at its Garwood, New Jersey, plant.

On November 1, 1942, the Company entered into an Agreement with the International Union, Aluminum Workers of America, C.I.O., covering Company plants in Alcoa, Tennessee; Badin, North Carolina; Bauxite, Arkansas; Detroit, Michigan; Drury, Arkansas; Edgewater, New Jersey; Fairfield, Connecticut; and New Kensington, Pennsylvania, for which plants the union had been certified by the National Labor Relations Board. It will be noted that the Garwood, New Jersey, plant was not included in the list of plants in the above Agreement with the Aluminum Workers of America, C.I.O., as it had been in the previous Agreement of November 11, 1939. The reason for this change was that the National Association of Die Casting Workers had become affiliated with the International Union, Mine, Mill and Smelter Workers, C.I.O., and a separate Agreement was signed with it covering the employees of the Garwood plant on December 22, 1942.

Following the signing of the Agreement on November 1, 1942, with the Aluminum Workers of America, C.I.O., bargaining rights were obtained by this union through N.L.R.B. elections at the Company's plants at Hurricane Creek, Arkansas; Jones Mills, Arkansas; Troutdale, Oregon; Mobile, Alabama; Mead, Washington; Trentwood, Washington; Cressona, Pennsylvania; Newark, Ohio; Chicago, Illinois; Phoenix, Arizona; Canonsburg, Pennsylvania; and Monroe, Michigan. It should be noted that the Company's plants at Hurricane Creek, Jones Mills, Troutdale, Mead, Trentwood, Cressona, Newark, Chicago, Phoenix, Canonsburg and Monroe were Defense Plant Corporation plants which the Company built and operated for the Government during the war period.

Under an Agreement dated July 18, 1944, in recognition of the amalgamation of International Union, Aluminum Workers of America, with the United Steelworkers of America, C.I.O., the Company agreed that the United Steelworkers of America, C.I.O., would assume the collective bargaining rights which were then held by the International Union, Aluminum Workers of America, C.I.O., in the Company's plants as listed above. At the time of the negotiation of the current contract of May 8, 1947, with the United Steelworkers of America, C.I.O., the Defense Plant Corporation plants mentioned above had been closed, leaving only the Company plants at Alcoa, Tennessee; Badin, North Carolina; Bauxite, Arkansas; Detroit, Michigan; Drury, Arkansas; Edgewater, New Jersey; Bridgeport-Fairfield, Connecticut; Mobile, Alabama; and New Kensington, Pennsylvania, for whom the International Union, United Steelworkers of America, C.I.O., had been certified as the exclusive bargaining agency.

Appendix

Following the signing of the current Agreement with the United Steel-workers of America, C.I.O., on May 8, 1947, the Company's plant at Richmond, Indiana, was certified by an N.L.R.B. election on August 12, 1947, and included in this Agreement. Similarly, as a result of an N.L.R.B. election, the Company's plant at Point Comfort, Texas, was certified on September 21, 1950, and included in this same Agreement.

The foregoing chronological record deals entirely with Alcoa's relations with the Aluminum Workers' Unions, A. F. of L., and with the United Steelworkers, C.I.O., the two unions that have bargaining rights at the majority of the Company plants. Other unions, however, have bargaining rights at some of the other Company plants, and their chronological records are shown in the paragraphs that follow.

As stated above, the International Union, Mine, Mill and Smelter Workers, C.I.O., became the bargaining agency at the Garwood, New Jersey, plant in 1942, and a separate Agreement was signed with that union covering the employees at Garwood on December 22, 1942. Later, on April 3, 1945, another Agreement was signed with the International Union, Mine, Mill and Smelter Workers, C.I.O., covering the Garwood plant along with the Cleveland, Ohio, plant. The current Agreement covering Garwood is dated May 19, 1947.

On April 28, 1941, the National Association of Die Casting Workers, C.I.O., won bargaining rights at the Company's plant in Cleveland. In August, 1942, this was changed to the International Union, Mine, Mill, and Smelter Workers, C.I.O. Later, on June 28, 1949, as a result of an N.L.R.B. election, the United Automobile Workers, C.I.O., Local No. 1050, was certified as the bargaining agency. The current Agreement between the Company and this union is dated May 1, 1950.

The United Automobile Workers, C.I.O., also hold bargaining rights at the Company's plants in Vernon, California, and Hillside, Illinois. Local No. 808 at Vernon was certified on June 17, 1941, and the current Agreement with this union is dated August 21, 1947. Local No. 1065 was certified on August 9, 1949, at Hillside, and the current Agreement with this union is dated September 2, 1949.

The United Automobile Workers, C.I.O., also held bargaining rights at two Defense Plant Corporation plants during the war period—namely,

282

the plants at Kansas City, Missouri, and New Castle, Pennsylvania. N.L.R.B. certification was obtained at Kansas City on November 5, 1943, and at New Castle on September 27, 1943. Local Agreements were signed between Alcoa and the union at these plants.

On October 14, 1941, District 50, United Mine Workers, was designated as the bargaining agency at the Company's plant in Buffalo, New York. The current Agreement between Alcoa and this union, Local No. 12285, is dated April 14, 1947.

District 50, United Mine Workers, is also the bargaining agency at the Company's plant at Rosiclare, Illinois. N.L.R.B. certification was obtained by Local No. 12590 first on September 21, 1942, and later on June 28, 1943, to cover the newly developed portion of the mine. The current Agreement between the Company and Local No. 1250, District 50, United Mine Workers, is dated September 27, 1947, having been extended twice since the original date by mutual agreement.

At the Company's plant in Vancouver, Washington, the Aluminum Trades Council, A. F. of L., was certified by the N.L.R.B. on November 20, 1942. The current Agreement between Alcoa and this union is dated July 11, 1947.

The United Furniture Workers of America, C.I.O., Local No. 34, holds the bargaining agency at the Company's plant in Jamestown, New York, as the result of already being there when the Company bought the plant in 1946. The current Agreement with this union is dated November 3, 1949.

During the war period, the Defense Plant Corporation plant at Torrence, California, was certified on September 13, 1943, to Local No. 609 of the Mine, Mill, and Smelter Workers, C.I.O. Similarly, the Defense Plant Corporation plant at Riverbank, California, was certified on October 25, 1943, to the Stanislaus County Central Labor Council, A. F. of L. Both of these plants were closed following the war period and the Company is not involved at either location today.

The International Die Sinkers Conference represents trade and apprentice die sinkers at the Cleveland, Ohio, and Vernon, California, plants. Local No. 10 was certified at Cleveland on August 5, 1942, and Local No. 220 at Vernon on June 17, 1941. The current Agreement at

Cleveland is dated August 27, 1948, and at Vernon, August 24, 1948.

The first, and, for a number of years, the only, office union dates back to October 10, 1938, at the East St. Louis plant. This union is the Aluminum Administrative Workers Union, A. F. of L. Since that time the Office Employees' International Union, A. F. of L., has obtained bargaining rights at the Mobile plant on February 18, 1944, and at the Massena plant on August 5, 1946. Also, the Association of Aluminum Salaried Employees, National Federation of Salaried Unions, obtained bargaining rights at New Kensington on August 4, 1945.

Index of Names

Sherman Act, 75-77, 80, 82, 201, 209,
225, 227, 234, 266
Sherman, John, 75
Shields, Thos. L., 41
Shipshaw project, 103, 189
Sholes, C. L., 59
Smallman Street Works, 17, 37, 42,
43
Smith, William Watson, 38, 49
Smith, Buchanan, Ingersoll, Rode-
wald & Eckert, 38
Southern Aluminium Company, 100-
102, 170, 178
Snoqualmie Falls Power Company,
120
Sparkes, Boyden, 109
Sprague Steamboat, 154
Stanley, George J., 133, 134
Stimson, Mrs. M. L., 9
Symington, W. Stuart, 256, 265, 266,
271
Stutz Motor Car Company, 214
Suriname, 72, 189
Surplus Property Act, 264
Surplus Property Administrator, 269-
272
Swan, Judge Thomas W., 215, 230

Taft, Judge William H., 53
Tallassee Power Company, 94
Taylor, J. G., vi
Templin, R. L., 143
Tennessee Valley Authority, 96-100,
173, 174
Tesla, Nicola, 59
Thorpe, J. E. S., 94
Thorpe Development, 94
Toronto, Ontario Works, 152, 187
Trentwood, Washington, Sheet Mill,
249, 273
Troutdale, Oregon, Works, 249, 272
Truman, President Harry S., 265, 269
Truman Committee, 235, 255
Tuckasegee Project, 95
Turner, R. C., 198
Twentieth Century Fund, 99

Uihlein, Robert, 171, 172
Underwood-Simmons Tariff, 166
United States Aluminum Metals Com-
pany, 57
United States Supreme Court, 229,
233
U. S. Bureau of Mines, 64, 239
United Smelting & Aluminum Com-
pany, 166
United Steel Workers, C.I.O., 198,
277-283

Vancouver, Washington, Works, 104,
248
Van Horn, Dr. K. R., 144

Wallace, Donald H., 177
Waltz, James L. T., 226
War Assets Administration, 235
War Industries Board, 150, 156
War Production Board, 144, 260, 267
War Property Committee, 268
Washington Monument, 119
Wear-Ever, 114, 115, 162
West Indian Court of Appeals, 172
Westinghouse, George, 59
White, Stanford, 90
Whitney, C. F., 112
Whitney, Eli, 59
Wickersham, Attorney General, 75,
81
Wilm, Alfred, 137, 151
Wilson, I. W., 92, 219, 248, 276
Wilson, J. H., 113, 114
Wilson Philip B., 144
Withers, Colonel R. E., 47
Wood, R. T., 245
Wöhler, Frederick, 3, 9
Wright, Orville, 59, 118
Wright, Wilbur, 59, 118

Yadkin River, 100, 102

Zeppelin Airships, 137
Ziegler, Dr. Charles E., 113, 114
Zimmerman, William, 27

290

Index of Subjects

☆ ☆ ☆ ☆ ☆ ☆ ☆ ☆ ☆ ☆